The Essential Bach Choir

The Essential Bach Choir

ANDREW PARROTT

THE BOYDELL PRESS

First published 2000
The Boydell Press, Woodbridge

ISBN 0-85115-786-6

The Boydell Press is an imprint of Boydell and Brewer Ltd.,
PO Box 9, Woodbridge, Suffolk IP12 3DF, UK
and of Boydell and Brewer Inc.,
PO Box 41026, Rochester, NY 14604-4126, USA
Website: http://www.boydell.co.uk

A catalogue record for this book is available from the British Library

Library of Congress Catalog card number 99-087035

Cover designed by Rowie Christopher
Music originated by Jeanne Fisher

Printed in Great Britain on acid-free paper by
Halstan and Co. Ltd., Amersham, Bucks

To my mother
and to the memory of my father

Contents

page

List of illustrations   ix
List of music examples   xiii
List of tables   xv

Prologue   1
Chapter 1   Introduction   3
Chapter 2   Bach as Cantor and *Director Musices* in Leipzig   7
Chapter 3   Repertoires   17
Chapter 4   Concertists and ripienists   29
Chapter 5   Copies and copy-sharing   43
Chapter 6   Bach's use of ripienists   59
Chapter 7   The *Entwurff*   93
Chapter 8   Additional resources   103
Chapter 9   Instrument/singer ratios   117
Chapter 10 Balance   131
Chapter 11 Conclusions   141
Epilogue   147

Acknowledgements   152

Appendices
1   Bach's written undertakings to the Leipzig Town Council (1723)   155
2   Bach's audition reports (1729)   159
3   The *Entwurff* (1730): text and translation   163
4   Some contemporary accounts of concerted music-making   171
5   Sources of Bach's concerted vocal music   177
6   Bach's chorus (1981) *by Joshua Rifkin*   189
7   Twentieth-century discussions of Bach's choir   209

Bibliography   213
Index   221

Illustrations

page

Illus. 1. Street singing: engraving, Germany, eighteenth century. **8**
H. Gärtner, *Johann Christian Bach*, 1989 (Nymphenburger in der
F. A. Herbig Verlagsbuchhandlung, Munich)

Illus. 2. Nikolaikirche, Leipzig: engraving after J. E. Scheffler, **10**
Nuremberg, 1749. Leipzig, Bach-Archiv

Illus. 3. Thomasschule and Thomaskirche, Leipzig: engraving by **11**
J. G. Krügner, Leipzig, 1723 (frontispiece to school *Ordnung*). Leipzig,
Bach-Archiv

Illus. 4. Violinist with horn, Hamburg, 1719 (detail of Illus. 21) **14**

Illus. 5. West galleries, Nikolaikirche, Leipzig: water-colour by **20**
C. B. Schwarz, *c*.1785. Leipzig, Stadtarchiv

Illus. 6. West galleries, Thomaskirche, Leipzig: conjectural plan by **21**
A. Schering. Schering 1936

Illus. 7. E. Bodenschatz, *Florilegium Portense* (Leipzig, 1618): first **23**
page of the Discantus partbook, showing Hans Leo Hassler, *Pater
noster*. London, The British Library, B67

Illus. 8. J. S. Bach, *Gott ist mein König* BWV71: first page of the **37**
autograph score. Berlin, Staatsbibliothek, Mus. ms. Bach P 45

Illus. 9. J. S. Bach, *Missa* BWV232(I): a page from the autograph **45**
'Tenore' copy. Dresden, Sächsische Landesbibliothek, Staats- und
Universitätsbibliothek, Mus. 2405-D-21

Illus. 10. J. S. Bach, *Lobe den Herrn, meine Seele* BWV69: last page of **47**
the autograph 'Alto' copy. Berlin, Staatsbibliothek, Mus. ms. Bach
St 68/2

Illus. 11. J. G. Walther, *Musikalisches Lexicon* (Leipzig, 1732): **50**
engraving by J. C. Dehné (frontispiece)

Illus. 12. Singers performing concerted music in church, Leipzig, **55**
1710 (detail of Illus. 18)

Illus. 13. Singers, Freiberg, *c.*1710–14 (detail of Illus. 19)   56

Illus. 14. Singers (apparently ripienists), Freiberg, *c.*1710–14 (detail   57
of Illus. 19)

*Illus. 15. J. S. Bach, *Dem Gerechten muß das Licht* BWV195: first page   60
of 'Soprano in Ripieno' copy. Berlin, Staatsbibliothek, Mus. ms.
Bach St 12/5

*Illus. 16. J. S. Bach, 'Entwurff einer wohlbestallten Kirchen *Music*',   100
23 August 1730: first page (autograph). Leipzig, Bach-Archiv

Illus. 17. '*Tabula musicorum* der löbl. großen *Concert*-Gesellschafft',   120
Leipzig, 1746–8: from J. S. Riemer's manuscript chronicle of events
in Leipzig 1714–50, vol. ii. Leipzig, Stadtarchiv

*Illus. 18. F. Groschuff, *Unfehlbare Engel-Freude* (Leipzig, 1710):   121
frontispiece (engraving) and title-page (cf. detail, Illus. 12). Halle,
Universitäts- und Landesbibliothek Sachsen-Anhalt

*Illus. 19. Musicians in the organ gallery, Freiberg Cathedral,   122
*c.*1710–14: engraving by J. G. Krügner after E. Lindner (cf. details,
Illus. 13 and 14). Freiberg, Stadt- und Bergbaumuseum

Illus. 20. Musicians in the gallery of the Kongregationssaal, Munich,   124
*c.*1715: engraving by J. A. Corvinus (detail). Munich, Stadtmuseum

Illus. 21. Jubilee banquet (*Jubelmahl*) of the Hamburger   124
Bürgerkapitäne, Drill-Haus, Hamburg, 1719: engraving by C. Fritzsch
(detail; cf. detail, Illus. 4). Hamburg, Staatsarchiv

*Illus. 22. Concerted music-making at court, ?Augsburg, *c.*1750:   125
engraving by G. B. Probst (cf. detail, Illus. 23). New York, Metropolitan
Museum of Art, gift of Harry G. Friedman, 1956

Illus. 23. Vocal concertists, ?Augsburg, *c.*1750 (detail of Illus. 22)   125

Illus. 24. An outdoor performance by the collegium musicum, Jena,   126
mid eighteenth century: water-colour (detail). Hamburg, Museum
für Kunst und Gewerbe

Illus. 25. A meeting of the collegium musicum, Jena, mid   126
eighteenth century: water-colour. Hamburg, Museum für Kunst
und Gewerbe

Illus. 26. Concerted music-making, ?Nuremberg, *c.*1775: gouache   127
(from a family album). Nuremberg, Germanisches Nationalmuseum

* Details of these illustrations also form part of the cover design

Illus. 27. Neue Kirche, Leipzig, after 1710: engraving by   137
J. C. Oberdörffer (detail). Leipzig, Stadtgeschichtliches Museum

Illus. 28. A meeting of the Leipzig Town Council, 1713: engraving by   154
J. C. Lünig. Leipzig, Stadtgeschichtliches Museum

Music examples

	page
Ex. 1. J. Handl, *Ecce quomodo moritur justus* (part 1), from *Florilegium Portense* (1603)	24
Ex. 2. J. Handl, *Beatus vir* (opening), from *Florilegium Portense* (1603)	26
Ex. 3. J. S. Bach, *Geschwinde, geschwinde, ihr wirbelnden Winde* (*Dramma per musica: Der Streit zwischen Phoebus und Pan*) BWV201/15, bars 9–16	63
Ex. 4. J. S. Bach, *Wir danken dir, Gott* BWV29/2, bars 1–18	65
Ex. 5a. J. S. Bach, *Gott ist mein König* BWV71/3, bars 1–13	66
Ex. 5b. J. S. Bach, *Gott ist mein König* BWV71/6, bars 3–10	67
Ex. 6. J. S. Bach, *Dem Gerechten muß das Licht* BWV195/1, bars 13–25	72
Ex. 7. J. S. Bach, *Ich hatte viel Bekümmernis* BWV21/6, bars 1–10	74
Ex. 8. J. S. Bach, *Ich hatte viel Bekümmernis* BWV21/11, bars 25–36	76
Ex. 9. J. S. Bach, *Unser Mund sei voll Lachens* BWV110/1, bars 24–32, 48–54, 67–73, 126–137	78
Ex. 10. J. S. Bach, *Jesus nahm zu sich die Zwölfe* BWV22/1, bars 7–20	81
Ex. 11. J. S. Bach, *Ich glaube, lieber Herr* BWV109/1, bars 17–24	82
Ex. 12. J. S. Bach, Mass in B Minor BWV232(II)/6 ('Et resurrexit'), bars 74–86	84
Ex. 13. J. S. Bach, *Dem Gerechten muß das Licht* BWV195/1, bars 13–44	85
Ex. 14. J. S. Bach, *Gottes Zeit ist die allerbeste Zeit* (*Actus tragicus*) BWV106/2d, bars 180–185	135

Tables

		page
Table 1.	Leipzig organists in Bach's time	12
Table 2.	Distribution of duties between choirs I and II	19
Table 3A.	Works by Bach with surviving copies for ripienists	61
Table 3B.	Further works by Bach with indications of ripieno participation	62
Table 4A.	Bach's ripieno writing	68
Table 4B.	Further ripieno writing indicated by Bach	71
Table 5.	Copies used in two of Bach's Passion performances	83
Table 6.	Deployment of Thomasschule pupils	97
Table 7.	Known additional performers	109
Table 8.	Annual numbers of additional performers	110
Table 9.	Instruments per voice in contemporary sources	128
Table 10.	Instruments per voice in selected works by Bach	128

Prologue

Quid uerum atque decens curo,
& rogo, & omnis in hoc sum.[1]

The central thesis of this book is one that was first put forward at a musicological gathering in Boston the best part of two decades ago. (Appendix 6 presents Joshua Rifkin's 1981 paper in published form for the first time.) Yet insofar as any of this new thinking may have filtered through to conductors, singers, and the listening public – to those most directly affected by the performance of J. S. Bach's choral music – it has emerged in such a distorted and simplistic form that disbelief has been all but guaranteed. With the 250th anniversary of Bach's death now upon us, the present aim therefore is to clarify the various issues and to give a richly rewarding subject the wider public attention it deserves.

Although the matter under discussion is nothing less than the essential nature of the medium used by Bach throughout his entire career and for what is arguably the core of his incomparable musical output, many people may well be somewhat bemused at the very suggestion that 'Bach's choir' might allow of any significant discussion at all. (Does it really matter what sort or size of choir sings his music? Isn't it just a matter of musical taste and judgement?) After all, it is not as if any urgent need for reassessment has arisen through the rediscovery of a major document from Bach's own hand, explicitly defining his choral ideal in unexpected ways. The critical sources remain the familiar ones, already picked over by generations of Bach

---

[1] 'The search of truth and decency hath fill'd my breast,/ Hath every thought and faculty possess'd' (Horace, *Epist.* 1.i.11) – a quotation chosen by Johann Abraham Birnbaum to head his (anonymously published) *Unpartheyische Anmerckungen* [1738], dedicated to and in defence of J. S. Bach; see Appendix 4, document 4.

scholars. Is there really any need to question their collective scholarly opinion, one which has served musicians well enough through most of the twentieth century?

The realization that a familiar object or concept may make much better sense when viewed in an entirely different way can happen in a blinding flash, or it may demand an arduous process of analysis. Like countless others, I initially reacted to Rifkin's challenge with some scepticism. But as a conductor – and as one engaged in making recordings (which by their very nature are likely to be more widely influential than occasional concert performances) – I felt a responsibility to wrestle with the newly raised issues until I was quite sure of what I thought. (Needless to say, I had never before given the subject any very serious consideration.) The more I pondered, the more it became apparent that this was no casual hypothesis but rather the inescapable product of a radical and brilliant re-examination of the central source material. Or, to put it another way, it became clearer at every turn that conventional theory and practice were resting on the flimsiest of foundations, on a simple assumption (albeit an entirely understandable one) which was proving all but impossible to substantiate. What was thereby revealed, after effectively lying hidden since the eighteenth century, was not a minor historical point, a detail of purely academic interest, but a fundamental principle of performance – and of composition – running right through Bach's (and others') creative output, and consequently something which would contribute to a significantly fuller understanding of his music.

Not everyone sees it this way, of course. Hence the present book, which aims above all to make the subject readily accessible to all those who wish to explore it seriously – by presenting all the salient material in a single place for the first time. In particular, the various appendices, tables and illustrations will, I hope, make this a useful work of reference. I have shamelessly plundered and recycled material from articles of my own which originally appeared in the Oxford University Press journal *Early Music*; in most cases, though, this material has undergone a process of substantial revision, reorganization, and, above all, expansion.

With the sudden intensification of millennial talk at the start of the New Year 1999 I became acutely aware that Bach celebrations in the year 2000 – which will inevitably help shape the listening habits and performance expectations of millions for decades to come – seemed destined to sidestep this whole area of research and performance, more out of sheer convenience and habit than for considered historical or musical reasons. The old half-truths would become even more deeply rooted. A short book might go at least some way towards salvaging the situation.

1

Introduction

What size of choir sang J. S. Bach's concerted church music? What vocal forces did he *really* want to perform those works? To the second question, at least, received wisdom has a ready answer: 'Bach speaks of three or four [singers] to a part in four-part writing as ideal.'[1]

In recent decades, performances of Bach's choral works on historical lines have been dominated by this image of a 12- or 16-strong choir. But behind that image lies another – the even more familiar one of massed voices (158 of them) at the 1829 'centenary' revival of the St Matthew Passion in Berlin under the direction of the 20-year-old Felix Mendelssohn.[2] Though the two images may appear quite different, they nevertheless depict one and the same medium; each is what we clearly recognize as a 'choir'. And, though it is rarely articulated, a defining characteristic of such a choir, large or small, is that each voice part is sung by at least two singers – and perhaps by 12 or 20 – but not by one. This definition of a choir seems self-evident to us today, as it undoubtedly did in Mendelssohn's time, almost eighty years after J. S. Bach's death.

Yet, if we look at the Lutheran traditions of the seventeenth century in which Bach's music has its roots, we find that the term 'choir' has a crucial-ly broader meaning, one which embraces not only an instrumental ensemble (*Instrumental Chor*) but also groups of just one voice (or instrument) per part – 'consorts', as they have recently (and usefully) come to be known. Heinrich Schütz, typically for his time, draws a clear distinction between

---

[1] Ellen T. Harris, 'Voices', chap. 5 in Brown/Sadie 1989, p. 114.

[2] Rehearsals had started, at the Mendelssohns' house, with some 12 singers, but numbers 'grew from one rehearsal to the next'; for Eduard Devrient's contemporary account, see *NBR*, pp. 509–19. See also Geck 1967.

two types of choral medium for certain of his *Psalmen Davids* (1619), in which

> the second choir is used as a capella and is therefore strong [in numbers], while the first choir, which is the *coro favorito* [literally, the 'favoured choir'], is by contrast slender and comprises only four singers . . .

> . . . wird *Coro secondo* für eine *Capell* gebraucht/ und dahero starck bestimmet/ weil aber *Choro 1.* welches ist *Choro Fauorito* hingegen schwach/ und nur von vier Sängern ist . . .[3]

In other words, capella sections are appropriate for several voices per part (or perhaps voices and instruments), but the remainder is intended for single voices.[4] While we may be tempted to associate the former with a 'real' choir and, subconsciously, to dismiss the latter as being for a mere vocal quartet and hence not strictly for a choir at all,[5] seventeenth-century usage is unambiguous: both groups qualify perfectly naturally as 'choirs'. Moreover, we should note that it is not the several-per-part choir that is 'favoured' in such works but the small élite group of solo voices – the vocal 'consort'. It is select choirs of this latter sort that are the chief protagonists of most seventeenth-century concerted music; capella writing need not appear at all, and when it does, it generally plays a subsidiary role.

The critical question is therefore this: which of these two types of choir was destined to become the essential vehicle for the concerted music of J. S. Bach?

The prime focus of our attention here will be the church music of Bach's Leipzig years, the best-documented phase of his career. But many of the conclusions we may draw will apply equally to his earlier works – and, indeed, to those of his Lutheran contemporaries; there is, after all, no reason to suppose that Bach's practices in Leipzig were exceptional for his time.

Not surprisingly, no single document tells us everything we might wish to know, and in this book we shall examine not only Bach's own writings and the key musical sources (especially the many surviving sets of original performing parts) but also a mass of other pertinent material – archival, theoretical and iconographic. And each step of the argument is to be taken with caution, since (as we have already seen) both unfamiliar concepts and treacherous terminology abound.

It may be as well to notice a few key terms at the outset:

Chor: a choir (of singers and/or instruments); a piece of choral music (a 'chorus'); a choir-loft

---

[3] Schütz 1619, Preface ¶3, referring to swv31, 33, 39 and perhaps 41.

[4] One writer imagines that 'it was not at all unusual for the *Favoritchor* to have more than one singer to a part' but presents no support for this notion (Smithers 1997, p. 22).

[5] Sure enough, a '*Chorus pro capella*' has recently been defined (in contrast to a '*Favoritchor*') as 'a *proper* choir of many voices': Smithers 1997, p. 22 (emphasis added).

concertiren: to perform (a principal role in) concerted music

Concertist: one who performs a principal role in concerted music (as opposed to a *Ripienist*, who performs a ripieno or 'filling-out' part)

figural: contrapuntal – generally used to denote music of a more elaborate or demanding nature than simple chorales, and thus often (but not always) concerted music

Kirchenstück: (specifically) a church cantata (literally, a 'church piece')

Motette: motet – as encountered here, most often used to denote a traditional repertoire of sixteenth- and early seventeenth-century motets, considerably simpler in character than the motets of Bach's own time

Music: music; music-making, or a piece of music, which involves instruments (such as a concerted work); a body of musicians (i.e. an ensemble)

musicalisch: (of a singer) musically literate – specifically, implying competence equal to the demands of the older *Motette* repertoire

musiciren: to perform music involving instruments

Orgel: organ; organ-loft

Singen: singing, especially of chorales and the simple *Motette* repertoire (as opposed to concerted works)[6]

The works Bach composed during his 27 years in Leipzig, like the documents concerning his activities there, arose for the most part in a specific institutional context. Chapter 2 of this book looks at the nature of his duties as Cantor of the Thomasschule and *Director musices* for the town, and surveys the varied range of musical tasks discharged by the pupils of the school under Bach's supervision. Chapter 3 examines the diverse repertoires in use there, from simple chorales to the most demanding new concerted music, and the differing technical demands they made on the performers.

Chapter 4 notes the specific vocal requirements of concerted music and elucidates the essential – and, in Bach's time, utterly conventional – distinction between 'concertists' and 'ripienists'. A secure grasp of that distinction is crucial to our perception of the character and composition of Bach's choir; to equate 'concertist' with modern 'soloist' and 'ripienist' with 'choir-singer', for example, would be sure to trigger a succession of misunderstandings.

The presence or absence of ripienists – which is clearly central to determining not only the size of Bach's choir but its very nature – hinges on the question of copy-sharing. To accept that three (or more) singers sang each vocal line in a work of Bach's, we are compelled to assume that each surviving copy was routinely shared by several singers, and/or that large numbers

---

[6] Thus, when we read of two 'persons' assisting at the Neue Kirche (*c*.1740) 'partly with the *Singen* and also with the *Music*' ('theils beym Singen oder auch bey der Music': Glöckner, p. 136), it may not be entirely clear whether those persons were singers who also played in the instrumental ensemble, or whether they were singers who were capable of singing concerted music as well as simple motets.

of extra copies have disappeared. Chapter 5 asks whether the available evidence supports either of these assumptions.

How often were ripienists available to Bach, and in what numbers? Chapter 6 focuses on their role, inspecting the handful of works which explicitly call for them, and the manner in which they are deployed.

The case in favour of the model of a 12- or 16-strong Bach choir has traditionally rested on the composer's *Entwurff* of 1730, addressed to the Leipzig Town Council.[7] We see in Chapter 7 that the purpose of this document is to set out the structure and operation of the musical institution in Bach's charge. However, it was written as an administrative memorandum – not as a musical treatise – and it will not directly tell us how many singers Bach required to perform a cantata or a Passion.

Additional musicians are known to have joined the Thomasschule pupils quite regularly in performing Bach's concerted music, and their presence has been used to bolster the idea that Bach used several singers on each voice part. Chapter 8 investigates how numerous these additional performers actually were and what role they played.

Chapter 9, which addresses the relative proportions of vocal and instrumental groups, challenges the (often unconscious) assumption that a large instrumental ensemble necessarily implies a large body of singers. Chapter 10 then explores related questions of balance between voices and instruments, as a practical matter of acoustics and musicianship.

Only after investigating all these issues with an open mind will we be able to frame responsible answers to the two questions with which we began. Those answers may well turn out to be different from those we take for granted; and the differences may help us to learn whether the questions themselves are matters of marginal academic interest or have the power to transform our conception of the music itself.

---

[7] 'Kurtzer, iedoch höchstnöthiger Entwurff einer wohlbestallten Kirchen *Music*', cited hereafter as *Entwurff*: *BD I*, pp. 74, 67 = *NBR*, pp. 158, 152. For a full text and translation of this document, see Appendix 3 below; for detailed discussion, see Siegele 1978 and Rifkin 1990.

2

Bach as Cantor and *Director Musices* in Leipzig

Much of the vital documentation that has come down to us from Bach's 27 years in Leipzig is concerned with the various administrative problems he encountered along the way, problems which sprang largely from tensions inherent in the 'exceptional' nature of his appointment in 1723 as Cantor of the Thomasschule and Director of Music for the town.[1] Let us therefore begin by looking at the institutional framework within which Bach's own church performances took place.

Bach's position was linked not directly to any of the town's churches, as one might imagine, but to its 'Latin school', the Thomasschule (see Illus. 3 below).

> In this school a number of scholars are supported with board and lodging by means of various generous bequests, [in return] for which they must provide the forces for church music and also accompany funerals and – three times a week (on Sundays, Mondays and Fridays) – go street singing, as the residents will then let them have something for their sustenance, as is usual in other towns.

[1] Those responsible in 1722–3 for selecting Johann Kuhnau's successor were aligned with one of two opposing parties with different objectives: the absolutist court party wanted a Capellmeister (which is what Bach's eventual title of *Director musices* implies), whilst the Estates' city party wanted a traditional Cantor (Siegele 1997, p. 22). The upshot was that, though the absolutists won their choice of candidate, they were 'unable to carry out the public and legal act of redefining the office'. Thus 'The post remained very much the traditional, conventional one of cantor, which was filled just this once by a Kapellmeister.' In other words, 'Bach's tenure in office was defined as an exception' (*ibid.* p. 25). This uneasy compromise was not helped by the fact that 'The rector . . ., as the Councillor responsible for the Thomasschule, . . . was aligned with the city party'; thus Rector and Cantor tended to pull in opposite directions (*ibid.*, p. 30).

Illustration 1. Street singing: engraving, Germany, eighteenth century. The singers are arranged in a 'half moon', as recommended for street singing by Printz (1678, p. 5)

> In dieser Schulen werden eine Anzahl *Discipuli* durch verschiedene reiche *Legata* mit Kost und Wohnung unterhalten, wovor sie die Kirchen-Music bestellen, auch die Leichen begleiten müssen, und wochentlich 3 mal, Sonntags, Mittwochs u. Freytags durch die Gassen singende gehen, da denn die Besitzer derer Häuser ihnen etwas zur *Sustentation*, wie in andern Städten üblich, reichen lassen.[2]

[2] *Das in gantz Europe berühmte, galante und sehens-würdige Königliche Leipzig* (1725); quoted in Knick 1963, p. 153.

Given that our interest lies predominantly with Bach's major church works and their performance, this usefully reminds us just how diverse and extensive were the school's musical activities. As the various school regulations (*Ordnungen*) show,[3] the pupils were much occupied with 'funerals, weddings and especially the evening street singing'[4] (see Illus. 1). These extra-liturgical duties afforded opportunities for the school and its pupils (under strict supervision) to earn a little money, while at the same time promoting Lutheran devotion in the daily life of the town.[5] Naturally enough, though, concerted music – our present concern – generally played no part in these activities.

The school differed in several other important respects from, for example, today's Anglican choir-schools, which typically support a single choir for a single church. As the 1733 *Ordnung* tells us, 'Our forebears have decreed that music be promoted at the Thomasschule and be taken care of by its resident pupils in *all* the town's churches' (emphasis added).[6] In Bach's time, the school accordingly provided not one but four separate choirs, serving five churches:

choir I   Nikolaikirche/Thomaskirche (in alternation with choir II)
choir II   Nikolaikirche/Thomaskirche (in alternation with choir I)
choir III   Neue Kirche
choir IV   Petrikirche and (on feast days) Johanniskirche

In addition, the Cantor had certain musical functions at the university church, the Paulinerkirche.[7]

In practice, Bach's energies were directed almost exclusively towards the musical activities of his first choir in the two principal churches, the Nikolaikirche and the Thomaskirche (see Illus. 2 and 3). To assist the Cantor, a prefect was assigned to each of the four choirs, 'because I cannot be in all the churches at the same time'.[8] The four prefects'

[3] Detailed and extensive regulations were issued in printed form in 1634, 1723 and 1733; they are reproduced in facsimile in a single volume, cited hereafter as *Ordnungen*.

[4] 'bei Begräbnissen, Hochzeiten und besonders bei den Abendkurrenden . . . vor den Häusern': *Ordnungen*, 1723 chap. 1 = Knick p. 147. See also (concerning funeral processions) *ibid*., chaps. 8, 12 = Knick pp. 147f, and Stiller 1984, p. 94.

[5] For accounts of the 'Kurrende' tradition, see Stemler 1765, and *MGG*, 'Kurrende' (entry by Franz Krautwurst). See also Kuhnau (1717) = Spitta 1889, p. 863. At Freiberg in 1744, Superintendent Christian Friedrich Wilisch wrote a 21-point 'Entwurf einer *Instruction*, wonach sich der Herr *Cantor* alhier mit seinen *Choralisten* und *Currendanern* zu achten hätte': Schünemann 1918–19, p. 195.

[6] 'Es haben unsere Vorfahren angeordnet, daß die Musik auf der *Thomas*-Schule getrieben, und von den dasigen *Alumnis* in allen Stadt-Kirchen besorget werden soll': *Ordnungen*, 1733 p. 22 (chap. 6 ¶1).

[7] The exact status of these was the cause of much vexation to Bach; see *BD I*, pp. 30–41, *BD II*, p. 155 = *NBR*, pp. 118—25.

[8] 'weil ich zugleich in allen Kirchen nicht seyn kan': *BD I*, p. 96 = *NBR*, p. 191.

Illustration 2. Nikolaikirche, Leipzig: engraving after J. E. Scheffler, Nuremberg, 1749

duties were broadly outlined by Rector Johann August Ernesti (in 1736)[9] as follows:

> For the prefects all have the same tasks, which are (1) to conduct the motets in church . . . (2) to lead the songs [i.e chorales] in church [and] (3) at New Year to conduct a group of singers in the house singing; the difference is purely that the First Prefect also does the latter at Michaelmas, and at weddings he has some motets sung at table, when he conducts; the second prefect, however, conducts the [concerted] music in the second choir on feast days.

> Denn die *Præfecti* haben alle gleiche Verrichtung, welche darinnen bestehet, daß sie 1) die *Motett*en in der Kirche *dirigi*ren . . . 2) die Lieder in der Kirche

---

[9] J. A. Ernesti was no relation to his predecessor but one, Rector Johann Heinrich Ernesti, who was over seventy years old at his death in 1729.

Illustration 3. Thomasschule and Thomaskirche, Leipzig: engraving by J. G. Krügner, Leipzig, 1723 (frontispiece to school Ordnung*). The left side of the school building was the Cantor's residence, the right side the Rector's*

anfangen 3) im Neuen Jahre eine *Canto*rey bey dem Singen in den Häusern *dirigi*ren; der Unterschied bestehet blos darinnen, daß der erste *Præfectus* das letztere auch in der *Michaëlis* Meße thut, und auf Hochzeiten bey Tische einige *Motette*n singen läßt, dabey er *dirigi*rt; der andere *Præfectus* aber, die *Music* im andern Chor an Festtagen *dirigi*rt . . .[10]

The First Prefect, moreover, had to be capable of standing in for the Cantor himself as occasion demanded.[11] Each of the churches (except the Petrikirche) also had its own organist (see Table 1).

Table 1.   Leipzig organists in Bach's time

Nikolaikirche	1721–9	Johann Gottlieb Görner
	1729–	Johann Schneider (†1788)
Thomaskirche	1701–1729	Christian Gräbner (†1729)
	1729–	Johann Gottlieb Görner (†1778)
Neue Kirche	1720–9	Georg Balthasar Schott (†1736)
	1729–	Carl Gotthelf Gerlach (†1761)
Petrikirche		[no organ until 1799]
Johanniskirche	1695–1731	Johann Michael Steinert (†1731)
	1731–47	Johann Gottlieb Reinicke
	1747–	Johann Georg Hille (†1766)
Paulinerkirche	1721–	Johann Christian Thiele (†1773)

For each of the four choirs, the school supplied not only sopranos (as we might expect) but also altos, tenors and basses. Most of the 55 or so *alumni* (resident pupils)[12] were much older than in today's Anglican choir-schools (where boys usually start at ages 8–10 and finish by about 14): Bach's pupils

---

[10] *BD II*, p. 274 = *NBR*, pp. 183f. See also *BD I*, pp. 35, 37, 83, 85, 88, 90, 95, 103; *BD II*, pp. 269, 272f, 275 = *NBR*, pp. 120, 122, 173, 177, 180ff, 185, 190; *Ordnungen*, 1723 chap. 14 = Knick, p. 148.

[11] *BD I*, p. 83, and Wollny 1997, p. 40 = *NBR*, pp. 173, 239f. It is hardly surprising that Bach was infuriated when in 1736 the new young Rector (J. A. Ernesti) took it upon himself to promote a musically 'unproficient' (Bach variously uses the words *untüchtig, nicht geschickt, Ungeschicklichkeit* and *incapacité*: see *BD I*, pp. 85, 87f, 95 = *NBR*, pp. 174ff, 190) senior pupil to the position of First Prefect. The outcome was the unseemly spectacle of Bach ejecting the unfortunate prefect from the choir loft not once but twice. 'As after lunch the two prefects had now each gone once again to the places assigned to them by me [Rector Ernesti], he [the Cantor] again chased Krause out of the choir-loft with much shouting and uproar' ('Da nun die beiden *Praefecti* nach Mittage wiederum jeder an den ihn von mir angewiesenen Orth gegangen waren, hat er [der *Cantor*] den Krausen wieder mit großen Schreyen u. Lermen von dem Chor geiagt'): *BD II*, p. 272 = *NBR*, pp. 180f.

[12] For the non-boarders (*externi*), see below, pp. 104f.

were already 13 or 14 when they were admitted (as sopranos and altos),[13] and they might remain at the school for at least six years and sometimes for as many as ten.[14] (When the 'unproficient' Gottfried Theodor Krause was appointed First Prefect in 1736, he was 22 years old.[15]) Voices also tended to break significantly later than today – at over 17, on average.[16] Bach himself, for example, was already 15 when he arrived in Lüneburg to take up a place as a soprano in the *Mettenchor* of the Michaeliskloster; his voice broke 'some time later'.[17] Martin Heinrich Fuhrmann remarks (1706) that the usual age at which an alto became a tenor was over 18,[18] and Christian Friedrich Schemelli, whom Bach decribes as a soprano, was already 17 (or perhaps 18) when he entered the Thomasschule in 1731.[19] Consequently, good, mature tenor and bass voices must often have been in short supply at the school (see below, p. 110).

Lastly – and perhaps most surprisingly – in concerted music several of the most able pupils took part not as singers but as instrumentalists (string-players):

> because the second violin has mostly had to be taken by pupils, and the viola, violoncello and violone always so . . .

> da die 2de *Violin* meistens, die *Viola, Violoncello* und *Violon* aber allezeit . . . mit Schülern habe bestellen müßen . . . (*Entwurff*, ¶14)

In the 1730s Maximilian Nagel, for example, apparently 'never did anything [as First Prefect] other than play the violin'.[20]

---

[13] See Appendix 2, below, and Richter 1907, p. 50; see also Butt 1994, pp. 31, 197.

[14] See Richter 1907, pp. 43f, 55.

[15] *BD I*, p. 85 = *NBR*, p. 174; *BD I*, p. 65.

[16] See Daw 1973, p. 14 (although Daw's methodology is questionable, his conclusions seem correct: see below).

[17] 'einige Zeit später': *BD II*, pp. 8f = *NBR*, p. 37; and *BD III*, p. 82 = *NBR*, p. 299. Johann Friedrich Doles junior is known to have sung as a soprano when approaching 17 (Schulze 1991, p. 25).

[18] Fuhrmann 1706, p. 36. Johann Friedrich Agricola writes that a male voice changes – or perhaps begins to change – at about age 13 ('daß . . ., ohngefähr um das vierzehnte Lebensjahr, die hohe Stimme sich in eine tiefere verwandelt'): Agricola 1757, p. 28 = Baird, p. 72.

[19] *BD I*, p. 145 = *NBR*, p. 208, where Schemelli's age is taken to be 'an explicit reference to his [Bach's] use of falsetto singers'. In France voices ordinarily broke between the ages of 15 and 20, according to Bénigne de Bacilly (1668, pp. 36, 81), and one writer advises parents to send their sons to Germany 'to retard the age of puberty by the rigours of the climate' (A. M. de Mirampole, *c.*1700, cited Daw 1973, p. 14).

[20] 'Der Vorige *Præfectus* Nagel hat nie was anders gethan, als die *Violine* gestrichen': memorandum by the Rector, J. A. Ernesti, 13 September 1736, *BD II*, p. 275 = *NBR*, p. 184; see also *BD III*, p. 118.

Illustration 4. Violinist with horn,
Hamburg, 1719: (detail of Illus. 21)

This practice was commonplace. Just as instrumentalists were often proficient on more than one instrument[21] – see Illus. 4 – so singers (including schoolboys) were often capable of serving as instrumentalists:[22]

- At Arnstadt, *c.*1689, all but two of the 11 singers doubled as string-players.[23]
- Five *Kapellknaben* at the Württemberg court in 1699 were said to be capable of singing and playing at least one instrument.[24]
- At Eisenach (*c.*1708) Georg Philipp Telemann was ordered 'to assign the necessary singers [to the new *Kapelle*], who could also be used as violinists'.[25]
- The four named singers of Leipzig's collegium musicum (in the late 1700s) 'also graced' its 'instrumental choir' (see below, p. 136)
- At Lüneburg all 20 of the Cantor's pupils were required to be 'musically proficient, both in singing and in playing.'[26]
- Johann Christoph Altnickol 'assisted' in Bach's first choir (1745–7) as both string-player and singer (see below, p. 109, and Table 7, where others who may have doubled are also listed).

[21] In order to become an assistant town piper Carl Friedrich Pfaffe was examined on 'violin, oboe, flute, trumpet, horn and . . . bass instruments': *BD I*, p. 147 = *NBR*, p. 220. See also *BD I*, p. 48 = *NBR*, p. 127, and *BD II*, pp. 407, 452. See also below, pp. 109f.
[22] For a splendid example of such versatility from Hanover in 1663, see Spitta 1889, i, p. 201 n. 37.
[23] Schiffner 1987, esp. p. 47; cf. below, p. 41. Similarly, two of Pfleger's three adult singers at Güstrow in the 1660s doubled as instrumentalists (see below, pp. 111f).
[24] Sittard 1890–1, i, pp. 68f.
[25] 'benöthigte Sänger zu verschreiben, die aber auch als Violinisten gebraucht werden könnten': Telemann [II], p. 203.
[26] 'Mein gantzer Schüler-Chor, welcher aus einigen 20. bestehet, muß musikalisch seyn, zugleich im Singen und Spielen': Johann Conrad Dreyer, in Mattheson 1740, p. 57.

- Five of the six singers listed as members (1746–8) of the 'große *Concert-Gesellschafft*' in Leipzig doubled as string-players.[27]
- One of Bach's prefects, Johann Nathanael Bammler, 'applied himself well both *vocaliter* and *instrumentaliter*' for ten years up to 1749.[28]

Instrumental tuition of course plays an important part in the musical education offered by many present-day choir-schools, although – since liturgical services nowadays routinely require a vocal choir but not an instrumental ensemble – only rarely would a pupil now be called on to play in a church service (unless as organist). By contrast, it was understood

> how the main intention in admitting and maintaining chapel boys is the [concerted] music: that we be trained and rendered capable of performing both as vocalists and as instrumentalists . . .

> wie aber das Hauptabsehen, warumb Cappellknaben auffgenommen und unterhalten werden, die Music ist, dass wir sowol *vocaliter*, als *instrumentaliter* dabey zu gebrauchen unterrichtet und fähig gemacht werden.[29]

The 'undertaking' which Bach gave in 1723 as the Thomasschule's new Cantor –

> Diligently [to] instruct the boys not only in vocal but also in instrumental music, so that the churches may not be put to unnecessary expense . . .

> Damit die Kirchen nicht mit unnöthigen Unkosten beleget werden mögen, die Knaben nicht allein in der *Vocal-* sondern auch in der *Instrumental-Music* fleißig unterweisen . . .[30]

– was entirely conventional. That is, 'unnecessary expense' in hiring additional instrumentalists could be avoided if some pupils were sufficiently skilled to play in concerted works. This was particularly relevant in the case of any musical boy whose voice had not yet settled after puberty:[31]

> because their [the school's youths'] voices also always break, and for many a year after losing their good treble [voice] they remain quite mute . . .

> weil sie [der Schul Jugend] auch immer die Stimme *mutir*et, und manche jahre nach dem verlohrnen guten *Discant* ganz stum bleibet . . .[32]

---

[27] See Illus. 17, p. 120 below, and see Schering 1941, p. 264.

[28] Wollny 1997, p. 38 = *NBR*, p. 239.

[29] From a document written by J. S. Kusser, relating to his duties as Capellmeister at the Württemberg court in 1700: Scholz 1911, p. 234.

[30] *BD I*, p. 177: see below, Appendix 1, document 2, ¶6.

[31] Agricola observes that 'around the time when the voice begins to change, hoarseness generally sets in, which often lasts half a year or even longer' ('um die Zeit da die Stimme verändert werden soll, meistentheils eine Heiserkeit einzustellen pflegt, welche öfters ein halbes Jahr und noch länger dauert'): Agricola 1757, p. 29 (= Baird 1995, p. 72).

[32] Kuhnau (1709), ¶12: Knick 1963, p. 126.

In practice, the focus of Bach's energies in Leipzig was always on his first choir, and on his own concerted music. And in this repertoire, where instruments and voices vie with one another in importance, a substantial portion of the choir did not sing at all but – contrary to our expectations – were put to use as instrumentalists.

3

Repertoires

The four choirs under Bach's supervision at Leipzig were responsible for several distinct categories of vocal music:

repertoire	choir I	choir II	choir III	choir IV
Bach's concerted works (with large instrumental ensemble)	✓	—	—	—
simple concerted works (with some instruments)	—	✓	—	—
motets (many of them *a8*)	✓	✓	✓	—
chorales (*a4*) and unison chant	✓	✓	✓	✓

As Bach explains to the Town Council, the pupils 'have partly to perform [concerted] music, partly to sing motets, and partly to sing chorales'.[1]

Each of the terms Bach uses – '*musiciren*', '*motetten*' etc. – refers to a distinct category of repertoire; and each category had specific functions in specific contexts, ranging from everyday street singing to liturgical celebrations of the year's major feasts in the town's principal churches. Consequently, each repertoire had its own hierarchical connotations, from humble unadorned chorale-singing at one extreme to the performance of sophisticated newly composed *Kirchenstücke* involving considerable instrumental display.[2] Thus, at Arnstadt, for example, the young Bach is said (in 1703) to have claimed – perhaps peevishly – that 'he was appointed only for chorales, not concerted music',[3] while as late as 1736, as Cantor in Leipzig, he was

---

[1] 'theils *musiciren*, theils *motetten* und theils *Chorale* singen müßen': *Entwurff*, ¶7.

[2] In 1708 Cantor Johann Samuel Beyer of Freiberg was insistent (for personal financial reasons) that music at weddings with thirty or more guests 'zu Tische' (at table) should always be performed *figuraliter*, but otherwise *choraliter*: Schünemann 1918–19, p. 191.

[3] 'er sey nur auff *Choral* nicht aber *musicali*sche stücke bestellet': *BD II*, pp. 17, 20 = *NBR*, pp. 45, 46.

chided by Rector J. A. Ernesti for believing 'that it was beneath his dignity to direct [the music] at a nuptial mass where only chorales were to be performed'.[4]

These various repertoires almost inevitably made quite diverse musical and technical demands. While all of the Thomasschule boys – perhaps even those Bach characterized as 'unproficient' (see below, p. 101) – presumably could sing a straightforward chorale tune in some fashion,[5] only the best were ever entrusted with Bach's own complex music. The four choirs were thus carefully graded, and their very different musical duties were carefully defined.[6]

At the low end of the spectrum, the fourth choir (which sang principally at the Petrikirche and, on feast days only, at the Johanniskirche) could consist of those 'who do not understand music at all but, rather, can just barely sing a chorale'.[7]

The third choir served the Neue Kirche,

> where the pupils have to sing nothing apart from motets and chorales, and have nothing to do with other concerted music . . .

> als woselbst die Schüler weiter nichts als Motetten und *Choræle* zu singen, mit anderer *Concert Musique* aber nichts zu thun haben . . . (Bach, 1736)[8]

The 'other concerted music' heard there – but only on high feasts and during the annual Fair – was supplied by an entirely separate musical body, the collegium musicum founded in 1702 by Telemann,[9] and was 'taken care of' ('besorget') by the Neue Kirche's own organist.[10]

The first and second choirs alternated between the town's two principal churches, the Nikolaikirche and the Thomaskirche (see Illus. 5 and 6), and performed concerted pieces in addition to chorales and motets (see Table 2). Only on feast days did the second choir perform concerted music.[11] More important, the works chosen for it, which were not by Bach, had to be rela-

---

[4] 'daß es ihm unanständig sey, bey einer Braut-Meß zu *dirigi*ren, wo nur *Choral musici*rt werden soll': *BD II*, p. 273 = *NBR*, p. 181.

[5] See Appendix 2, document 2, ¶5.

[6] Cf. the distinctions drawn by, for example, Pfleger and Kuhnau between the required skills of concertists and ripienists: see below, pp. 112 and 114.

[7] 'so keine *music* verstehen, sondern nur nothdörfftig einen *Choral* singen können': *Entwurff*, ¶7. Their chorale singing was nevertheless presumably *a4*, as the choir was meant (in 1729) to comprise two each of soprano, alto, tenor and bass: *BD I*, p. 250 = *NBR*, p. 142.

[8] *BD I*, pp. 87f = *NBR*, p. 175.

[9] See the reminiscences of G. H. Stölzel, quoted Mattheson 1740, p. 118; see also below, p. 136.

[10] *BD I*, p. 88.

[11] *Entwurff*, ¶14, and *BD I*, p. 88 = *NBR*, p. 176 (quoted below). See also Stiller 1984, pp. 74–95.

Table 2.   Distribution of duties between choirs I and II

		choir I	*choir II*
SUNDAYS	(a.m.)	motet & cantata (*church A*)	motet (*church B*)
	(p.m.)	—	—
FEAST DAYS	(a.m.)	motet & cantata (*church A*)	motet & simple cantata (*church B*)
	(p.m.)	motet & cantata (*church B*)	motet & simple cantata (*church A*)

church A and *church B* = the two principal churches, in alternation

---

tively simple.[12] Bach's own elaborate works thus remained the exclusive province of his élite first choir, which accordingly needed the best musicians:

> above all, because the musical church pieces [i.e. cantatas] which are done in the first choir, and which are mostly of my own composition, are incomparably harder and more intricate than those which are performed in the second choir – and then only on feast days, when I am principally obliged to choose the same [i.e. the concerted music] according to the capabilities of those who are to execute it.

> zumahlen die *musicali*schen Kirchen Stücke so im ersteren Chore gemachet werden, u. meistens von meiner *composition* sind, ohngleich schwerer und *intricat*er sind, weder die, so im anderen [i.e. zweiten] *Chore* und zwar nur auf die FestTage *musicir*et werden, als wo ich mich im *choisir*en selbiger nach der *capacitè* derer, so es *executir*en sollen, hauptsächlig richten muß. (Bach, 1736)[13]

(Whatever the limitations and difficulties of his job, Bach claims that he selects music – at least for his second choir – primarily '*according to* the capabilities' of the available performers, rather than, as the received Romantic notion would have it, being forced by circumstance to tolerate weekly travesties of music *beyond* their grasp.[14])

---

[12] Disappointingly little is known about this repertoire.

[13] *BD I*, p. 88 = *NBR*, p. 176.

[14] Cf. Kuhnau (1709), ¶11 = Knick 1963, p. 126. Similarly, Kuhnau points out that 'for better or worse, one . . . has to organize the musical material according to the inferior capabilities of the individuals [*subjecta*]' ('man . . . die *Musicalien* nach der schlechten *Capacität* der *Subjectorum* schlecht genug einzurichten hat'). Newer music tended to be more demanding, and in 1733 Cantor Simon Vatke of Osnabrück writes: 'For, in addition, the music of today has risen to such perfection and pre-eminence that a young person could sooner be brought to the point where he should be able on his own to construct a Latin or even a Greek oration than sing a fine piece of music straight off' ('Da über das die Musik heutiges Tages zu der Vollkommenheit und Hoheit gestiegen, daß ein junger Mensch ehender so weit könnte gebracht werden, daß er proprio ausu eine Lateinische, ja wohl gar Griechische Oration verfertigen solle, als ein vollkommen gutes Musicalisch Stück so gleich weg singen'): Bösken 1937, p. 178.

Illustration 5. West galleries, Nikolaikirche, Leipzig: water-colour by C.B. Schwarz, c. 1785

Even more critical for our present purpose than the distinction between these two types of concerted music is the difference between concerted works (especially Bach's own) and motets. It must be emphasized that the broad motet repertoire shared by the Thomasschule's first, second and third choirs comprised *not* Bach's own elaborate motets but much older and simpler compositions, generally in Latin and often for double choir (probably with organ when sung in church).[15] It was almost certainly the fundamental

[15] 'If J. S. Bach used the term "motet" in written documents in only one of its eighteenth-century senses [that is, to refer to pieces in Latin of the type just described], in musical sources he used it in the others' (Melamed 1995, p. 21).

Illustration 6.　West galleries, Thomaskirche, Leipzig: conjectural plan by A. Schering (Schering 1936)

distinction between 'exclusive' new concerted music, on the one hand, and chorale or *stile antico* idioms, on the other, that Christoph Graupner had in mind when he commended Bach to Leipzig's Town Council as 'expert in church works and *Capella* pieces'.[16]

In 1729 the school recorded a payment of 12 thaler

> To Cantor Bach for a *Florilegium Portense* which the pupils need in the churches and for musical performance . . .

[16] 'erfahren in Kirchensachen und Capell-Stücken': letter from Graupner (4 May 1723) confirming that he was no longer a candidate for the office of Cantor in Leipzig: *BD II*, p. 98 (cf. *NBR*, p. 103).

Dem Herrn *Cantori* Bachen vor ein *Florileg: Portense* welches die Schüler in denen Kirchen und zur *Music* brauchen . . .[17]

Already more than a century old, Erhard Bodenschatz's popular anthology *Florilegium Portense* (i, 1603/1618; ii, 1621) contains works in four to eight parts (mostly the latter); Handl, Lassus and German composers such as H. Praetorius predominate in the first part, and Italians including Croce, G. Gabrieli, Marenzio and Viadana in the second.[18] Illus. 7 shows the first page of the collection in one of the partbooks, and Ex. 1 gives the opening of Jacob Handl's *Ecce quomodo moritur justus*,[19] which in Leipzig was sung at Vespers on Good Friday, following the conclusion of the Passion setting.[20] A more typical double-choir work is Handl's setting of *Beatus vir*, which was sung at weddings: see Ex. 2 (p. 26).

Collections of this sort had been 'the bread and butter of the cantor's art throughout the seventeenth century'[21] and remained so for much of the eighteenth. At Leipzig the *Florilegium* seems to have been the principal source of motets and as such must have been in constant use.[22] (An inventory drawn up by Johann Schelle at the Thomaskirche in 1678 includes 'Florilegium Portense 9 Stück' (i.e. one complete set),[23] and the copies later bought by Bach were evidently still in use as late as 1770.[24]) The pieces chosen probably formed a limited and unvarying repertoire:

> In addition, a *Chorstück* [i.e. motet] can be repeated by the choir more than ten times in a week, and therefore more than a hundred times in a quarter of a year, whereas the majority of *Kirchenstücke*, and especially those for feast days, can be done in total just once in each church . . .

> Es kömmt hinzu, daß ein Chorstück kann in einer Woche im Chor mehr als Zehnmal, und also in einem ¼Jahr mehr als 100 mal repetirt werden, dahingegen die meisten Kirchen, sonderlich Feststücke im gantzen nur einmal in jeder Kirche kann gemacht werden . . .[25]

Friedrich Erhard Niedt (*c*.1708) was one of those who expressed disdain for this old-fashioned repertoire:

---

[17] *BD II*, p. 199; see also *ibid*., p. 294.

[18] For a complete list of contents, see *Grove 1*, 'Bodenschatz'.

[19] Also found, with German text, in the *Neu Leipziger Gesangbuch* (1682) and the *Privilegirte Ordentliche und Vermehrte Dreßdnische Gesangbuch* (1725); see Melamed 1995, pp. 143f.

[20] Butt 1997, p. 99; see also *BD II*, p. 141 = *NBR*, p. 115, and Stiller 1984, p. 60. The work was also sung annually at one of the memorial services for the Rettenbach family; see *BD II*, p. 131 = *NBR*, p. 111.

[21] Webber 1996, p. 42.

[22] See Schering 1936, pp. 121–9 (chap. 27, 'Das Motettensingen und das Florilegium portense').

[23] Richter 1907, p. 38.

[24] *BD II*, p. 199; see also *ibid*., p. 133.

[25] Bösken 1937, p. 179.

Illustration 7. E. Bodenschatz, Florilegium Portense *(Leipzig, 1618): first page of the* Discantus partbook, *showing Hans Leo Hassler,* Pater noster

The explanation of motets I leave to Thuringian peasants, who retain things of that sort by Hammerschmidt all their life long.

Die Explication über die Moteten überlasse ich denen Thüringischen Bauern/ als welche solche von dem Hammerschmid Zeit ihres Leben . . . behalten werden.[26]

A generation later, however, Johann Adolf Scheibe hotly defended 'this . . . most splendid ornament of the church service'[27] and warned against the

[26] Niedt 1717, p. 34.
[27] 'diese . . . so prächtige Zierde des Gottesdienstes': Scheibe 1745, p. 185 (first published 1737).

Ex. 1. J. Handl, *Ecce quomodo moritur justus* (part 1), from *Florilegium Portense* (1603)

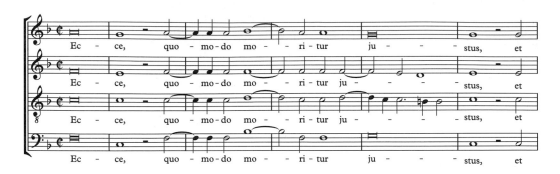

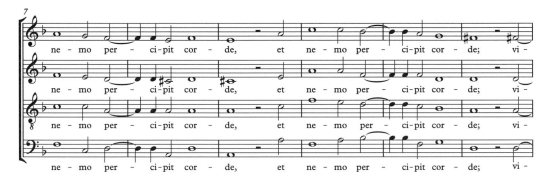

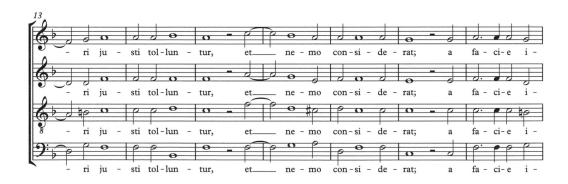

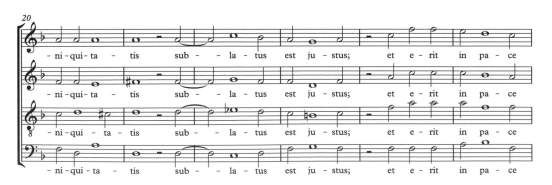

patronizing attitudes of many 'accomplished' ('geschickte') singers towards motet performance.[28]

The motet repertoire was much less demanding technically than most concerted music, and this clear distinction formed the basis of Bach's categorization of his singers; the twenty 'not yet usable' ('noch nicht zu gebrauchende') pupils listed at the end of his *Entwurff* were

> motet singers, who first have still to perfect themselves further, so that in time they can be used for figural [i.e. more elaborate] music . . .

> *Motetten* Singer, so sich noch erstlich mehr *perfectioniren* müßen, üm mit der Zeit zur *Figural Music* gebrauchet werden zu können . . . (*Entwurff*, ¶¶20)

Bach's overwhelming concern was for concerted music. At Leipzig responsibility for directing motets – even in the first choir – customarily lay with the prefect,[29] whereas only a cantor would normally have responsibility for

> full-voiced church pieces [i.e. cantatas] which are as hard again, because of the artifice of the writing, and are much more extensive because of the musical instruments needed for them; how much more [readily] can choir pieces [?motets], which are always easier, be brought off by a prefect who may be on duty in choir.

> vollstimmige Kirchenstücke . . ., die doch wegen der künstlichen Composition noch mal so schwer, auch wegen der musikalischen Instrumenta, so dabey gebraucht werden, viel weitläufiger sind; wie vielmehr kann ein Praefectus, wenn er sein Devoir thun will im Chor ein Chorstück, welche alleweil leichter sind, zu Wegne bringen.[30]

Whatever his own attitude towards this conservative motet repertoire, Bach took care to emphasize that the demands of his own concerted music were of a very different order.

---

[28] *Ibid.* See also Bösken 1937, p. 185 (Osnabrück's *Chorordnung* of 1731, chap. 2 ¶7), and Agricola 1757, p. 148 = Baird 1995, pp. 169f.

[29] See *BD I*, pp. 35, 37 = *NBR*, pp. 120, 122; *BD I*, p. 85 = *NBR*, p. 174; *BD I*, p. 90 = *NBR*, p 182; *BD II*, pp. 274f = *NBR*, pp. 183f; Wollny 1997, p. 40 = *NBR*, p. 239.

[30] Letter to the Osnabrück Town Council (1733) from Cantor Simon Vatke: Bösken 1937, p.179.

Ex. 2. J. Handl, *Beatus vir* (opening), from *Florilegium Portense* (1603)

4

Concertists and ripienists

Traditional motet repertoire and new concerted works clearly required very different levels of musical skill. They also demanded essentially different types of vocal choir.

Motets certainly lent themselves to – even if they did not necessarily demand – performance by several voices per part.[1] 'For motets there must be as many again' as in concerted music, wrote Thomas Selle (1642).[2] Wolfgang Caspar Printz (1678: see below, p. 33) and Johann Adolph Scheibe (1737)[3] confirm the point, each seeming to imply a contrast with the requirements of concerted music.

---

[1] As Bach himself clearly suggests, motets can perfectly well be sung by single voices; even if fewer than 12 singers are available, he tells us, 'at least a two-choir motet can be sung' ('wenigstens eine 2 *Chörig*te *Motette* gesungen werden kan'): *Entwurff*, ¶8. See also below, p. 95. (A full 12 singers could not in any case double *all* the parts, while even a total of 16 would allow a maximum of only two per part – or, alternatively, one choir of single voices and one with three singers per part.)

[2] 'Zu Muteten müssen derer noch einmal so viel sein': quoted Krüger 1933, p. 69. For concerted music-making ('Zu einer Concertat-Musik') Selle wanted a larger than usual group of 10 singers (4s, 2A, 2T, 2B), specifically 'because the churches in Hamburg are spacious and large, and the whole power of music depends on the text' ('weil die Kirchen in Hamburg weitläuftig und gross sein, und die ganze Kraft der Musik in dem Text beruht'); Krüger 1933, pp. 68f.

[3] 'And therefore one should also, wherever possible, use a very strong contingent of singers for motets; otherwise the expression will nevertheless remain weak and feeble, even though the composer has taken great trouble to prevent this' ('Und man muß dahero auch die Motetten, wo es nur möglich ist, sehr stark von Sängern besetzen, sonst wird der Ausdruck dennoch schwach und matt bleiben, wenn schon der Componist alle Mühe angewendet hat, dieses zu verhindern'); 'each voice part must also have several people on it' ('es muß auch jedwede Stimme mehr verschiedenemal besetzet seyn'): Scheibe 1745, pp. 182, 185.

One might be tempted to conclude from this simply that a motet choir could be – and generally was – larger than a 'cantata' choir. But there is a much more fundamental difference.

For *Kirchenstücke* (i.e. cantatas), Bach tells us, 'the vocalists must be divided . . . into two sorts, viz. concertists and ripienists'.[4] This simple and conventional distinction introduces a principle that is fundamental to any understanding of how concerted music of Bach's time works. Modern preconceptions may well tempt us to equate the vocal ripienist with today's choral singer, and the concertist with the soloist – someone who sings solo movements and perhaps occasional solo passages within choral movements but who is essentially quite independent of the 'choir'. However, in Lutheran choirs from the time of Michael Praetorius – and until well after Bach's death – concertists' responsibilities embraced both solo *and ensemble* (i.e. choral) singing equally: concertists were thus 'the foundation of the whole *concerto*', as Praetorius puts it.[5] The role of ripienists, who were often dispensable, was merely to *reinforce* – and not to replace – the concertists at certain points.

> For *concerti* and *cantiones* such as these can be performed completely with just these [concertato] voice parts alone, without adding other vocal capellas or instruments (especially as they are not available everywhere). Therefore one must select the best *cantores* and singers for these voice parts . . .

> Denn solche *Concert* und *Cantiones* mit denselben [*Concertat*-]Stimmen gantz allein/ ohne zuthun der andern *Vocal*-Capellen oder Instrumenten (bevorab weil die nicht allenthalben vorhanden) . . . volnkömmlich *musicirt* werden können. Darumb muß man zu diesen Stimmen die besten *Cantores* und Sänger außlesen . . .[6]

The practices Praetorius and others so enthusiastically adopted were, of course, Italian in origin, and, while it is clearly beyond the scope of the present book to attempt a comprehensive account of this background, a brief look at four Venetian publications will help pinpoint some abiding performance principles of concerted vocal music:

(1) Giovanni Croce, *Sacre cantilene concertate a tre, a cinque et sei voci, con i suoi ripieni a quattro voci* (Venice, 1610)[7]

---

[4] 'müßen die *Vocali*sten . . . in 2erley *Sorten* eingetheilet werden, als: *Concerti*sten und *Ripieni*sten' (*Entwurff*, ¶3).

[5] 'des gantzen Concerts Fundament': Praetorius 1619, p. 196.

[6] *Ibid.*, p. 196; see also *ibid.*, pp. 126f [*recte* 106f], etc.

[7] A note 'to the gentle reader' ('A virtuosi lettori') at the end of each partbook reads: 'Then there are the four-part ripieno parts to all of the said *Cantilene*: these ripieno parts may be used again in two or three choirs as wished, because they create a very beautiful and elegant *concerto*' ('Vi è poi li Ripieni à Quattro à tutte le dette Cantilene: quali Ripieni si possono replicare in due, & tre Chori, come si voranno, perche fanno vaghissimo, & soauissimo Concerto').

(2) Francesco Usper, *Salmi vespertini . . . parte concertati al'vso moderno, & parte alla breue* (Venice, 1627)
Seven of the 22 items are variously labelled (and variously spelt):
'Alla Breue'
'da Capella' (×2)
'Alla Breue da Capella' (×2)
'da Capella alla Breue'
'da Capella si placet'
The significance of these indications to the performer is outlined in an 'Auertimento sopra li Salmi notati Alla Breue':

> If the singer intends to sing the present psalms *alla semibreve* – that is, *alla battuta ordinaria* – he will be well satisfied; but take note that they work both more harmoniously and more melodiously if they are sung *alla breve* with the voices doubled and tripled, together with proportionate instruments on each part, as is done in the most famous city of Venice.[8]

(3) Lorenzo Calvi, *Quarta Raccolta de Sacri Canti* (Venice, 1629)
A note at the end of the 'Basso per l'organo', relating to a five-part piece by Monteverdi included in the collection, reads:

> This vocal piece *Exultent caeli* can be doubled, that is, copied out again, and played by instruments and sung at the same time by voices; this way it will make a good body of sound. The remainder, though, are to be sung as written.[9]

(4) Claudio Monteverdi, *Selva morale e spirituale* (Venice, 1640/1)
The following rubrics are found:
'a 3 voci con 5 altre ne' ripieni'
'a 5 voci concertato con due Violini et un choro a quattro voci qual potrasi e cantare e sonare con quattro Viole o Tromboni et anco lasciare se acadesse il bisogno' ('. . . a four-part choir which can be sung and played by four *viole* or trombones, or omitted as necessary')
'concertata/o' (×9)

---

[8] 'Potrà benissimo compiacersi il Cantore intendente di cantar i presenti Salmi alla Semi-breue, cioè, alla battuta ordinaria; ma auuerta però, che riusciranno e più armoniosi, e più melodici se saranno cantati alla Breue con duplicate, e triplicate voci con i suoi proportionati Stromenti sopra ogni parte, come s'vsa nell'inclita Città di Venetia.'
[9] 'Questa Cantada di Exultent caeli si puol [*sic*] radoppiare, cioè ricopiarla, & farla sonare da gli Istromenti, & cantare insieme con le voci, acciò faccia un bel corpo di Musica, il rimanente poi, và cantato nel modo che stà scritto.' The piece is published in Monteverdi, *12 composizioni vocali profane e sacre (inedite)*, ed. W. Osthoff (Milan, 1958; R/1966), pp. 39–44, and in *Tutte le opere di Claudio Monteverdi*, ed. G. F. Malipiero, 'Supplemento' (Venice, 1966; R/Vienna, n.d.), pp. 15–21.

> 'a 5 voci qual si può cantare ridoppiato et forte o come piacerà' ('. . .
> which can be sung with the parts doubled and loudly, or as you
> please')
> 'da Capella' (×3)
> 'in genere da Capella'

From these sources alone we learn that works labelled 'alla breve'/'da
capella' are different in kind from those designated 'concertato' (nos. 2 and
4 above) and that, implicitly, they require a different mode of performance.
In the former, two or three voices per part plus instruments (as in Venice)
may be desirable (2). In concerted music, on the other hand, solo voices
form the basic medium; performing the piece 'as written' means without
additional voices or instruments (3), and any 'doubling' – meaning literally
two voices per part (2) – implies the need for additional parts to be copied
out (3). Occasional parts for *ripieni* (1, 4) have a wholly subsidiary role and
may well be optional (4). In exceptional cases these fundamental distinctions do not apply – hence Calvi's note (3) and the designations 'da Capella
si placet' (2) and 'with the parts doubled and loudly, or as you please' (4).

It has been observed that 'performing polyphony with single voices (concertists), occasionally and often selectively supported by a second rank of
(single) voices or instruments (ripienists), . . . has quietly become something
of a norm in recent recordings of German sacred music from the 17th century'.[10] Scholars too have begun to acknowledge that in Lutheran Germany
'Concertato sacred music was written in essence for solo voices'[11] and that
'the new German church concerto . . . was essentially music for skilled
soloists',[12] sometimes with optional extra voices for simpler or fuller sections:

> The author has expanded the small few-voiced concertos, which to some ears
> may sound all too bare in large churches, with string and vocal capellas, so
> that they make a fuller impression and so that the instrumental musicians (of
> whom there are quite a number here in Hamburg), as well as the other singers,
> might also have something to do.

> Die kleinen Concerten mit wenig stimmen, die in etlichen Ohren in grossen
> Kirchen allzu bloß klingen wollen, hat der Autor vermehret mit Capellis
> fidiciniis und Vocalibus, damit sie desto völliger hereintreten u. die Musici
> Instrumentales, deren hier in Hamburg eine Zimbliche anZahl, neben den
> übrigen Vocalisten auch mögen zu thun haben. (Selle, 1663)[13]

Subsequent generations of German composers, as represented for example in the Düben and Bokemeyer collections, adopted the very same principles:

[10] Van Tassel 1999, p. 148.
[11] Webber 1996, p. 176.
[12] Butt 1994, p. 110.
[13] Thomas Selle, MS *Opera Omnia* (1663), quoted Webber 1996, p. 103.

- Crato Bütner (1616–79), *Frohlocket mit Händen* – 'A 8 voci con li stromenti e 6 capella'
- Johann Sebastiani (1622–83), *Ad sacram mensam* – ssatb 'con la Capella se piace a 5'
- Joachim Gerstenbüttel (*c*.1650–1721), *Dazu ist erschienen der Sohn Gottes* – 'for 10 or 15 or more' ('a 10 l. 15 l. plur')
- Johann Förtsch (1652–1732), *Ich vergeße was dahinten ist* – 'à 10, 15 et 20', including ssatb voices 'in Concerto' and a further (optional) ssatb group 'pro Ripieno'[14]

(For an explanation of formulas such as 'à 10, 15 et 20', see below, p. 36.) Not least, Dieterich Buxtehude (*c*.1637–1707) 'intended the majority of his works for four voices not for chorus but for an ensemble of soloists', i.e. for a chorus of concertists (without ripienists).[15]

Concerted music and 'da capella' writing continued to imply differing performing forces, as this observation on breathing suggests:

> When several . . . sing one voice part, as customarily happens in full-voiced motets or *Capella* parts, they should start, proceed and stop together, but not take breaths together.

> Wann . . . etliche eine Stimme singen/ wie in Vollstimmigen *Motet*ten oder Capell-Stimmen zu geschehen pfleget/ sollen sie zugleich anfangen/ fortgehen/ und aufhören/ nicht aber zugleich Athem holen.[16]

And within one and the same piece these distinctions continued to hold good. Johann Mattheson, early in the new century, differentiates in the clearest terms between the two types of vocal choir commonly employed in pieces written for three or four 'choirs':[17] one type '– with its own instrumental support – called *Capella*',[18] the other

---

[14] See Webber 1996, pp. 104f, 177.

[15] This is the 'inescapable' conclusion reached by Kerala Snyder (1987, p. 366). She also points out that Buxtehude – an organist and not a cantor – 'did not normally have a choir [of multiple voices] at his disposal'. This leads Smithers – who acknowledges that 'Buxtehude's cantatas are the most famous and very possibly the best seventeenth-century German works of this genre of Lutheran church music' – to query whether they are necessarily 'the most representative' (Smithers 1997, pp. 15f). However 'representative' or otherwise they may be, these are nevertheless conspicuous examples of a genre widely believed to be a modern invention – 'choral' concerted works intended for one voice per part. Nor is there any reason to suppose, with Smithers, that Buxtehude – 'had he been, like Bach, the director of a large choir school' – would simply have caused these works to be sung with multiple voices on each part in and throughout all choruses. (After all, the performance of a string quartet requires only four players, whether or not additional string-players are available.) The *stile antico* writing of the *Missa brevis* attributed to Buxtehude would, on the other hand, have been wholly appropriate for a large vocal ensemble; see Webber 1996, pp. 131, 177, 211.

[16] Printz 1678, p. 22.

[17] 'Stücke mit 3. à 4. Chören': Mattheson 1713, p. 158.

[18] 'mit zugehörigen *Accompagnement*, welches *Capella* heist': *ibid.*

a choir of singers which forms the principal choir and [which] consists of concertists, who are the selected best singers; this is where the chief performers are
[located] and [where] the [musical] direction is given.

ein Chor Sänger/ welches das Haupt-Chor ist/ und aus *Concerti*sten/ die der
Auszug der besten Sänger seyn/ bestehet; allda sind die vornehmsten
*Symphoni*sten und wird die *Direction* geführet.[19]

The chief singers are not discrete 'soloists', involved only sporadically for
whatever solo movements there happen to be: they constitute a choir –
indeed, the work's 'principal' choir, the very centre both of the composition
and of its performance.

Despite continuing shifts in musical taste and fashion, there is little reason
to believe that these general principles did not continue to obtain throughout the first half of the eighteenth century and thus throughout Bach's
working life.

   In larger vocal ensembles, the concertist – far from being a soloist who
might (or might not) happen to join in with a separate and self-contained
choir – was clearly viewed as the principal ensemble singer of a particular
voice-type, in exactly the same way that an obbligato violinist is (and was)
also a section-leader. (In the Mass in B Minor, the violin obbligato in the
'Laudamus te' is correctly understood to be intended for the principal player of that instrument within the ensemble, rather than for a 'soloist' who
would take no further part in the performance.) According to Georg
Friedrich Wolf, as late as 1787,

'Concertist' . . . means that singer or player who, on the one hand, executes the
sections and entire pieces which are sung or played alone [i.e. solos] and
[who], on the other hand, is responsible for the whole [of his] part [i.e. choruses as well as solos]. The expression is in use especially [in connection] with
vocal choirs.

Konzertist . . . bedeutet denjenigen Sänger oder Spieler welcher theils die
Stellen und ganzen Stücke, welche allein gesungen oder gespielt werden,
vorträgt, theils für die Ausführung der ganzen Stimme sorgen muß. Der
Ausdruck ist besonders bey den Singechören gebräuchlich.[20]

   This principle is by no means unknown, but its practical significance has
consistently been overlooked. Through the assumption of an ever-present,
multi-voiced choir singing throughout all choruses, the presence of con-

---

   [19]   *Ibid.* Cf. Praetorius on the term *Concertando*: 'When you seek out a few – and especially the best and most distinguished fellows – from a whole company of musicians . . .'
('Wenn man unter einer gantzen Gesellschafft der *Musicorum* etzliche/ und bevorab die
besten und fürnembsten Gesellen heraus sucht . . .'): Praetorius 1619, p. 5.
   [20]   Wolf 1787, p. 110, quoted Butt 1994, p. 215 n. 13.

certists within a choir has seemed to be a mere historical detail and of no real musical significance.

Bach's *Entwurff* flatly states that for *Kirchenstücke* (i.e. cantatas as opposed to motets) 'the vocalists must be divided . . . into two sorts, viz. concertists and ripienists', but otherwise reveals little more than that the concertist – unlike today's soloist – was counted as a member of the choir and not as a supernumerary. Johann Gottfried Walther (1732) borrows Mattheson's turn of phrase (see above, p. 34) when defining vocal concertists as 'a selection of the best singers',[21] a definition which seems to reflect this collective (non-soloistic) function. The adjective 'Concertante', he also tells us,

> is applied to all reciting [i.e. solo] voices, in order to distinguish them from those that sing only in the large choir or capella.

> wird zu allen *Recitir*enden Stimmen gesetzt, um sie von denen, so nur im grossen Chor, oder *à Capella* singen, zu unterscheiden.

(While others sing *only* in the large choir, concertists additionally form an implied small choir.) A one-to-a-part ensemble of these concertists constitutes the direct successor to the seventeenth-century *choro favorito* as defined in, for example, Gengenbach (1626), Demantius (1632), Erhardi (1660) and Falck (1688).[22]

The nature of the concertists' role is also implicit in Walther's definitions of the complementary ripieno group or capella:

> [Capella] . . . that special or large choir which in a musical [i.e. concerted] piece joins in only occasionally as strengthening.

> [Capella] . . . denjenigen besondern oder grossen Chor, welcher in einem musicalischen Stücke nur bißweilen zur Verstärckung mit einfällt.

> [Ripieno] . . . those voices which are added only for filling out and strengthening a musical ensemble.

> [Ripieno] . . . diejenigen Stimmen . . ., welche nur zur Ausfüll- und Verstärckung einer Music beygefüget werden.

(Later still, Georg Joseph Vogler describes 'Voci ripiene' in similar terms as 'the entire company of singers who function as a filling out [of the texture]'.)[23] Ripienists do not constitute 'the choir' in concerted choral writing; their function is merely to *reinforce* an ever-present concertists' choir. (In Agricola's view, 'all the refinement of solo singing cannot of course be

---

[21] 'ein Auszug der besten Sänger': Walther 1732. (Walther's mother was a close relative of Bach's family, and, according to the Leipzig *Post-Zeitungen* for 18 April 1729, Bach acted as an agent for the first instalment of Walther's book; see *BD II*, p. 191 = *NBR*, p. 139.)

[22] Cf. Butt 1994, pp. 109f, 207.

[23] 'das ganze Heer von Sängern, die zur Ausfüllung dienen': Vogler 1780, p. 125.

applied in a ripieno part'; nevertheless, 'Loudness and softness of tone, especially on long and solemn notes, must also be observed and applied even by those who sing choruses and the strengthening parts within them.'[24])

Walther's choice of words (*besondern, bißweilen, Verstärckung, mit einfällt, Ausfüllung, beygefüget*) unambiguously conveys the ancillary or supplementary nature of the ripienists' function: in fact, he falls only a little way short of describing the ripienists as optional.

And for most choral works a self-contained ripieno group or *Capella* was indeed optional, either explicitly or implicitly so. Expressions such as 'ad libitum' or 'se piace'[25] were one obvious way in which this could be expressed; another – less familiar to musicians today – was by means of formulas such as 'à 16 ò 21'.[26] (This particular inscription, which baffled Schering,[27] comes from *Machet die Tore weit* by one of Bach's predecessors, Sebastian Knüpfer, Thomascantor 1657–76.) In such a formula, as Praetorius explains,

> the first number means the concertato voices which are the foundation of the whole *concerto*; the following numbers, however, indicate [i.e. also include] the additional instrumental voices or capella [parts] which are there only *per accidens, ornatus & plenioris concentus gratiâ* [as circumstances allow, for adornment and a fuller ensemble] and which can be completely omitted if musicians are lacking.

> der erste *Numerus* die *Concertat*-Stimmen/ so des gantzen Concerts Fundament seyn/ bedeutet: Die folgende *Numeri* aber bezeichnen die *Instrumental*-Stimmen oder Capellen/ welche nur *per accidens, ornatus & plenioris concentus gratiâ* ... darzu kommen/ unnd in mangelung der *Musicorum* gantz aussengelassen werden können.[28]

The two forms of rubric are combined in Bach's heading for *Gott ist mein König* BWV71, 'âb 18. è se piace 22' (see Illus. 8). Bach could not have announced the optional nature of the ripienists more clearly.

The limited function of a ripieno group meant that in most circumstances it was considered optional. The point was sufficiently well understood to require little elaboration. Gottfried Ephraim Scheibel (1721) expresses it very simply:

---

[24] 'Die Stärke und Schwäche des Tones, muß auch, absonderlich auf langen und ernsthaften Noten, so gar von denen wohl beobachtet und angebracht werden, welche Chöre, und darinne Verstärkungstimmen singen . . . Freylich kann bey einer Ripienstimme nicht alle Feinheit des Sologesangs angebracht werden': Agricola 1757, p. 147 = Baird, p. 169.

[25] Johann Sebastiani's *Ad sacram mensam*, for example (cf. above, p. 33), is marked 'Con la Capella se piace': cited Webber 1996, p. 104.

[26] See also the Gerstenbüttel and Förtsch works listed above, p. 33.

[27] See Rifkin 1983, p. 162.

[28] Praetorius 1619, p. 196.

Illustration 8. J. S. Bach, Gott ist mein König BWV71: *first page of the autograph score, showing the super-scription 'âb 18. è se piace 22' and, beneath the basso continuo stave, a wavy line marked 'Capella'*

even if tuttis . . . do occur, it is enough if the principal voices – even though they consist of single persons – do their [job].

kom̄en . . . *tutti* gleich vor/ so ist es genung/ wenn die Haupt-Stimmen ob sie gleich aus eintzeln Personen bestehen/ das ihrige thun.[29]

(Scheibel, who is said to have studied in Leipzig in the late 1710s, and whose book was warmly praised by Mattheson,[30] may simply be explaining here that, unlike the older musical idioms, the newer (more intricate?) ones generally did not benefit from the participation of one or more ripieno groups.[31])

The same point apparently still needed to be made a decade or so later. In a letter written just a month after Bach's death, Johann Christian Strodtmann, as Rector of the Ratsgymnasium in Osnabrück, specifically insists that his conservative Cantor,

if he finds a tutti [i.e. a 'choral' movement] in the new musical material, [i.e. some newly acquired works by Telemann] should use just one – and of course the best one – of each voice. It sounds beautiful if one hears just one bass, tenor, alto and treble; whereas if everybody is shouting indiscriminately it is nothing but the bleating of a flock of sheep . . .[32]

wenn er ein Tutti in den neuen Musikalien findet, von jeder Stimme nur einen und zwar den besten nehme. Es klingt schön, wenn man nur einen Bassisten, Tenoristen, Altisten und Discantisten höret; hingegen ist es nichts als ein Geblöke, wenn alle durcheinander schrein . . .[33]

And, at the time when Bach was just beginning his career, Fuhrmann (1706) gives this revealing definition of the term *Capella*:

'Capella' is [used] when, in vocal music, a separate choir joins in in certain sections for the splendour and strengthening of the music [or musical ensemble]; [it] must therefore be separately positioned in a place apart from the concertists. With a shortage of people, however, these capellas can even be left out, because they are in any case already also sung by the concertists.

Capella ist/ wenn in einer *Vocal-Music* ein absonderlich *Chor* in gewissen *Clausuln* zur Pracht und Stärckung der *Music* mit einfällt/ muß dahero an einem *a parten* Ort von den *Concerti*sten abgesondert gestellt werden. Es können aber diese *Capellen* in Ermangelung der Personen wol ausgelassen werden/ weil sie von dem *Concerti*sten ohne dem schon mitgesungen werden.[34]

[29] Scheibel 1721, pp. 54f (in a chapter entitled 'Von der Bestellung eines *Chori Musici* in der Kirchen').

[30] Mattheson 1722, p. 96. For an outline of Scheibel's book, see Walther 1732, p. 547.

[31] Butt's interpretation of the passage is that Scheibel 'objected to the trend towards adding extra voices to vocal lines' (in Boyd 1999, p. 98), while Smithers sees in it merely the 'suggested reforms' of a young theologian (Smithers 1997, pp. 16f).

[32] Cf. Smithers 1997, pp. 17ff, who argues that 'the situation at Osnabrück speaks rather loudly *against* one-on-a-part performances of cantatas' (emphasis added).

[33] Bösken 1937, p. 143; see also *ibid.*, pp. 142, 144.

[34] Fuhrmann 1706, p. 80.

This usefully reminds us that

- concertists sing throughout;
- ripienists do not (often) sing throughout;
- ripieno parts are (usually) optional;
- ripienists are placed apart from concertists (and therefore require separate copies).

The evidence points unerringly towards these principles' obtaining equally in Bach's own work. Certainly, the surviving performance materials (discussed in Chapter 6 below) strongly imply that in practice Bach – for whatever reasons – used ripienists on only the very rarest of occasions. Moreover, there is, as we shall see, very little justification for assuming that, but for some imagined 'shortage of people', he would have preferred to have (multiple) ripienists singing throughout (all) choruses.

In fact, the very term 'ripienist' need not always imply a 'choral' singer, in the modern sense of one who shares a vocal line with at least one other singer. We have already noted (p. 29 note 1) a possible implication in the *Entwurff* that ripienists might sing one to a part in the motet repertoire; in his own concerted music, Bach can use the term *Ripieni* to denote single voices (in non-soloistic roles) – as a cluster of four Leipzig works shows.[35] Each is a solo cantata ending with a four-part chorale (in which instruments double the vocal lines), and the wrappers of the surviving sets of parts bear the following autograph inscriptions:[36]

Gott soll allein mein Herze haben BWV169	'à Alto Solo è 3 Voci Ripieni'
Ich will den Kreuzstab gerne tragen BWV56	'S. A. T. et Basso Conc:'
Ich armer Mensch, ich Sündenknecht BWV55	'à 4 Voci, ò vero Tenore Solo è 3 Ripieni'
Ich bin vergnügt mit meinem Glücke BWV84	'à Soprano Solo è 3 Ripieni'

In each case a single concertist sings throughout the work, evidently not just as soloist but also as the only voice on that part in the chorale, while three ripienists – presumably one to a part, matching the concertists – have nothing but the straightforward chorale setting to sing. Thus in the final chorale of BWV55 the tenor concertist, rather than simply resting after his four solo movements (or, alternatively, merging with a choral ensemble of a dozen or so voices), is joined by three other singers (soprano, alto and bass) to form a vocal quartet. In other words, there is – in the modern sense – no choir at

---

[35] See also Appendix 6, pp. 198f below. Three of the cantatas were first heard within a month of each other, in October–November 1726, the fourth probably early the following February.

[36] The wrappers of two of these cantatas (BWV55 and 56) are illustrated in Parrott 1996, p. 558.

all. Two important inferences may thus be drawn from Bach's terminology: (1) that such simple, unspecific designations as 'Voci' or 'S. A. T.' should not be presumed to imply several voices per part[37] (here they apparently imply one to a part); (2) that the term 'Ripieni' (which always indicates a subordinate role) can, in this repertoire, perfectly well imply single voices – and not necessarily even *extra* voices doubling others.

Elsewhere in Bach's music, ripienists clearly form a self-contained group, strengthening the concertists in choruses (see below, Chapter 6). Is there any reason, though, to imagine that more than one ripienist per part is implied? Bach's own specification in the *Entwurff* of eight ripienists ('two for each voice') is, alas, surrounded by ambiguity.[38] But on those rare occasions when we know for certain that Bach did have more than eight singers at his disposal – for the St John and St Matthew Passions – the surviving materials show that the extra singers were not used as additional ripienists (see below, pp. 80f).[39] Certainly, the possibility that he used *more* than two ripienists per part (in conjunction with a concertist) is very remote, for a variety of reasons.[40]

We are thus left with an apparent maximum of just two, and a natural minimum of one. As Scheibel and Bach himself have shown, a one-to-a-part ripieno group, far from being in any way exceptional, must have been the norm in this repertoire – if ripienists were used at all.[41]

---

[37] This point has been misunderstood on occasion: cf Parrott 1998, p. 638 and n. 9.

[38] Having first distinguished between concertist and ripienist, Bach then specifies four (or more) concertists: 'Concertists are ordinarily four [in number], indeed even five, six, seven [and] up to eight – if one wishes, that is, to perform music *per choros* [i.e. for more than one choir]' ('Derer *Concerti*sten sind *ordinaire* 4; auch wohl 5, 6, 7 biß 8; so mann nemlich *per Choros musiciren* will'): for detailed discussion of this passage in the *Entwurff* (¶¶4f), see Rifkin 1990. Bach continues, 'Ripienists must also be at least eight [in number], namely, two for each voice' ('Derer *Ripieni*sten müßen wenigstens auch achte seyn, nemlich zu ieder Stimme zwey'). Again, Bach's requirements for an appropriate pool of singers do not necessarily translate directly to any individual cantata performance: there is surely an implication that each concertist would be matched not by two ripienists but by one.

[39] Rifkin 1982, Table III, p. 749.

[40] The passage quoted in note 38 above concerns Bach's 'choirs for cantatas' – that is, both his first and second choirs – and could even be taken to indicate not that each choir should include 'at least eight' ripienists, but that the student body as a whole should contain that number to be distributed between the first two choirs. In addition, Bach's strategic intentions in the *Entwurff*, the singers' instrumental duties and absences, the musical requirements of particular cantatas – all must be taken into consideration. Certainly, to infer from this passage a single vocal choir of about 16 ('up to eight' concertists plus 'at least eight' ripienists) singing cantata choruses would, in the context of the *Entwurff*, be unsafe.

[41] For Telemann's practice, see Swack 1999. For what it is worth, the practice of (literally) doubling four singers with another four can be traced right back to the beginning of what we label 'the Baroque', to Emilio del Cavalieri's *Rappresentatione di Anima, et di Corpo* (1600): 'when the music for the choir is in four parts, whoever so wishes will be

Around 1689 there was just such a group at Arnstadt, where two relatives of Bach's were employed:[42] besides the seven principal singers (SATTTBB – clearly a pool to be drawn upon, rather than a fixed line-up required to sing in every piece) there were a further four (SATB) from the local school who could serve 'Zur Capella oder Zum Complimento'.[43] Accordingly, when Fuhrmann (1706) touches on a practical matter relating to vocal doubling, he writes not of several but of just two singers sharing a line, confirming in an aside that such doubling occurs in capella (as opposed to *concertato*) writing, and 'often', though not always,

> if two singers sing one voice part together (which one often causes to happen in capella [passages], so that it sounds the more penetrating at that point) . . .

> wenn 2. Sänger zugleich eine Stimme singen (welches man offt in *Capella* thun läst/ damit es desto durchdringender daselbst klinge) . . .[44]

Such vocal forces would not, in Scheibel's view, be considered unduly 'modest':

> If each part or voice comprises one or at most two individuals [*subjecta*] who pull their weight, then a choir is well set up.

> Wenn jede *Partie* oder Stimme mit einem oder auffs höchste zweyen *Subjectis* versehn/ die das ihre *præstir*en/ so ist ein Chor gutt bestellt.[45]

At the Württemberg *Hofkapelle* (1714) we find just such a 'well-set-up' ensemble of precisely eight singers. This was viewed neither as an extremely small choir nor as a group of four soloists plus a 'minimal' choir (of just four) but – in the evocative terms of one document – as a 'quartet with its ripieno'.[46]

---

able to double the voices, so that sometimes four are singing and at other times [all of them] together, if the platform has space for eight' ('essendo la musica per il Choro à quattro voci, si puotrebbe, chi volesse, raddoppiarle, cantando hora quattro, & alcuna volta insieme, essendo il palco però capace di otto'): Cavalieri 1600, 'Avvertimenti per la presente Rappresentatione . . .'

[42] See above, p. 14.
[43] Schiffner 1987, pp. 46f.
[44] Fuhrmann 1706, p. 77. See also Webber 1996, pp. 176f.
[45] Scheibel 1721, p. 54.
[46] '*quator* mit seiner *Ripien*': Owens (forthcoming).

5

Copies and copy-sharing

Arguments in support of the traditional modern view – 'that Bach's chorus normally consisted of 12 singers, three to a part' – depend, effectively, on two strands of evidence: on one side Bach's written remarks, especially in the *Entwurff* of 1730, and on the other the surviving scores and parts used by Bach in his performances.[1] We shall examine the *Entwurff* in due course (see below, Chapter 7), but first we should look more closely at those performance materials and, in particular, at the question of copy-sharing.

The image of eighteenth-century choral singers routinely sharing copies – with two or three reading from a single copy in performance – is so deeply rooted in our consciousness[2] that we hardly think of questioning it.[3] Yet we must not leave it unexamined, for it forms a cornerstone of the historical argument that endorses the use of several voices per part in Bach's – and indeed in all Baroque – music. Where a complete set of parts survives, it is assumed that each vocal copy will have served two or three (or more) singers at the same time. Thus the mere existence of 'separate solo and ripieno parts' amongst a work's original performance materials (i.e. one concertist's and one ripienist's copy for each voice part) has, in at least one instance, been taken by a leading Bach scholar as proof positive of 'a chorus of 12–16', and thence of Bach's 'standard ensemble'.[4]

Yet it was those same strands of evidence – an unbiased rereading of documents, including the *Entwurff*, and in particular a careful analysis of the

---

[1] Marshall 1983, p. 21.

[2] See Schering 1936, pp. 30f.

[3] The image of such copy-sharing is powerfully reinforced in, for example, Hogarth's splendid 1732 engraving which shows about 14 singers at work on De Fesch's oratorio *Judith* – reproduced, for example, in Young 1949, facing p. 64; *New Grove*, iv, p. 350 ('Chorus'); *Early Music*, 12/1 (Feb 1984), p. 7.

[4] Wolff 1998; see also Rifkin 1998b.

surviving performance materials of Bach's church music – that led Joshua Rifkin towards his conclusion – first made public in the paper reproduced as Appendix 6 below – that from Schütz to Mozart vocal ripienists 'did not read from the same music as . . . concertists'.[5] And a recent study of 'one of the largest and most significant collections of primary sources of cantata performance material in the time of J. S. Bach', the *c.*800 cantatas by Telemann preserved at Frankfurt am Main, confirms 'that only one singer sang from each part, and that concertists and ripienists did not share parts'.[6]

In Bach's case, *solo/tutti* markings certainly 'remain notoriously absent . . . where the assumption of shared parts would seem most to demand them';[7] in other words, if a ripienist were to read from the same copy as a concertist he could expect no guidance from the page itself in judging exactly where to start and stop singing (see, for instance, Illus. 9). Nor are there any other unambiguous indications (verbal instructions, *divisi* writing) that the surviving vocal copies – including those for ripienists – were ever shared.

Explaining away this sort of evidence 'simply takes one too far beyond the bounds of reasonable scholarship'.[8] Thus, if a complete set of parts includes no ripieno copies, performance by just one voice per part is the only plausible inference.

Undoubtedly it is no easy matter to prove conclusively, on the basis of internal evidence, that a specific copy of music was *not* shared – even in the absence of indications to the contrary. Equally, though, it may well seem that 'there is no way of establishing whether or not Bach's singers shared their individual parts purely on the basis of *external* evidence'.[9] Yet other factors do have a direct bearing on the same question: the structure of vocal choirs, the positioning of performers, and iconographic evidence. And, as we shall see, each challenges our usual understanding and points firmly in the same direction as the other evidence reviewed here.

First, a look at the musical sources themselves. The overwhelming majority of Bach's church music survives in sets of parts, and these almost always have just a single copy for each voice part; see Table 3A (p. 61 below) for the extant ripieno copies, and Appendix 5 for a complete list of surviving vocal material.[10] A soprano copy, for example, will contain not only any recitatives and arias for that voice but also the soprano part of all choruses. Thus, the

---

[5] Rifkin 1995a, p. 223. Rifkin has since enlarged upon his thesis in various articles: see Appendix 7 below, and the Bibliography to this book.

[6] See Swack 1999.

[7] Rifkin 1995a, p. 227.

[8] Butt 1998, p. 101. Rifkin's critics 'tend to discount his examination of the original parts without even attempting to address the very convincing arguments he has developed from their internal coherences' (Butt 1994, p. 208 n. 55).

[9] Butt 1998, p. 100 (emphasis added).

[10] Appendix 5 is based on Dreyfus 1987, App. A (pp. 183–207), which also gives details of surviving instrumental as well as vocal copies.

Illustration 9. J. S. Bach, Missa BWV232(I): *a page from the autograph 'Tenore' copy, showing (at the end of the second stave) the transition from the ST duet 'Domine Deus' to the chorus 'Qui tollis' (unmarked except by the change of key- and time-signatures)*

musical content of the double sheet (bifolium) marked simply 'Alto' from the surviving set for *Lobe den Herrn, meine Seele* BWV69 is as follows:

[1]	[Coro]	[complete alto part]
[2]	Recit Canto	tacet
[3]	Aria [Alto]	[complete solo part]
[4]	Recit Tenore	tacet
[5]	Aria Basso	tacet
[6]	Choral	[complete alto part]

The last page of this autograph part is shown in Illus. 10. For virtually every work, then, there are four vocal copies (one each of SATB), and four only.

If we are to rely solely upon the evidence of this surviving performance material, the thesis that most of Bach's choral works were originally sung without ripieno doubling, i.e. by one-to-a-part concertists alone, will rest on two premises: first, that the extant parts mostly represent complete sets which Bach himself used; second, that the concertists' copies were not intended to be shared by other singers. If both premises are correct, we are forced to conclude that where we find one copy of each voice part, there must have been one singer for each voice part.

At this point the sceptic may understandably ask whether the near-total absence of surviving extra parts is the whole story: 'do we know how much has been lost?'[11] It has been proposed (though not, I believe, in print) that vocal ripieno parts, and any duplicates of them, would routinely have been discarded rather than preserved with a set of parts. Quite apart from the apparent absence of any clear evidence for such 'pruning', various factors argue against it: Bach's personal ownership of such material, the evident care taken (not least by Bach himself) to preserve the family's musical inheritance,[12] and in particular the survival of numerous duplicate violin parts (doublets)[13] which, if the 'pruning' hypothesis is sound, should also have been discarded. (Friedemann and Emanuel inherited most of their father's church music, a set of parts typically going to one brother while the other got a score and any duplicate or ripieno parts; each therefore possessed the work in question, albeit in a different format.)

These sources – their authorship, chronology and transmission – have for several decades been the subject of intense scrutiny by a succession of Bach scholars, and their studies have produced a clear (if tacit) consensus that the general lack of ripieno parts is not a mere accident of survival – that the surviving materials are indeed effectively complete. Thus Robert Marshall:

> the vast majority of [Bach's] surviving vocal compositions were written during the first three and a half years . . . at Leipzig . . . and . . . most of these works were composed – and performed – at the almost unimaginable rate of one per week. That is, between one typical Sunday and the next during those few years, Bach normally conceived the music for a new cantata, wrote it down in score, and marshalled a crew of copyists from among his pupils and family to prepare a complete (i.e. a functionally adequate if minimal) set of parts for his singers and players.[14]

In other words, the contention is that a surviving set of parts which is 'functionally adequate' (albeit – as Marshall claims – 'minimal') is likely to be the 'complete' set prepared and used under Bach's supervision.

The absence of additional vocal parts (containing choruses), it has been argued, is merely a notational detail: once he had established certain practices at Leipzig, Bach 'no longer had the time – or perhaps the need – to spell

[11]   Koopman 1996, p. 614.
[12]   The Alt-Bachisches Archiv is a 'collection of music by members of the Bach family, owned and probably assembled by J. S. Bach' (Boyd 1999, p. 11). In 1999 the collection, lost since 1945, was rediscovered in Kiev.
[13]   See Dreyfus 1987 as cited in note 10 above.
[14]   Marshall 1983, pp. 21f.

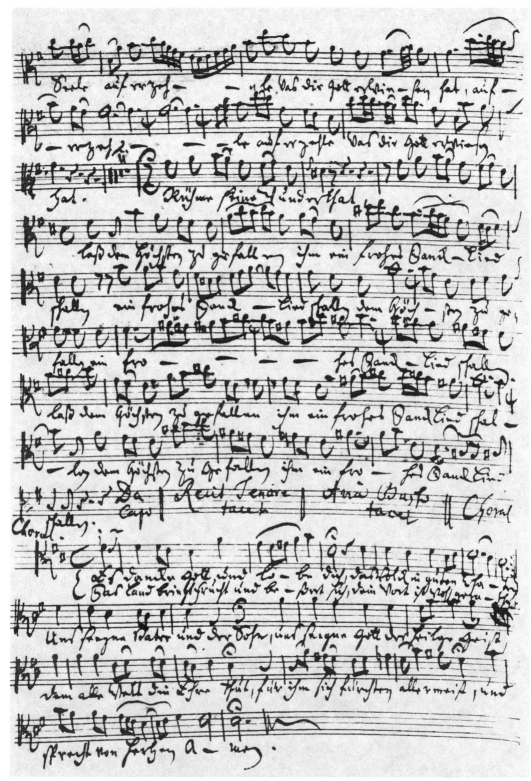

Illustration 10. J. S. Bach, Lobe den Herrn, meine Seele BWV69: *last page of the autograph 'Alto' copy, showing part of the alto aria and the final chorale*

them all out', and in performance his practice remained consistent – and consistently involved ripienists.

> Understandably, in such circumstances, there was not even always time available for such desirable tasks as adding performance indications . . . into the principal parts, still less time for copying out separate duplicate parts for *every singer* in the chorus . . . [Bach's] indications are more complete for these first Leipzig works [BWV75, 76, 21 and 24] than they would normally be later on . . . I believe this tells us . . . that Bach . . . no longer had the time – or perhaps the need – to spell them all out.[15]

From this, Marshall infers that Bach 'would have loved to provide ripieno parts for every cantata . . . had time permitted, and had he had sufficient copyists at his call',[16] and reaches the conclusion that each copy that Bach did provide was routinely shared by two or three singers.

This brings into focus the question of copy-sharing, on which such an hypothesis self-evidently hinges: did a single ('minimal') set of vocal parts allow 'every singer in the chorus' of at least 12 to participate?[17] Is it safe to assume that in concerted music-making, no less than in street singing, the sharing of copies by two or even three singers was commonplace?

We may begin by examining three specific pieces of evidence which have been thought to lend weight to the idea that such copy-sharing was routine. First, a passage from Printz (1678):

> The most experienced singer of each voice part should carry his part[-book] himself and promptly turn to the piece which the prefect indicates . . .

> Der geübteste Sänger von jeder Stimme sol seine *Partem* selbst tragen/ und das Stück/ welches der *Præfectus* andeutet/ fein zeitlich aufschlagen . . .[18]

---

[15]   *Ibid.*, p. 22 (emphasis added).

[16]   *Ibid.* Marshall appears not to have elaborated on this hypothesis elsewhere.

[17]   Printz rules out singing from memory (Printz 1678, p. 9). Smithers nevertheless argues: 'it is not beyond the bounds of probability that many performers at the time of Bach actually played or sang their parts from memory' (Smithers 1997, p. 30; see also pp. 47f). Here it would seem prudent to recognize the distinction, described in Chapter 3 above, between a brand-new and decidedly 'intricate' concerted work by Bach on the one hand and the recurring repertoire of chant, chorales and traditional motets on the other (see also Osnabrück's *Chorordnung* of 1731, chap. 2 ¶¶1, 3: Bösken 1937, p. 185). In support of his conjecture Smithers points to 'the want of musical parts in many iconographic sources from the period, not the least of which is the title-page engraving from the *Unfehlbare Engel-Freude*' (p. 30), where in contrast to the singers 'none of the instrumentalists . . . are shown with any musical parts' (p. 29); see Illus. 18, p. 121 below. I suggest that instrumentalists are visually identified by the instruments themselves, and the artist can safely omit desks and copies to avoid undue clutter; however, if singers are to be identified as such they positively must be depicted holding sheets of music.

[18]   Printz 1678, pp. 5f.

But this instruction is specifically directed at prefects in charge of street and house singing; it has nothing whatsoever to do with the elaborate concerted music performed in church.[19]

Second, a drawing by Ludwig Richter (1803–84) of Thomasschule boys sharing copies.[20] Quite apart from the fact that the illustration dates from the nineteenth century, the subject once again appears to be street singing (directed by a prefect), an activity of no relevance to Bach's concerted music.[21]

Third, a 1723 Thomasschule ordinance, echoing an earlier one (in Latin) from 1634,[22] which probably concerns chant or chorales sung from a single 'text' (a choir-book);[23] according to this the pupils, when in church, should

> Remain quietly seated on their benches until they are called to the desks, but then position themselves in front of them in such a way that each can see the text that has been put out, and no one can interfere with anyone else's singing.

> So lange auf ihren Bäncken stille sitzen, bis sie zu denen Pulten geruffen werden, so dann aber sich dergestalt vor dieselbe stellen, damit ein ieder den aufgelegten Text sehen, und keiner den andern im Singen hindern möge.[24]

Chant and chorales presumably continued to be sung in similar fashion in Bach's time. In any case, what this 1723 regulation does *not* refer to is concerted music – as is clear from both context and terminology.[25]

Underpinning the notion of copy-sharing by singers in Bach's concerted music are two broad assumptions. First, since instrumentalists sometimes shared copies, singers must have done so too. Second, ripienists (without copies) would naturally be sure to cluster around concertists (with copies).

The well-known frontispiece to Walther's *Musicalisches Lexicon* (1732: see Illus. 11) has been invoked as support for the first of these two propositions.[26] In fact, neither copy-sharing singers nor even copy-sharing instrumentalists are depicted; contrary perhaps to initial impressions, the two standing

---

[19] At Leipzig, some concertists were in fact given special dispensation from street singing at New Year: see below, p. 95 note 11.

[20] Cited and reproduced in Boyd 1984, p. 431.

[21] See Rifkin 1984, p. 591.

[22] 'Furthermore, each should stand at his desk in such a way that one does not obstruct another's view or in any way distract or impede him while he is singing' ('Pulpitis verò ita adstent singuli, ne alter alterius prospectui officiat, eumq́; in canendo qvovis modo turbet aut impediat'): *Ordnungen*, 1634 fol. G4ʳ (chap. 19 ¶4).

[23] The singing of motets would presuppose not one book but as many as eight.

[24] *Ordnungen*, 1723 p. 72 (chap. 13 ¶1).

[25] The terms *Singen* and *Gesang* are used here, rather than *Music* or *Kirchenstück*. In any event, the 1634 ordinance pre-dates the introduction of elaborate concerted music in Leipzig on any regular basis; see Rifkin 1995a, pp. 224f.

[26] Koopman twice misreads this picture as evidence that *instrumentalists* shared copies: see Koopman 1996, p. 614, and Koopman 1997, p. 541.

string-players are shown reading from *separate* music stands, and there are no other obvious candidates for copy-sharing.[27]

In the second assumption, two or three singers of, for example, a tenor part are visualized standing together and thus able to read from a single copy.[28] Yet the conventional practice was apparently to place any ripieno group some distance away from the concertists (cf. Fuhrmann on p. 38 above): this positively precludes copy-sharing and demands the provision of separate copies.

As we have seen, the Italian editor and singer Lorenzo Calvi (1629) directly equates 'doubling' with 'copying out again': 'radoppiare, cioè ricopiar[e]' (see above, p. 31). In Germany this convention can be traced back at least as far as Praetorius (1619), whose definition of the term *ripieno* makes it abundantly clear that large forces are to be deployed in discrete, separated choirs – a practice demanding multiple copies:

> When a large company of musicians is on hand, one can thus also have such ripieno parts copied out two or three times and distributed and divided into sundry widely separated choirs; these I have then mostly called *chorus pro capella* . . . And so the ripieno [sections] are nothing other than certain *clausulae* [sections] or *particulae* [small pieces] of a *concerto* which are sung and played in the other choirs at certain moments – [together] with the principal choir – in order to make a full-voiced musical ensemble. 'Ripieno' therefore does not actually mean *chorus plenus* [full chorus] but rather *reiteratae plenitudines* [reiterated full sections], the *clausulae* which are taken from the principal voices of the *concerto* and allocated to sundry other separated choirs, in order to make a complete and full-voiced *concerto*.

> So kan man auch/ do eine grosse *Compagny* von *Musicis* vorhanden/ solche *Ripieni* zwey: oder dreymahl abschreiben lassen/ und in unterschiedene weit von einander abgesonderte *Chor distribuiren* uñ abtheilen: welches ich dañ meistentheils *Chorum pro Capella* genennet habe . . . Uñ sind also die *Ripieni* nichts anders/ alß gewisse *Clausulæ* oder *parriculæ* [sic] aus einē *concert,*

---

[27] There seem to be six identifiable instrumentalists, a director, and a possible eight others whose copies/stands/musical functions are simply not identifiable. In any case, the face, body, bowing hand and bow of the standing string-player on the right are all shown unambiguously *behind* a music stand, while the bow and instrument of the one on the left are *in front of* the same stand, thus effectively making sharing a physical impossibility. (A second stand is partially visible on the extreme left of the picture; if both the left-hand player and the 'violone'-player are meant to be using it, they would presumably be reading from different parts.)

[28] This proposition seems to have originated with Arnold Schering: 'There could be at most two of them [i.e. ripienists]; the one looked at the copy from the right, the other from the left of the concertist': Schering 1920, p. 81. See also Rifkin 1999b.

Illustration 11.   J. G. Walther, Musikalisches Lexicon *(Leipzig, 1732): engraving by J. C. Dehné (frontispiece). The original is printed with the image reversed*

welche in dē andern Chorē zu gewissen zeitē eine vollstiṁige *Music* zu machē/ mit dē Häupt-*Chorē* gesungē uñ geklungē wird. Heist derowegē RIPIENO eigentlich nicht *Chorus plenus*, besondern *Reiteratæ plenitudines*, die *clausulæ*, welche aus den Häupt-Stimmen des *Concerts* genommen/ und in andern unterschiedenen abgesonderten *Choren* auffgesetzet werden/ einen volligen und vollstimmige *Concert* zumachen.[29]

In his subsequent definition of 'capella' Praetorius repeats the same point:

> And so . . . anyone can, as he pleases, extract . . . from . . . all concertos . . . one or two four-part capellas and, where the word *omnes* or *chorus* is marked, have the same written out on separate sheets . . . And then in performance this *chorus pro Capella* will be set up and positioned in a separate place.

> Und kan also . . . aus . . . allen . . . *Concerten*, ein jeder nach seinem gefallen/ . . . eine oder zwo Capellen mit 4. Stimmen herausserziehen/ und das jenige/ darvor das Wort *omnes* oder *Chorus* gezeichnet stehet/ . . . uff absonderliche Bletter/ . . . heraus schreiben lassen . . . Und derselbe *Chorus pro Capella* alsdann zum *musiciren* an einen absonderlichen ort geordnet und gestellet werden.[30]

And Schütz (1636) writes in very similar terms:

> From these six *concertato* voice parts, six other voice parts can be copied out additionally (where the word *Capella* stands) . . . and thereby another separate choir or capella can be set up and introduced with them.

> Aus diesen sechs *Concertat*Stimmen können ferner (wo das Wort *Capella* stehet) Sechs andere Stimmen . . . abgeschrieben/ und also noch ein absonderlicher *Chor* oder *Capella* mit angestellet und eingeführet werden.[31]

Where space permitted (Mattheson tells us), there was also the possibility of adding – 'in *Ripieno*' – a second group of '*Capellistē*' in the organ gallery.[32] Such an arrangement, he emphasizes, was entirely optional.[33] What Mattheson does *not* suggest is that extra singers be drafted into the first capella.

This 'additive' way of expanding a vocal ensemble has been seldom acknowledged – and rarely adopted in performance – in our own time. Yet

---

[29] Praetorius 1619, p. 131 [*recte* p. 111].

[30] *Ibid.*, pp. 134f [*recte* 114f].

[31] Preface to Schütz 1636; cf. the prefaces to Schütz 1619 and Schütz 1650. See also Rifkin 1995a, p. 226.

[32] 'So far as the [physical] circumstances of the place allow' ('Nach Gelegenheit des Ortes') and 'if everything works' ('wenn alles gehet'): Mattheson 1713, pp. 158f. Cf. Cavalieri above, p. 40 note 41.

[33] 'What I am giving here is only a rough outline of everything; I introduce it only by way of example, without [wishing] to prescribe anything to anyone, yet alone preclude better ideas' ('Ich mache hier nur von allen Sachen einen ohngefehren Entwurff/ und führe es nur *Exempels* weise an/ ohne jemanden was vorzuschreiben noch sonst seine bessere Meinung zu benehmen'): Mattheson 1713, p. 159.

it was a central feature of a continuous tradition from Schütz to Bach – as BWV71 clearly attests (see below, p. 134) – and was evidently still a norm for concerted music in the middle of the eighteenth century. Thus, in a '*Specification*' of the lavish forces heard at Stadtilm in 1742 (see below, pp. 118f), the names of the 12 singers are listed neither in a single block nor as 'soloists' plus 'choir' but as three separate choirs/quartets:[34]

Sänger. 1. Chor	
	H. Köster
	H. Streicher
	H. Völkner
	H. Sorge
	Summa 4
	H. Otto, von Merseburg
	H. Cantor Kiesewetter
	H. Langstedt
	H. Horn
	Summa 4
	Biel ein Schüler
	Arnold "
	Thon "
	Walther "
	Summa 4
	Summa 12

(An arrangement of this sort is most probably what Niedt has in mind when he writes of 'a whole choir of eight, 12 or more voices'.[35])

By contrast, one little-known comment by Mattheson does seem, on the surface, to point towards the modern multi-voice choir:

> Otherwise one would always, as much as possible, place the best singers in the middle, particularly the most delicate voices – and not, as custom would have it, on the right hand. The basses and strong voices can more readily be separated and can more readily work on the left as well as the right on both sides.

---

[34] Engelke 1918–19, p. 604.
[35] 'ein gantzer Chor von 8/ 12 oder mehr Stimmen': Niedt 1706, p. 121.

Ubrigens stelle man die besten Sänger, so viel möglich, allemahl in die Mitte, absonderlich die zartesten Stimmen; nicht aber, nach dem alten Herkommen, zur rechten Hand. Die Bässe und starcken Stimmen können sich ehender theilen, und so lincks als rechts auf beiden Seiten schicken.[36]

The passage is scarcely unambiguous, though; we cannot even be certain what repertoire Mattheson has in mind (secular concerted music or liturgical motets?). One thing, however, is quite clear: any spatial separation of, say, two or more bass singers would inevitably preclude their sharing a single copy.[37]

Two valuable iconographical sources from early-eighteenth-century Saxony appear to illustrate the convention of positioning any ripieno group 'in a separate place' from the concertists. The first of these is the frontispiece to *Unfehlbare Engel-Freude* (1710),[38] which Schering analyses in the following terms:

The right-hand side [see Illus. 12] belongs to the singers, who are divided into three groups of four. Each quartet has two older and two younger singers. The younger [and shorter] ones (sopranos and altos) are marked out by their black gowns and boys' wigs [*Knabenperücken*] as pupils of the Thomasschule, while the older ones are identified as youths by their men's clothes and full-

---

[36] Mattheson 1739, p. 484: chap. 26 ('Von der Regierung, An- Auf- und Ausführung einer Musik'), §31.

[37] Mattheson's second sentence may even relate to *instrumental* 'voices', to be disposed on either side of the centrally placed singers. Alternatively, the passage might mean that outside of opera (which Mattheson has just discussed) one would always try to place the best singers (the concertists) in the middle, particularly the 'most delicate voices' (e.g. soprano and alto) and not on the right; the (two or more) basses and any other strong voices (e.g. tenors) could more readily be separated – i.e., the bass concertist and ripienist(s) could be farther from each other than, say, the soprano concertist and ripienist(s) – and could more readily work on both sides. This would seem to relate to a practice described over a century earlier by Daniel Friderici: 'Auch sollen nicht alleine die *Chori*, wann unterschiedene *Chori* seynd, Sondern auch die gleichen Stimmen beyderseits Choren jegen einander gefüget und gestellet seyn, Doch also, daß die Fundament Stimmen ein wenig weiter von einander stehen, und die *Resonantz* besser zu den Zuhörern kommen könne. Als: *in Cantionibus 8. Voc.*

	Chori Primi	Chori Secundi	
	Cantus	Cantus	
	Altus	Altus	
	Tenor	Tenor	
	Bassus	Bassus'	

('Also, when there are separate choirs, not only the choirs but also the corresponding voices in each choir should be disposed and placed opposite one another with the 'fundamental' voices standing a little further from one another and in such a way that the resonance can come to the listeners better. Viz. in *cantiones a8* [see diagram above]'): Friderici 1618/1624, pp. 45f, rule 12. Cf. Michael 1637, preface to *Quinta vox*, quoted Butt, p. 206 n. 41.

[38] Groschuff 1710: see Illus. 18, p. 121 below. This is, incidentally, the only depiction of a choir of any kind included in the *c.*350 illustrations in *BD IV*.

Illustration 12. Singers performing concerted music in church, Leipzig, 1710 (for Schering's description, see text): detail of Illus. 18

bottomed wigs [*Allongeperücke(n)*]; the one standing at the front on the right, moreover, [is identified] by his dagger as a student.[39]

Here, then, is a 'choir' set up not as a single block but evidently in discrete, self-contained units of four singers: three separate vocal quartets can be

[39] Schering 1926, pp. 153f.

discerned (as can some individual copies), the singers apparently positioned in such a way as to prevent two singers of any one voice part from sharing a single copy.[40] (This total of 12 singers, incidentally, makes this the largest number shown in any of the known – and pertinent – iconographical sources.)

The second source is a contemporary illustration of the Freiberg Cathedral organ loft – a valuable addition to the disappointingly small number of relevant church scenes generally known. This shows the second-largest number of singers that I am aware of: probably 11.[41] A possible seven singers are shown grouped around the central figure (apparently the director), two to the left and five to the right;[42] although only five copies are visible, there is no obvious suggestion of any copy-sharing (see Illus. 13). A further group of four on the right may with reasonable confidence be identified as vocal ripienists (Illus. 14).[43] In any case, what is *not* shown – either

Illustration 13. Singers, Freiberg, c.1710–14: detail of Illus. 19

[40] Smithers takes a different view, seeing 'a number of singers, some of whom are reading from shared parts' (Smithers 1997, p. 48 n. 84), and offering another interpretation: 'the angle of several of the visible singers' parts suggests that they may not be individual parts but opposite pages of a book, perhaps a hymnal' (*ibid.*, p. 29). He nevertheless accepts that 'this engraving does show . . . a performance of concerted music', without making clear how a hymnal would have been used in concerted music.

[41] The suggestion that these forces were meagre by the standards of the day – 'Freiberg was only a provincial town' (Koopman 1998, p. 117) – contrasts with the view that 'For centuries Freiberg shared first place amongst the great musical centres of Saxony' (Schünemann 1918–19, p. 179).

[42] Koopman (1998, p. 116) states that four of the figures (but which four?) are 'solo singers' (i.e. concertists).

[43] *Pace* Koopman (1998, p. 117), these four are not 'next to' the other singers but are very clearly separated by two or possibly three trumpeters and a timpanist (see Illus. 19, p. 122 below). Moreover, to claim that from 'the direction of their gaze, it is clear that they are singing from one or two parts at the most' not only is wholly fanciful but would lead one to conclude that these 'ripienists' are singing only 'one or two' (of four or more) vocal lines. Such an arrangement (which would be anything but typical) hardly supports the contention that *each* chorus part was normally taken by three or four singers.

Illustration 14. Singers (apparently ripienists), Freiberg, c.1710–14: detail of Illus. 19

here or (to the best of my knowledge) anywhere – is ripienists reading from concertists' parts (or even ripienists sharing ripienists' parts).[44]

In short, the case for today's conventional choir is heavily dependent on what is widely believed to have been commonplace in eighteenth-century Lutheran Germany: the practice of copy-sharing by singers in concerted music. Yet the claim that 'many' illustrations show this[45] proves very wide of the mark; not a single example has yet surfaced. Indeed, I know of *no* iconography from Bach's Germany that depicts what most people today would consider to be a Bachian 'choir' – at least 12 singers (and usually more than 20), supported by an instrumental ensemble and positioned as a single group.

In sum, copies were shared by singers in some contexts but evidently not in others; different circumstances produced different conventions. In simple and familiar repertoires (chorales, for example) copy-sharing would have been quite practicable; but the idea of four (or more) ripienists' necessarily standing next to concertists at the front of a mixed ensemble in order to be able to share (undifferentiated) parts in a new cantata by Bach – at 7.30 or so on a Sunday morning[46] and perhaps by candlelight – is surely quite another matter. I am not aware of any evidence that suggests such a practice. Nor do I know of any reason to imagine that Bach's own practices constituted a special case.

[44] See also Illus. 24 and 25 below, p. 126. Various iconographical sources presented as pertinent evidence of copy-sharing fail to live up to claims made for them. One illustration in Koopman 1998 (his illus. 2), for example, shows unaccompanied outdoor singing from long before Bach's time (*c.*1650). In another (his illus. 4: Zurich, 1769) there are in any case probably just five singers *in toto*, with the three smaller figures sharing a desk on which there seem to be at least two copies.

[45] Koopman 1998, p. 116.

[46] Boyd 1990, pp. 120f.

6

Bach's use of ripienists

How often, and in what ways, did Bach make use of vocal ripienists?

There are almost 150 extant original sets of parts to church works by Bach. Of these sets, no more than nine include ripieno parts supporting the concertists;[1] and in one of the nine – the sumptuously scored Mühlhausen cantata *Gott ist mein König* BWV71 (1708) – the ripienists are explicitly optional ('se piace': see above, p. 36). These nine works are listed in Table 3A, and Table 4A shows how the ripienists are actually used in the same group of works. Wherever original ripieno parts survive, there is only one such copy for each voice part[2] – which seems to be the usual pattern in the German Baroque.[3] (For an example of such a ripieno part, see Illus. 15.) In a handful of further instances, markings found in scores or in concertists' parts may imply the intended participation of a ripieno group: see Table 3B.[4]

---

[1] (The count of nine does not include the four solo cantatas discussed above, pp. 39f.) By comparison, there are also some 26 surviving sets of parts, evidently complete or substantially complete, which are associated with the Neue Kirche's organist Carl Gotthelf Gerlach; only two of these sets include vocal ripieno parts: Glöckner 1990, pp. 97f, 131.

[2] There is a single exception: BWV76 has two soprano ripieno copies (see Appendix 5 below, p. 181 note 6). For two instances of what may be duplicate soprano concertist's copies, see BWV121 and 134 on p. 183 below.

[3] For example, 'all the Capella parts which survive in the Düben collection [from the second half of the seventeenth century] are single parts', with the exception of one double set: Webber 1996, p. 176. A generation or so later, 'the evidence of the vocal parts to Telemann's cantatas in the Frankfurt collection seems to point most often to performances with four singers, one per part. Somewhat less often the soprano part was provided with a ripieno part, and in much of the 1716–17 Jahrgang all four vocal parts had single ripienists': Swack 1999.

[4] See Rifkin 1983.

Illustration 15.   J. S. Bach, Dem Gerechten muß das Licht BWV195: *first page of 'Soprano in Ripieno' copy (cf. Ex. 13, p. 85 below)*

Table 3A.   Works by Bach with surviving copies for ripienists

BWV	title	first perf.	occasion	brass, timp	ripieno parts
71	Gott ist mein König	1708 Mühlhausen	Inauguration of Town Council	3 tpt timp	SATB 'se piace'[a]
63	Christen, ätzet diesen Tag	1714 ?Weimar	Christmas Day	4 tpt timp	– AT –[b]
76	Die Himmel erzählen die Ehre Gottes	1723 Leipzig	Trinity II	tpt	S(×2)A – –
21	Ich hatte viel Bekümmernis	1714 Halle	Trinity III *per ogni tempo*	3 tpt timp	SATB, added Leipzig 1723[c]
245	St John Passion	1724 Leipzig	Good Friday	—	SATB
110	Unser Mund sei voll Lachens	1725 Leipzig	Christmas	3 tpt timp	SAT, added c.1728–31
201	Geschwinde, ihr wirbelnden Winde (*Der Streit zwischen Phoebus und Pan*)	1729 Leipzig	[secular *dramma per musica*]	3 tpt timp	SA only[d]
29	Wir danken dir, Gott	1731 Leipzig	Inauguration of Town Council	3 tpt timp	SATB
195	Dem Gerechten muß das Licht	?c.1727/32 Leipzig	wedding	3 tpt (2 horns) timp[e]	SATB, added c.1742

[a] BWV71: 'âb 18. è se piace 22.': see above, p. 36. A wavy line (~~~) marked 'Capella' appears at the foot of the autograph score wherever the ripienists sing (see Illus. 8)
[b] BWV63: On the ambiguity surrounding these two copies, which are not labelled 'ripieno', see Rifkin 1996a, p. 599 n. 33
[c] BWV21: Also ?3/4 trombones *colla parte* added 1723: see Rifkin 1996a, *passim*
[d] BWV201 has six named characters, producing an unusual SATTBB scoring for the two choral movements (see p. 63, Example 3). As the two vocal bass parts move in octaves and unisons, only the two independent tenor parts effectively remain undoubled.
[e] BWV195: 3 tpts and timp in mvts 1 & 5; 2 horns in mvt 6

Of the fourteen works listed in Tables 3A and 3B (*over*),

- eleven employ an instrumental ensemble which includes one or more trumpets;
- four are for events outside the routine of Sundays and feast days;[5]
- three are proper to Christmas Day;
- four date from Bach's first weeks in office at Leipzig, May—June 1723;[6]
- at least two seem to have had no ripieno parts when first performed.

[5] BWV71 and BWV29, for town council installation ceremonies; BWV201, a secular *dramma per musica*; and BWV195, a wedding cantata.
[6] One or both of Bach's test pieces, performed in February 1723, may also have involved ripienists. See Wolff 1996, p. 135; Rifkin 1998a, p. 380 and n. 5; Wolff 1998, p. 540; and Rifkin 1998b.

TABLE 3B.   **Further works by Bach with indications of ripieno participation**

BWV	title	first perf.	occasion	brass, timp	'solo'/'tutti' indications
22	*Jesus nahm zu sich die Zwölfe*[a]	1723 Leipzig (a test piece)	Quinquagesima	—	in score
75	*Die Elenden sollen essen*[b]	1723 Leipzig (Bach's inauguration)	Trinity I	tpt	in score
24	*Ein ungefärbt Gemüte*[c]	1723 Leipzig	Trinity IV	tpt ('clarino')	in concertists' parts
234	Mass in A	*c.*1738 Leipzig; also *c.*1743/46 & *c.*1748/49	—	—	in score
191	Gloria in excelsis Deo (cf. BWV232(1))	*c.*1743/46 Leipzig	Christmas	3 tpt timp	[d]

Inscriptions by Bach are also found on the following works:
- 'S. A. T. et B. e 4 Ripie:', Bach's autograph score (1716) of J. C. Schmidt, *Auf Gott hoffe ich* (*motetto*)[e]
- 'Quatuor Voces in Concerto/ et/ Quatuor in Ripieno', Bach's autograph title-page (*c.*1740) to a score of G. B. Bassani's *Acroama missale.*[f]
- A. Lotti, *Missa sapientiae* (1730s), SSAATTBB; 'tutti' cues to ss only[g]
- Anon., Mass in G, BWV Anh.167 (1730s), 8 *concertato* voices and 4 ripienists[h]

[a] BWV22: See Rifkin 1990
[b] BWV75: See Rifkin 1990
[c] BWV24: See Rifkin 1990
[d] BWV191: The words 'solo'/'tutti' do not appear. However, in mvt 3 a wavy line (〜〜〜) appears from time to time at the foot of the autograph score, probably – by analogy with BWV71 (cf. Table 3A note *a*) – indicating passages where ripienists would sing
[e] See Melamed 1995, p. 22
[f] See *BD I*, p. 238
[g] See Rifkin 1990
[h] See Rifkin 1990

Together, the works in these lists give us valuable insight into Bach's conception of how ripienists could be used; and in this respect his explicit practice conspicuously fails to conform to today's expectations. Only in the St John Passion and at most two cantatas (BWV29 and 63) do ripienists sing throughout all the choruses to produce anything resembling the unvariegated 'choral' texture we are now accustomed to. At the other extreme, BWV71 includes an entire choral movement in which – unambiguously – the ripienists take no part at all.[7] (Bach's intention for the opening movement of the Mass in A Major BWV234 may well have been exactly the same.)

[7] See Ex. 5a below.

Ex. 3. J. S. Bach, *Geschwinde, geschwinde, ihr wirbelnden Winde (Dramma per musica : Der Streit zwischen Phoebus und Pan)* BWV201/15, bars 9–16

Wir danken dir, Gott BWV29 neatly illustrates the two main contexts in which the full participation of a ripieno group, if available, was entirely natural: the two choruses are an *alla breve* movement and a closing chorale. Chorale singing was part of the ripienist's stock-in-trade;[8] moreover, the instrumental doubling that was conventional in cantata (and Passion) chorales itself creates a ripieno effect. The first chorus is more familiar to us

---

[8] As Bach's designations in BWV55, 84 and 169 confirm; see above, p. 39.

in its later guises as the 'Gratias' and 'Dona nobis pacem' of the Mass in B Minor (see Ex. 4); with its fairly restrained use of eighth-note (♪) figuration and total avoidance of smaller note values, it stretches only a little Walther's definition of the 'serious style' of writing known as 'da Capella':[9]

> It is thus an accepted fact, then, that if many voices and instruments are to do one and the same thing accurately together, the composition must also be designed so that this can happen properly. Accordingly one finds that good and experienced masters employ only whole-, half- and quarter-notes [𝅝 𝅗𝅥 𝅘𝅥] in an *alla breve*, but dispose them in sundry ways with such great artistry and skill . . .

> Wobey es denn wohl eine ausgemachte Sache ist, daß, wenn viele Vocal- und Instrumental-Stimmen einerley *accurat* zusammen heraus bringen sollen, die *Composition* auch so beschaffen seyn müße, damit es füglich geschehen könne. Diesem nach findet man, daß gute und gewiegte Meister nur gantze, halbe, und viertel *Tact* Noten im *alla-breve*-Tact brauchen, aber in solchen grosse Kunst und Geschicklichkeit auf allerhand Art anbringen . . .[10]

In other words, large forces are best suited to music that is not unduly florid or elaborate.

A corollary of this principle is presumably that 'more intricate' music (to use Bach's own phrase) is essentially intended for smaller ensembles. The second and third choruses of BWV71 seem differentiated in just this way (see Exx. 5a and 5b), the one for concertists alone using supple counterpoint, the other (trills notwithstanding) with ripienists and predominantly in stately homophony.

Schematic plans of ripieno participation are given below in Tables 4A and 4B (which parallel Tables 3A and 3B). These plans cannot easily suggest either the inventiveness with which Bach deploys his vocal forces or the detailed modifications to vocal lines and text underlay that enable ripienists to enter and exit smoothly (as they do in Ex. 6, especially s part bar 17, SA parts bar 22, SAT parts bar 25). What these plans do convey, however, is the central importance of the concertists in each and every chorus.

Very broadly speaking, two underlying principles are at play. With the first, ripienists reinforce the full ensemble as it takes up musical ideas first introduced by concertists: see Ex. 7. In the case of *Die Himmel erzählen die Ehre Gottes* BWV76, where the bass concertist delivers the opening phrase alone, there is a definite echo of the traditional practice of having the first line or verse of a congregational chorale sung over by a single voice, usually the prefect.[11] Similarly, in fugal sections (as in BWV21, movement 11), a first exposition is typically sung by concertists alone (with continuo), and a

[9] On the term *capella*, see also pp. 4 and 35 above.
[10] Walther 1732, p. 139. See also Mattheson 1713, p. 145.
[11] See above, p. 10.

Ex. 4. J. S. Bach, *Wir danken dir, Gott* BVW29/2, bars 1–18

second exposition is then distinguished by the introduction of instrumental doubling: see Ex. 8. Vocal ripienists simply enhance the effect of forward momentum already created by successive instrumental entries

In concerto-like ritornello forms, on the other hand, ripienists join the full instrumental ensemble in acting as a foil to the concertists; see, for instance, Ex. 9. Indeed, fugal principle and ritornello principle can operate side by side, as in the opening chorus of BWV195 (see Ex. 6, p. 72 below; and cf. Ex. 13, pp. 85ff below). In such ways Bach uses his ripienists to clarify his musical structures still further, while remaining within the technical

Ex. 5a. J. S. Bach, *Gott ist mein König* BVW71/3, bars 1–13

Ex. 5b. J. S. Bach, *Gott ist mein König* BWV71/6, bars 3–10

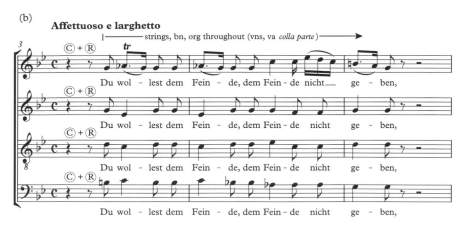

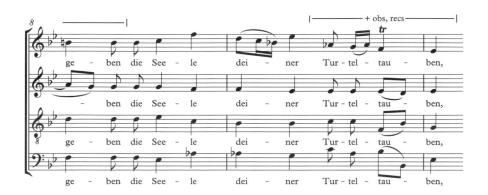

Table 4A.   Bach's ripieno writing

Ⓒ = concertists; Ⓡ = ripienists
Ⓡ〰➤ = passages in which the ripieno voices enter one by one

BWV71 *Gott ist mein König*

mvt	bars	concertists	ripienists	
1	1–7	Ⓒ	Ⓡ	
	7–13	Ⓒ	—	
	14–15	Ⓒ	Ⓡ	
	16–29	Ⓒ	—	
	29–36	Ⓒ	Ⓡ	
3	*passim*	Ⓒ		
6	*passim*	Ⓒ	Ⓡ	
7	1–32	Ⓒ	—	
	33	Ⓒ	Ⓡ	
	34–35	Ⓒ	—	
	35–39	Ⓒ	Ⓡ	
	40–64	Ⓒ	—	
	64–76	Ⓒ	Ⓡ〰➤	
	76–88	Ⓒ	Ⓡ	
	88–96	Ⓒ	—	
	96	Ⓒ	Ⓡ	
	97–98	Ⓒ	—	
	98–102	Ⓒ	Ⓡ	

BWV63 *Christen, ätzet diesen Tag*

1	*passim*	Ⓒ	Ⓡ[a]	
7	*passim*	Ⓒ	Ⓡ[a]	

[a] See Table 3A note *b*

BWV76 *Die Himmel erzählen die Ehre Gottes*

1	12–16	B only	—	
	20–59	Ⓒ	Ⓡ	
	67–93	Ⓒ	—	
	94–108	Ⓒ	Ⓡ〰➤	
	109–137	Ⓒ	Ⓡ	
7	*passim*	Ⓒ	Ⓡ	chorale
14	*passim*	Ⓒ	Ⓡ	chorale

BWV21 *Ich hatte viel Bekümmernis* (as performed in 1723)

2	*passim*	©	—
6	1–4	©	—
	5–43	©	®
	43–53	©	—
	59–75	©	®
9	1–116	©	T only[b]
	116–216	©	®
11	1–11	©	®
	12–25	©	—
	26–35	©	®⤳
	36–68	©	®

[b] Tenor has chorale melody in long note values

BWV245 **St John Passion** (as performed in 1724)[c]

	concertists	ripienists
— All choral writing —	©	®

[c] See Appendix 6, pp. 204ff

BWV110 *Unser Mund sei voll Lachens* (as performed *c.*1728—31)[d]

1	24–46	©	®	
	48–67	©	—	
	67–128	©	®	
	128–147	©	—	
	147–169	©	®	
7	*passim*	©	®	chorale

[d] There are surviving 'in Ripieno' parts for SAT but not for B; the 'con/senza ripieni' indications in *NBA* are editorial

BWV201 *Geschwinde, geschwinde, ihr wirbelnden Winde*[e]

1	*passim*	©	®
15	*passim*	©	®

[e] There are SA ripieno parts only: see Table 3A note *d*

BWV29 *Wir danken dir, Gott, wir danken dir*

2	*passim*	©	®	*stile antico*
8	*passim*	©	®	chorale

BWV195 *Dem Gerechten muß das Licht* (as performed *c*.1742)

2	13–14	©	®	
	14–16	©	s only	
	16–18	©	®	
	18–21	©	sa only	
	22	©	®	
	22–24	©	sat only	
	25	©	®	
	25–30	©	—	
	30–40	©	®⤳	
	41–52	©	®	
	52–72	©	—	
	72–83	©	®⤳	
	84–120	©	®	
5	21–28	©	—	
	33–54	©	®	
	57–76	©	—	
	77–78	©	®⤳	
	79–98	©	®	
	99–110	©	—	
	123–134	©	®	
	1–99 (*da capo*)	(*as before*)		
6	*passim*	©	®	chorale

Table 4B.   Further ripieno writing indicated by Bach

BWV22 *Jesus nahm zu sich die Zwölfe* (as performed in 1723)

1	7–55		
	56–62	'tutti' ⟿	successive entries
	62–85	[tutti]	
5	*passim*		chorale

BWV75 *Die Elenden sollen essen* (1723)

1	1–68		
	68–80		
	83–90	⟿	successive entries[a]
	91–105	[tutti]	
7	*passim*		chorale
14	*passim*		chorale

[a] 'tutti' marked only against B

BWV24 *Ein ungefärbt Gemüte* (1723)

3	1–37	[tutti]	s only: 'Tutti' at start
	37–54	'solo'	'solo' marked in s only
	54–69	'tutti' ⟿	successive entries
	69–104	[tutti]	
6	*passim*		chorale

BWV234 Mass in A Major (as performed in 1723)

1	*passim*		
2	*passim*		
6	1–6		
	7–24	'tutti'	except against B
	27–30	'solo'/'tutti'	B: 'tutti' throughout
	30–41	'tutti'	
	41–48	'solo'/'tutti'	inconsistently indicated
	48–53	'tutti'	against s only

BWV191 *Gloria in excelsis Deo* (1723 source)

1	*passim*	—
3	[b]	[b]

[b] A wavy line is drawn beneath the lowest system where the texture is full: see Table 3B note *d*, and cf. Illus. 8, p. 37 above.

Ex. 6. J. S. Bach, *Dem Gerechten muß das Licht* ʙᴠᴡ195/1, bars 13–25; in the passages shaded grey, ripienists join the concertists

Ex. 7. J. S. Bach, *Ich hatte viel Bekümmernis* BVW21/6, bars 1–10: in the passage shaded grey, ripienists join the concertists

limitations of his less skilled singers, who most often are merely duplicating the instruments' occasional reinforcement of the vocal concertists.

Most important of all, these elaborate movements with surviving ripieno parts give the overwhelming impression of being, above all, *for* concertists. Whether or not a particular ripieno group is strictly optional, its music mostly duplicates what is already there in the instrumental writing, and – in line with the definitions encountered earlier – it performs a role wholly subordinate to that of the concertists. Put most simply, the concertists are essential, the ripienists not. This, it will be recognized, is the exact reverse of today's preconception that chorus writing is obviously intended for a 'choir' (as opposed to a vocal quartet), and that it is of little consequence whether or not soloists choose to sing along.

This essential role played by concertists in choral movements could scarcely be more vividly illustrated than in the first 50 or so bars of the first Bach chorus that Leipzig will ever have heard – the opening of *Jesus nahm zu sich die Zwölfe* BWV22, performed as a test piece in the Thomaskirche on

7 February 1723 (see Ex. 10). Here there is every reason to suppose that a single tenor sings the introductory first phrase (effectively, as Evangelist) and that a single bass responds (as Christus), joined in due course (from bar 42) by a single soprano and a single alto.[12] Ripienists enter only for the final third of the movement (see Table 4B). A 'choir' (in the modern sense) – albeit one of probably no more than eight singers – is thus heard for a mere 23 bars in all.

While patently soloistic writing of this sort may easily be dismissed as atypical – as a particular response to a specific text – it is by no means uncommon. Indeed, it also characterizes Bach's second test piece, *Du wahrer Gott und Davids Sohn* BWV23, performed on the same day as BWV22; in his edition Christoph Wolff accordingly suggests that more than half the vocal passages of the choral third movement be sung 'solo'.[13] Similarly, *Ich glaube, lieber Herr, hilf meinem Unglauben* BWV109, written just a few months later, opens with another chorus which is persistently soloistic (see Ex. 11).[14] By this time Bach may already have abandoned the regular use of a ripieno group – and any such use would almost certainly not have extended to much of the quoted soprano part.

Nor is soloistic choral writing limited to early and pre-Leipzig works. Towards the very end of his life (1748–9) Bach wrote one of his most notorious solo/choral passages, in the Credo of the Mass in B minor (see Ex. 12). Few today would claim that Bach intended this passage to be sung by multiple basses, yet there is equally little authority for the modern custom of assigning it to an independent soloist who plays no further role in the movement.

Over a period of some thirty or more years, it was evidently Bach's usual practice to use ripienists to 'strengthen' his concertists only intermittently in the course of a movement. Except in chorales, continuous doubling is anything but a norm in his mature cantatas.[15] The surviving examples do

---

[12] The question has nevertheless been asked: 'Why should the Cöthen Capellmeister for his audition have risked introducing a vocal quartet in place of a chorus . . . ?' (Wolff 1998).

[13] See *NBA* I/8.1. Wolff editorially designates the opening phrase – bars 9–17 – to be sung *tutti*; my own impression, however, is that any ripieno parts prepared under Bach's supervision would have begun later, with the instrumentally doubled repetition of this phrase at bar 24. See also Rifkin 1998a, p. 380 and n. 5; Wolff 1998 (and Rifkin 1998b); and Parrott 1998, p. 653 n. 22.

[14] The movement has been recorded by Koopman using solo voices throughout, 'and very fine it sounds too' (Butt 1999). Also first heard in Bach's first few months at Leipzig, *Christus, der ist mein Leben* BWV95 opens with a chorus containing an extended passage for tenor alone (bars 64–88).

[15] For BWV63, see Rifkin 1996a, p. 599 n. 33.

Ex. 8. J. S. Bach, *Ich hatte viel Bekümmernis* BVW21/11, bars 25–36: in the passages shaded grey, ripienists join the concertists

Ex. 9. J. S. Bach, *Unser Mund sei voll Lachens* BVW110/1, bars 24–32, 48–54, 67–73, 126–137: in the passages shaded grey, ripienists join the concertists

very little to validate the current practice of singing all choruses 'chorally' from start to finish; nor are there any good reasons to consider these works exceptions to Bach's usual compositional practices. The assumption that all stylistically comparable choruses *require* ripienists – let alone undifferentiated doubling of the vocal lines from start to finish – is without foundation.

When concerted music was performed outside the normal routine of Sundays and feast days, Bach could (if he chose) assign more Thomasschule pupils to his first choir. This was obviously a possibility on occasions like weddings and civic ceremonies; it was also an option at Vespers on Good Friday, when in the second church only 'Lieder' (i.e. Passion chorales) were sung,[16] while the first choir performed a full Passion setting. (But it is unlikely that everyone in the second choir would be equal to the demands of Bach's concerted music.) When the St John Passion was first presented in 1724, there was a mix-up about the intended venue; Bach complied with the Town Council's last-minute instruction to transfer the service from the Thomaskirche to the Nikolaikirche – where the choir loft was apparently smaller – but

> He . . . asks that at all events certain provisions be made in the choir loft, so that he might properly accommodate the persons to be used in the ensemble.

> Er . . . bittet allenfalls ihme auf den Chor noch einige Gelegenheit, damit er die bey der *Music* zu gebrauchende Personen wohl *logir*en konte, machen . . . zulaßen.[17]

The performing forces on this occasion presumably exceeded those previously used by Bach for all works presented in each of the principal churches. The presence of vocal ripieno parts among the performance materials of the St John Passion is thus not unexpected.[18]

With its two choirs and two orchestras, the St Matthew Passion is without question a special case, and its instrumental requirements make it fairly clear that rather more players than usual were available to Bach. But there is certainly no reason to imagine that either of the two instrumental ensembles would – taken by itself – have been larger than for any of the cantatas; nor, of course, should we expect either of the vocal choirs to have been larger than usual. (The 'current orthodoxy', in presupposing a normal chorus of 12–16, expects Bach to have mustered 24 or even 32 sufficiently skilled singers

---

[16] Schering 1936, pp. 165f.

[17] *BD II*, p. 140 = *NBR*, p. 116. In 1709 Kuhnau too had requested improvements there (for reasons of safety) – to the 'steps . . . on which the town pipers stand' ('. . . eine Ausbeßerung derer Tritte . . ., worauff die StadtPfeiffer stehen'): Knick 1963, p. 124.

[18] For more on the St John Passion, see Rifkin 1996b.

for this work.[19]) The evidence of the surviving performance material for the St Matthew Passion is unequivocal: choirs I and II have just four copies each.[20] (The 'Soprano in Ripieno' part, with its two simple chorale melodies, and the nine small solo roles are distributed across separate self-contained copies in which all the other movements are marked 'tacet': see Table 5.) Thus only eight singers were needed for the choruses – just as, most probably, in the St John Passion and in those cantatas for which ripienists were demonstrably available. The essential difference would have been in the distribution of the eight singers: as four concertists doubled by four ripienists in the St John, and as two groups of four concertists each in the St Matthew. And, of course, when the latter's two groups of concertists combine in four-part writing – not only in all the chorales but at several points during double-chorus movements – the effect is identical to that of concertists doubled by (one-to-a-part) ripienists.

The Mass in B Minor is even more obviously a special case, if only because it most probably never received a complete performance in the composer's

Ex. 10. J. S. Bach, *Jesus nahm zu sich die Zwölfe* BWW22/1, bars 7–20

---

[19] Boyd 1996, p. 717; see also Schulze 1991, p. 24.
[20] See Appendix 6, p. 200 below; and see Rifkin 1982, p. 749.

Ex. 11. J. S. Bach, *Ich glaube, lieber Herr* BVW109/1, bars 17–24

Table 5.   Copies used in two of Bach's Passion performances

© = concertist's copy   ® = ripienist's copy

⊕ = additional copy

St John Passion BWV245 (1724 version)

S	A	T	B		S	A	T	B
©	©	©	©		®	®	®	®
		Evang.	Jesus				Petrus	

		T	B
		⊕*a*	⊕*b*
		Servus	Pilatus

St Matthew Passion BWV244 (1736 version)

		choir I					choir II	
S	A	T	B		S	A	T	B
©	©	©	©		©	©	©	©
		Evang.	Jesus		Testis 1	Testis 2		

S
®
Soprano
in Ripieno

S	B	B
⊕	⊕	⊕
Ancil.1/	Judas/	Petrus/
Ancil.2/	Pontif.1	Pontif.[Caiaphas]/
Uxor Pilati		Pontif.2/
		Pilatus

a BWV245 'Servus' part = lost copy
b BWV245 'Pilatus' part = fragmentary copy

Ex. 12. J. S. Bach, *Mass in B Minor* BWV232(II)/6 ('Et resurrexit'), bars 74–86

lifetime. Yet several of its choruses are taken more or less directly from pre-existing Leipzig church works,[21] and absolutely nothing in the music itself implies vocal performing forces in any way different from those discussed above. But because Bach sent a set of parts for the Kyrie and Gloria (a self-contained *Missa*) to Dresden in 1733, it is often argued that performances of the Mass in B Minor should be judged by the standards of the Dresden court. There, it has often been supposed, such music would routinely have been sung by a large vocal choir – 16 strong at the very least. In practice, though, the largest recorded number of singers in the Dresden chapel seems to be just eleven.[22]

---

[21]   See, for example, Butt 1991, pp. 42–59.

[22]   Rifkin 2000, pp. 246–50; in the Dresden *Hofkapelle* in 1733 there were no more than 11 singers (3S, 4A, 2T, 2B), and thus a double quintet would have been feasible only if one of the altos sang a soprano part (SII?).

The sheer scale and exceptional variety of the choral writing in the B Minor Mass – along with the double-choir writing in the 'Osanna' and the likelihood that ripicnists were used in the model for the 'Cum Sancto Spiritu', BWV191 (see Table 4B) – arguably render the Mass an apt candidate for the selective addition, on Bach's own principles, of ripieno parts. (Such a selective application is demonstrated in my 1984 recording of the Mass with the Taverner Consort and Players (originally EMI 7 47293 8, reissued as Virgin Veritas 7243 5 61337 2 3).) It cannot be assumed, though, that the same is necessarily true of other large-scale works; surprisingly, perhaps, the nature of the choral writing in the Magnificat BWV243, for example, does not seem to lend itself at all easily to such treatment.

It has been objected that the use of one-to-a-part concertists – with or without ripienists – makes implausible demands on the concertists' stamina, but this overlooks the incontrovertible fact that concertists in any case sang throughout all choral movements, whether doubled by ripienists or not.

Ex. 13. J. S. Bach, *Dem Gerechten muß das Licht* BVW195/1, bars 13–44

Ex. 13. *cont.*

7

The *Entwurff*

At this stage of the argument we must return to key passages in Bach's *Entwurff*.

In August 1730, exasperated and humiliated by 'one unmerited affront or another' from a Town Council 'little interested in music',[1] Bach drafted a lengthy memorandum (see Appendix 3), which 'addresses troublesome aspects of the organizational structure of the Leipzig church music'.[2] This *Entwurff* explains that

- Bach was responsible for the music at five churches with different musical requirements;
- for this purpose, the 55 resident pupils of the Thomasschule were divided into four choirs, but
- those pupils varied considerably in musical ability, and only some were able to perform elaborate concerted pieces (such as Bach's own cantatas);
- such pieces often required more instrumentalists than the eight paid by the Town Council for such service, so that
- some Thomasschule pupils were needed as instrumentalists, and the number of pupils available as singers was diminished to that extent.

This document has been the prime source for the model of an 'ideal' Bach choir of three or four singers per part. Does the *Director musices* himself not say (to quote the 1966 *Bach Reader*) that 'it would be still better if . . . one could have [not three but] 4 singers on each part and thus could perform every chorus with 16 persons'?[3]

---

[1] 'ein und ein andere Bekränckung unverschuldeter weise', 'eine . . . der *Music* wenig ergebene Obrigkeit': *BD I*, pp.74, 67 = *NBR*, pp.158, 152.

[2] Wolff 1998, p.540. On Bach's strategy in the *Entwurff*, see also Appendix 6 Table IV, p. 195 below.

[3] *BR*, p. 121.

In short, no, he does not. While the 1998 *New Bach Reader* gives an accurate rendering of the clause just quoted,[4] its influential predecessor's poor translation of the passage reflected – and has perpetuated – a crucial misconception. This is what Bach writes:

> Each 'musical' choir must have at least three sopranos, three altos, three tenors, and as many basses . . . (NB though it would be better still if the student body were composed in such a way that one could take four individuals [*subjecta*] for each voice and thus set up each choir with sixteen persons.)

> Zu iedweden *musica*lischen *Chor* gehören wenigsten 3 *Sopran*isten, 3 *Alti*sten, 3 *Tenor*isten, und eben so viel *Baß*isten . . . (*NB.* Wiewohln es noch beßer, wenn der *Coetus* so beschaffen wäre, daß mann zu ieder Stimme 4 *subjecta* nehmen, und also ieden *Chor* mit 16. Persohnen bestellen könte.) (*Entwurff*, ¶8)

The problem lies with the word *Chor* (chorus), which at its first appearance here clearly refers to a body of performers, rather than to a musical movement. At its second appearance its sense is surely the same (*pace* the old *Bach Reader*), as the verb *bestellen* confirms ('to set up', 'to order', rather than 'to perform').[5] Far from specifying the number of singers needed to 'perform every chorus' in his cantatas, Bach is simply urging that at least 12 singers be assigned year-round to each of his first three *choirs*. These choirs should in any case be viewed as 'pools' of performers from which Bach could draw differing performing forces appropriate to each repertoire. (If a professional football/soccer club is to have the capability of fielding full and balanced teams of skilled and fit players throughout a whole season, it must employ a 'pool' or squad well in excess of the 11 players who take the field as a team at the start of a particular game.[6]

By statute, just eight Thomasschule pupils were allocated to each of the four church choirs (see Table 6 below). Bach's desire to increase these numbers was not new, as a document from the previous year shows. Submitted to the Leipzig Town Council as an enclosure with a letter of 18 May 1729 from the chairman of the school board, Christian Ludwig Stieglitz, is a plan in Bach's own hand showing the distribution of 44 singers in four choirs:

In the Nikolaikirche to the first choir belong	In the Thomaskirche to the second choir	In the Neue Kirche to the third choir
3 sopranos	3 sopranos	3 sopranos
3 altos	3 altos	3 altos
3 tenors	3 tenors	3 tenors
3 basses	3 basses	3 basses

[4] *NBR*, p. 146.
[5] See Rifkin 1990, n. 55. The first published English translation gets the passage right: Spitta 1889, p. 248.
[6] This useful analogy is borrowed from Rifkin: cf. Appendix 6, pp. 197f.

to the fourth choir

2 sopranos

2 altos

2 tenors

2 basses[7]

But such numbers can be misleading; Kuhnau explains that,

> because some of them are often either out of town or ill, the number can almost never be complete . . .

> weil deren einige öfters entweder verreiset oder kranck sind, der *Numerus* fast niemahls *complet* seyn kan . . .[8]

As a majority of *alumni* came from outside Leipzig (cf. Appendix 2, below), home visits and other absences had to be carefully regulated.[9] Illness was a constant problem;[10] the rigours of the New Year singing took their toll each year,[11] and there were also occasional deaths.[12]

The reasoning behind Bach's stated minimum of three singers of each voice type for each group turns out to be eminently practical:

> so that even if one person falls ill (as very often happens, and particularly at this time of year [late August], as the prescriptions written by the school doctor for the apothecary must show), at least a two-choir motet can be sung.

> damit, so etwa einer unpaß wird (wie denn sehr offte geschieht, und besonders bey itziger Jahres Zeit, da die *recepte*, so von dem Schul *Medico* in die Apothecke verschrieben werden, es ausweisen müßen) wenigstens eine 2 *Chörig*te *Motette* gesungen werden kan. (*Entwurff*, ¶8)

---

[7]   *BD I*, p. 250 = *NBR*, pp. 141f; see also *BD II*, p. 192.

[8]   Kuhnau (1709), ¶8 = Knick 1963, p. 125.

[9]   See *Ordnungen*, 1733 pp. 34ff (chap. 11).

[10]   Kuhnau too refers to 'ill or scabious pupils' ('kranck- und kräzigten Schülern'): Kuhnau (1709), ¶8 = Knick 1963, p. 126. (See also Kuhnau (1717) = Spitta 1880, p. 862.) In 1749 Jacob Born noted that 'a long time ago sick singers were sent to the Nikolaikirche' ('geraume Zeit her in die Kirche zu St Nicolai elende Sänger geschickt worden'): Fröde 1984, p. 53. See also Held 1894, p. 90, and Owens (forthcoming).

[11]   In 1736 Maximilian Nagel, then the first choir's prefect, 'complained that because of a weak constitution he was not in a state to hold out' ('sich beklagete, wie daß wegen überbeschaffener Leibes*constitution* nicht im Stande sey es auszutauern') through the New Year singing (*BD I*, p. 88 = *NBR*, p. 176). Under an arrangement dating back to at least 1694 (see Fröde 1984, p. 54), Bach regularly received annual sums 'for the concertists who have been excused the New Year singing on account of the [concerted] church music, as a reward' ('vor die *Concertist*en, so beym NeuJahr singen zur Kirchen *Music* geschonet worden, zur Ergötzlichkeit'): *BD II*, p. 135 (see also *ibid.*, pp. 134, 136, 335; Kuhnau (1717) = Spitta 1880, p. 863; and Fröde 1984, pp. 53f). (Where the Thomaskirche records use the term '*Concertist*en', those of the Nikolaikirche use '*Discantist*en'.) Cf. Held 1894, pp. 70f.

[12]   During Bach's 27 years in Leipzig there were reportedly 17 such deaths: Richter 1907, p. 47.

This is hardly the stuff of an artistic manifesto. And, once again, the context accords central importance not to the special demands of Bach's concerted music – the prime focus of our attention – but to the humbler motet repertoire common to choirs I–III.

Bach must have known that he would never be granted as many as 16 singers for each of these three 'musical' choirs. His was simply a time-honoured negotiating tactic: asking for 16 gave him a better chance of actually ensuring a workable pool of 12.

> Accordingly, the number of those who must understand *musica* works out at 36 persons.

> Machet demnach der *numerus*, so *Musicam* verstehen müßen, 36 Persohnen aus. (*Entwurff*, ¶9)

(Those remaining, 'who do not understand music at all' ('so keine *music* verstehen'), were assigned to the fourth choir.)[13] Even this total of 36 qualified singers, forming three balanced choirs of 12 each, was hard enough to achieve from a student body of 55: Table 6 sets out various possible deployments.[14] Only a year after the *Entwurff* was written there were, for example, just 10 singers at the Neue Kirche: four basses, and two each of soprano, alto and tenor.[15]

Such choir sizes may all seem to us puzzlingly modest, if not downright 'minimal'; yet in the context of eighteenth-century Leipzig they may actually have represented something of an expansion. New regulations for the Thomasschule, issued in 1723 (the year Bach took up office there), show that only 32 of the 55 or so boys were expected to take part in the school's singing activities,[16] with just eight allocated to each of the four choirs:

> whereas also nowadays the schoolboys who are in attendance at divine service are divided into four *Cantoreien*, into each of which eight are admitted . . . by the Cantor . . .

> Dieweil auch ietziger Zeit die Schul-Knaben, welche den Gottesdienst abwarten, in 4 Cantoreyen eingetheilet, in deren ieder von dem *Cantore* . . . ihrer acht angenommen . . .[17]

---

[13] *Entwurff*, ¶7. Bach's list of 17 'usable' pupils (*Entwurff*, ¶19) has on occasion been taken as representing the first choir (see, for example, Koopman 1998, p. 111); yet three of those named are prefects, at least two of whom would have been needed to supervise other choirs (see above, pp. 9f and 12). Moreover, it would make little sense to imagine Bach's having to plead for choirs of 12 or 16 if his first choir already exceeded that number.

[14] On the possible involvement of the school's *externi*, see below, pp. 104ff.

[15] See Schulze 1977, p. 75; see also Rifkin 1995a, p. 229.

[16] The allusion to '55 choral stipends' in Wolff 1998 (p. 540) gives the misleading impression that all 55 boarders were used as singers.

[17] *Ordnungen*, 1723 pp. 73f (chap. 13 ¶8).

Table 6.   Deployment of Thomasschule pupils

source

c.55 pupils

choir I	choir II	choir III	choir IV	non-singers	
Nikolaikirche & Thomaskirche (in rotation)		Neue Kirche	Petrikirche (& Johanniskirche)		*a*
works by Bach (+ motets, chorales etc.)	simple cantatas (+ motets, chorales etc.)	motets (+ chorales etc.)	chorales (etc.)		
8	8	8	8	[*c.*23]	*b*
12	12	12	8	[*c.*11]	*c*
12 (16)	12 (16)	12 (16)	[?8 (*c.*7)]	[?11 (0)]	*d*
17 'usable'	20 'not yet usable'		17 'unproficient'		*d*
?	?	10	?	?	*e*

a See Table 2, p. 19 above
b *Ordnungen*, 1723, 1733
c Bach, 1729 plan, pp. 94f above
d *Entwurff*, ¶7 (1730)
e See text, note 15

This regulation seems to have held good for some time and was reiterated by the Town Council in a decree of 1737.[18]

'The figure of eight singers to a choir seems to have represented something of a traditional norm', as one writer has observed, 'no doubt because it encompassed virtually every vocal scoring common at the time.'[19] This is the number found in 1714, for example, in the Württemberg *Hofkapelle* at Stuttgart.[20] Telemann's vocal resources in Frankfurt seem to have fallen below this level; in 1717 he drew the Town Council's attention to the fact

[18]   *BD I*, pp. 99, 105 = *NBR*, p. 189; see also *BD II*, p. 269 = *NBR*, p. 177.
[19]   Rifkin 1982, p. 750.
[20]   Owens (forthcoming), where we also learn that the *Hofkapelle* comprised 35 musicians in all, and that by 1717 the number of singers for 'the Church Music' had increased

that before this there were already voices *in duplo* [i.e. two of each], not to mention that the instrumental choir then also contained far more individuals [*subjecta*] than currently . . .

daß schon vor diesem die Singe-Stimmen *in duplo* besetzet gewesen, zu geschweygen daß auch damahls der *Instrumental-Chor* weit mehr *Subjecta*, als gegenwartig, begriffen . . .[21]

According to Scheibe (1737), a double quartet was a working minimum:

A complete choir of singers, for use both in the theatre and in church and chamber, cannot consist of fewer than eight persons. These I break down in the following way: first a pair of sopranos, [then] a pair of altos, a pair of tenors, and a high bass or so-called baritone and finally a low bass. But these eight persons must all be skilled people. However, as the choruses could still be filled out, one would quite easily be able – at courts – to add the chapel boys, [or] – in towns – some schoolboys.

Ein vollständiger Singechor, der so wohl zum Theater, als zur Kirche und zur Kammer zu gebrauchen ist, kann aus nicht weniger, als aus acht Personen bestehen. Diese theile ich folgendermaßen ein. Erstlich zweene Diskantisten, zweene Altisten, zweene Tenoristen, und ein hoher Baßist, oder so genannte Baritonist, und endlich ein tiefer Baßist. Diese acht Personen aber müßen alle geschickte Leute seyn. Da aber annoch die Chöre würden auszufüllen seyn, so könnte man an Höfen gar füglich die Capellknaben, in Städten aber einige Schulknaben, darzu anführen.[22]

Thus a pool of singers might be expanded from eight to perhaps 12, or even to 16.

Having stated in the *Entwurff* that 36 pupils (forming three choirs of 12) 'must understand *musica*', Bach turns to the question of his instrumental needs and resources. As we have already learnt, whenever concerted music was performed by the first 'choir', some portion of the pool of boys served not as singers but as instrumentalists:

because the second violin has mostly had to be taken by pupils, and the viola, violoncello and violone always so . . .

da die 2de *Violin* meistens, die *Viola*, *Violoncello* und *Violon* aber allezeit . . . mit Schülern habe bestellen müßen . . . (*Entwurff*, ¶14)

Separate stipends (*beneficia*) which had enabled Bach's predecessors to make use of a few university students – 'a bass and tenor, and even an alto . . . [and]

to 10 through the addition of another pair of female sopranos (girls singing 'Ripieno'). At Lüneburg, in Cantor Johann Conrad Dreyer's time, there were to be at least eight 'proficient singers' ('tüchtige Sänger'): Küster 1996, p. 86.

[21] Telemann [I], p. 26. See also Swack 1999, as quoted above, p. 59 note 3.
[22] Scheibe 1745, p. 156 (first published 1737).

particularly two violinists' – had (he claimed) 'been completely with-drawn'.[23] Moreover,

> cooperation from the *studiosi* has disappeared too; for who will work or render services for nothing?[24]

> so hat . . . sich auch die Willfährigkeit der *Studiosorum* verlohren; Denn wer wird ümsonst arbeiten, oder Dienste thun? (*Entwurff*, ¶14)

This was perhaps Bach's most pressing complaint in the *Entwurff* (see below, p. 108).

The use of pupils as instrumentalists must effectively have ruled out a vocal ripieno group on many occasions:

> [Thus] it is easy to imagine what the vocal choir has thereby lost.

> So ist leicht zu erachten was dadurch dem *Vocal Chore* ist entgangen. (*Entwurff*, ¶14)

And, as Bach was at pains to point out, his logistical problems were obviously most acute on feast days, 'on which I have to look after the music in both principal churches at the same time'[25] – i.e. when the second choir too was performing concerted music (see Table 2, p. 19 above).

What this all amounts to is that the *Entwurff* cannot be construed as a plea for a full complement of 12 (let alone 16) pupils to be deployed as a purely 'vocal choir' when instruments were also involved. At the very least, three of his musically most able boys were 'always' required to play rather than sing; and as many as five to eight boys might be needed to bring the string group up to the 11 players specified elsewhere in the same document.[26] And on feast days, at least two pupils – a pair of violinists, perhaps – had to be reallocated to the second choir. Under such circumstances, and allowing for absence through illness 'as very often happens', Bach can never have used as many as 12 pupils as singers in his cantatas. Moreover, the chances of forming a balanced SATB group from those singers who were not needed as instrumentalists cannot have been particularly good. If, then, he had chosen to compose in a way that not only called for several voices per part but also required equal numbers of each voice-type, he would have been exacerbating what was in any case a considerable organizational problem.

---

[23] *Entwurff*, ¶¶16, 14. Cf. Kuhnau (1709), ¶12: Knick 1963, p. 126.
[24] For more on Bach's relationship with the university students, see *BD II*, p. 95 = *NBR*, p. 103, and *BD I*, pp. 35, 38 = *NBR*, pp. 120, 122f. For Kuhnau's accounts, in 1709 and 1720, of difficulties in attracting *studiosi*, see Knick 1963, pp. 125f and pp. 127f respectively.
[25] 'als an welchen [ich] in denen beeden HauptKirchen die *Music* zugleich besorgen muß': *Entwurff*, ¶14.
[26] As Siegele has shown (1978, pp. 334f), the implied disposition of strings is 3-3-2-2-1 where there is one viola part, and 2-2-2-2-2-1 where the violas are in two parts. Thus 11 rather than 13 string-players are called for.

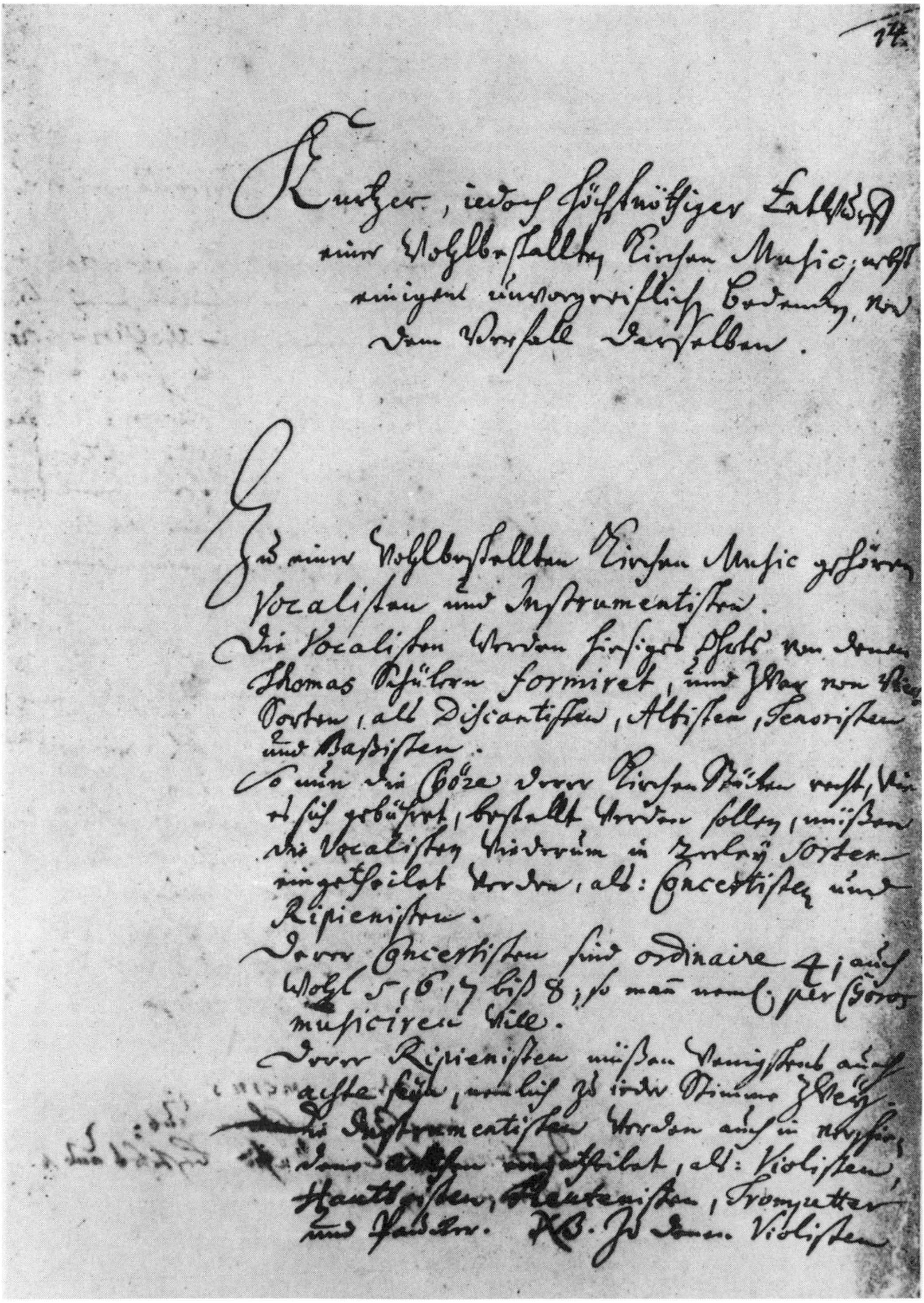

14.

Kurtzer, iedoch höchstnöthiger Entwurff einer Wohlbestallten Kirchen Music; nebst einigen unvorgreiflichen Bedencken, von dem Verfall derselben.

Zu einer Wohlbestallten Kirchen Music gehören Vocalisten und Instrumentisten.

Die Vocalisten werden hiesiges Orthes von denen Thomas Schülern formiret, und zwar von vier Sorten, als Discantisten, Altisten, Tenoristen und Bassisten.

So nun die Chöre derer Kirchen Stücken recht, wie es sich gebühret, bestellet werden sollen, müßen die Vocalisten wiederum in 2erley Sorten eingetheilet werden, als: Concertisten und Ripienisten.

Derer Concertisten sind ordinaire 4; auch wohl 5, 6, 7 biß 8; so man nemlich per Choros musiciren will.

Derer Ripienisten müßen wenigstens auch achte seyn, nemlich zu ieder Stimme zwey.

Die Instrumentisten werden auch in verschiedene Sorten eingetheilet, als: Violisten, Hautboisten, Fleutenisten, Trompetter und Paucker. NB. Zu denen Violisten

Illustration 16. J. S. Bach, 'Entwurff einer wohlbestallten Kirchen Music', *23 August 1730: first page (autograph)*

Numbers were not the only issue. There was also the question of the boys'
sheer musical ability:[27]

> Besides, it cannot remain unmentioned that, as a result of the admission
> hitherto of so many unproficient and musically quite untalented boys, music
> has necessarily had to deteriorate and decline.

> Hiernechst kan nicht unberühret bleiben, daß durch bißherige *reception* so
> vieler untüchtigen und zur *music* sich gar nicht schickenden Knaben, die
> *Music* nothwendig sich hat vergeringern und ins abnehmen gerathen müßen.
> (*Entwurff*, ¶15)[28]

In other words, the policy of admitting a quota of boys purely on the basis
of their academic ability left Bach with fewer musical boys to choose from,
and overall standards in church music were bound to suffer. It may be that
some of those cantatas in which the chorus sings nothing more than a simple concluding chorale – for example, five out of twelve cantatas from
between Easter and Trinity Sunday 1725[29] – represent one way in which Bach
could circumvent problems of this sort. (Carl Heinrich Graun implies, however, that the general standard of singing may have been high.[30])

Bach pointedly concludes his *Entwurff* by listing 17 pupils (almost one-
third of the student body) whom he classes as 'unproficient'.[31] But within a
few years things were to get worse still, under the 'progressive' new Rector,
J. A. Ernesti, who challenged the central role played by music in the
Thomasschule's curriculum. 'Do you want to become an alehouse fiddler
[*Bierfiedler*] as well?', he would reportedly demand of any pupil found prac-
tising an instrument.[32]

In both tone and content, the *Entwurff* as a whole makes it abundantly
clear that Bach's purpose in detailing the size and composition of his musical resources as he did was to make the members of the Leipzig Town
Council aware of the severe organizational difficulties under which he
was labouring, rather than to instruct them in the fundamentals of musical

[27] Kuhnau considered that his first choir 'on the other hand, however, is [only] as
good as the second choir has been in Herr Schelle's time' ('doch aber eben so gut ist, aß
zu Herrn Schellens Zeiten der andere *Chor* gewesen'): Kuhnau (1709), ¶11 = Knick 1963,
p. 126.

[28] Under the terms of Bach's 1723 contract, boys without musical talent and/or train-
ing would not be admitted to the school: *BD I*, p. 177. A century earlier, Seth Calvisius
'found that the boys he had accepted on musical grounds were turned down by the rector' (Butt 1994, p. 30).

[29] Cf. Boyd 1990, p. 125.

[30] In 1756 Graun wrote to Telemann describing a performance in Berlin of his Passion
Der Tod Jesu: 'The instrumental music was well executed, but the singers in every little
town in Saxony and Thuringia would have done it better' ('Die Instrumental Music
ward gut executiret, aber die Sänger in allen Sächsischen und Thüringischen Städtgen
würden es beßer gemacht haben'): Telemann [I], p. 293.

[31] 'untüchtig': *Entwurff*, ¶22.

[32] Köhler 1776; *BD III*, p. 314 = *NBR*, p. 172. See also above, p. 12 note 11.

performance practice. He may not have relished the task of explaining – in writing and to non-musicians – the logistical intricacies of the music-making for which he was responsible; but, although the *Entwurff* may not always be a model of clarity, its purpose seems clear enough. Bach was telling the Town Council that his three principal choirs had to discharge a wide range of musical tasks, and that he wished to be able to allocate 12 (or even 16) persons to each of those choirs in order to perform those varied duties more effectively and consistently.

If Bach had just wanted to single out his first choir as needing a bigger vocal group – to balance the instruments in his own concerted music or to project better in Leipzig's two principal churches, or perhaps to praise God more splendidly[33] – he could surely have found ways of saying so.

[33] Mattheson, perhaps with Hamburg's capacious principal churches in mind, suggests that a large ensemble including two 'capella' groups (probably two ripieno quartets), 'if well directed, is certainly something which contributes quite noticeably to devotion' ('wenn sie wol *dirigi*rt wird/ ist gewiß eine Sache/ die gar mercklich zur Andacht *contribui*ret'): Mattheson 1713, p. 159. Kuhnau, after asking that certain stipends for additional musicians be made available once more, concludes his 1709 *Erinnerung* to the Leipzig Town Council thus: 'By these means the praise and glory of God would be furthered, many devout students (who prefer studying to hanging about with merrymakers all the time) would be helped, and perhaps God's blessing might also be increasingly felt' ('Hiedurch würde Gottes Lob und Ehre befördert, manchem frommen, und lieber studirenden alß der lustigen *Compagnie* immer anhangenden Studenten geholffen, auch vielleicht Gottes Seegen immer mehr und mehr gespüret werden'): ¶12 = Knick 1963, p. 126.

8

Additional performers

The current orthodox view of the size of Bach's chorus has always relied heavily on what the *Entwurff* appears to be saying.[1] Yet it is appropriate to warn against 'see[ing] evidence of Bach's forces in the prescriptions for the organization of choirs with which he begins the *Entwurff*. Whatever his remarks do or do not mean . . ., they surely do not allow us to draw firm conclusions about his actual performances.'[2] While concurring with Rifkin that the document 'simply does not allow for a reconstruction of the composition of the actual vocal—instrumental ensemble',[3] Wolff also invokes 'the considerable alternative resources available to Bach as well as to his predecessors and successors'.[4] From the existence of resources outside the Thomasschule, we are meant to infer that Bach could readily call upon many more singers of adequate proficiency, and to believe that the very availability of such performers necessarily indicates that Bach's concerted choral music was originally sung by several singers per part.[5]

As the *Entwurff* and other documents show, the backbone of Bach's instrumental ensemble consisted of the *Stadtpfeifer* and *Kunstgeiger*, two

[1] See, in particular, Schering 1920, p. 78.

[2] Rifkin 1982, p. 751 n. 34. See also Rifkin 1998b.

[3] Wolff 1998, p. 540. This, of course, begs the question: if 'a chorus of 12–16' as Bach's 'standard ensemble' for church music in Leipzig (*ibid.*, p. 541) is *not* implied by the *Entwurff*, whence does it arise?

[4] Wolff 1999; see also Koopman 1998, pp. 111, 113, and Smithers 1997, *passim*. Wolff suggests that 'naming and enumerating these alternative resources would have defeated the purpose' of the *Entwurff*; presumably Bach intended his omissions to pass unnoticed by the Town Council. This might be a reasonable hypothesis if it were a matter of two or three extra performers; it is far less plausible with the more numerous additional resources that Wolff proposes.

[5] Alternative conclusions drawn from the *Entwurff* have been mistakenly characterized as the product of 'arithmetic exercises based solely on the names of choristers and town musicians listed' there (Wolff 1998, p. 540).

small groups of professional musicians employed for this purpose by the Town Council. It is clear that, along with these municipal musicians and the Thomasschule pupils, Bach could also draw upon various additional performers. But how numerous were they, and what was their role?

It has been argued that the *Entwurff* substantially underrepresents the forces regularly available to Bach, because 'three essential groups of musicians are not included': the Thomasschule's *externi* (non-resident pupils), university students, and apprentices and journeymen.[6] The issue, though, is significantly less clear-cut than may at first appear. With regard to the last of these categories, for example, Bach – like Kuhnau before him – explicitly mentions the inclusion of one or more apprentices (*Gesellen*) within the total of the eight municipal musicians who took part in church services. Kuhnau refers to 'the town pipers, string-players and apprentices, comprising eight persons in all',[7] and Bach enumerates them as follows:

> The number of persons appointed to the church musical establishment[8] consists of eight persons, viz. four *Stadtpfeifer*, three string-players and one apprentice.

> Der *Numerus* derer zur Kirchen *Music* bestellten Persohnen bestehet aus 8 Persohnen, als 4. StadtPfeifern, 3 KunstGeigern und einem Gesellen. (*Entwurff*, ¶11)

(In the list (*Plan*) that then follows, 'Der Geselle' (unnamed) appears again – as bassoonist.) The fact that one apprentice *is* mentioned tends to suggest that if others of similar status had 'typically' been available, they would also have been mentioned – at least, in a detailed memorandum of this sort.[9]

Similarly, university students *are* included in the *Entwurff*, though they are neither named nor enumerated for the very good reason that their participation could no longer be relied upon: 'cooperation from the *studiosi* has disappeared too'.[10]

Of these three categories, the largest by far is the school's *externi*, who by 1733 evidently outnumbered the *interni* (or *alumni*) in the upper school by

---

[6] See *ibid.* Along with the category of university students Wolff mentions 'Adjuvanten and volunteers recruited primarily from the local *collegia musica*'.

[7] 'die aus 8 Personen zusammen bestehenden Stadt Pfeiffer Kunst Geiger und Gesellen': Kuhnau (1709), ¶12 = Knick 1963, p. 126.

[8] On the term *Music*, see p. 5 above.

[9] Wolff argues that the town musicians 'typically brought along and played with their usually unspecified and variable entourage of apprentices and journeymen' (Wolff 1998, p. 541 n. 3); little justification for this claim is found in the one source cited by Wolff, namely Werner 1933.

[10] 'so hat . . . sich auch die Willfährigkeit der *Studiosorum* verlohren': *Entwurff*, ¶14. (The context in which students are mentioned is – perhaps significantly – that of instrumental rather than vocal resources.) For more on the role played by students, see below, pp. 106ff, and Table 7.

some two to one.[11] But these *externi* are also the least likely to have had any direct impact on the performance of Bach's own music, simply because – unlike the select group of *alumni* – they did not constitute a *musical* body. Even the New Year singing – which probably made only modest musical demands – did not involve them; while 32 of the boarders were thus occupied, all the remaining pupils (*inquilini* and *externi*) were to attend classes.[12] The only likely involvement of an individual *externus* in any musical activity was not as an extra but, rather, as a substitute for an absent *alumnus* – and then probably more often in street singing or at funerals than in Bach's music.[13] Any musically talented boy amongst their number is almost certain, at the earliest opportunity, to have sought one of the highly prized free residential places which the school offered;[14] and, indeed, whenever a place became vacant, preference was explicitly given to a boy who was already an *externus*.[15] The *alumni* – or at least those who had been admitted on the Cantor's recommendation (see above, p. 101) – formed the musical core of the larger school body, and in return for their considerable duties (see above, chapter 2) they received not only full board and lodging but also certain financial privileges (which were jealously guarded).[16]

It is unsurprising, therefore, that the *externi* were specifically excluded from membership of the prestigious first choir under a 1723 regulation:

> none apart from boarders must be admitted to the first *Cantorey* . . .

> müssen in der ersten *Cantorey* keine andere als *Inquilini* . . . *recipir*et werden . . .[17]

In any case, it seems highly unlikely that there would ever have been numerous musically skilled *externi* who were capable of performing elaborate concerted music alongside the élite of the first choir.[18]

---

[11] 'Whereas, however, the number of *externi* in the four upper classes has grown so much that there are twice as many again of them as of *alumni*' ('Dieweilen aber die Zahl der *Externorum* in den 4 Obern *Class*en so angewachsen ist, daß deren wohl noch zweymal soviel als der *Alumnorum* sind'): *Ordnungen*, final part p. 16 (J. A. Ernesti, '*Addenda* zu den Geßnerischen Anmerckungen', Anhang B: *c*.1736).

[12] *Ibid.*

[13] See *Ordnungen*, 1733 p. 19 (chap. 4 ¶6), p. 34 (chap. 11 ¶2), and p. 37 (chap. 12 ¶2).

[14] See, for example, *BD I*, p. 66 (Christian Gottfried Hesse). See also *Ordnungen*, 1733 p. 37 (chap. 12 ¶3).

[15] See *Ordnungen*, 1723 p. 38 (chap. 6 ¶1).

[16] Likewise, any competing musical activity that might involve *externi* was closely monitored. 'Whereas also this private house singing has hitherto been very much misused by some *externi* and in particular such beggar-boys as pass themselves off, falsely, as Thomasschule pupils . . .' ('Dieweil auch das Singen in denen *Privat*-Häusern von einigen *Externis*, und insonderheit solchen *Bettel*-Knaben, welche sich fälschlich für *Thomas*-Schüler ausgeben, bißher sehr gemißbraucht worden . . .'): *Ordnungen*, 1723 p. 57 (chap. 8 ¶15) = Knick 1963, p. 151.

[17] *Ordnungen*, 1723 p. 74 (chap. 13 ¶8).

[18] It has nevertheless been claimed that Bach had at his disposal both 'singers and

The status of Bach's own sons is intriguing. Although they attended the Thomasschule (where they almost certainly received a free education), the fact that they were evidently classified not as *inquilini* but as *externi*[19] indicates that they did not also receive board and lodging from the school, and thus that they did not occupy any of the coveted free residential places. (The Cantor's living quarters were under the same roof as the school but in a separate part of the building; see Illus. 3, p. 11 above.) One may easily imagine, though, that their status as the Cantor's sons might have allowed – even obliged – them to take part, at least on occasion, in the first choir's concerted music-making. (Interestingly, C. P. E. Bach is silent on the subject in his autobiographical sketch.[20]) Yet theirs would clearly have been a very special case. More particularly, any musical contribution they may have made is just as likely to have been instrumental as vocal. (In 1726 Friedemann was sent away to Merseburg for almost a year to study the violin with no less a figure than Johann Gottlieb Graun.) Their participation is also more likely to have had qualitative than quantitative significance, as no more than two of Bach's sons attended the school at any one time.

By contrast, the role played by Leipzig's university students – the *studiosi* – appears to have been vital to a 'properly constituted church musical establishment', and specifically to its first choir. Thus, in concluding the meeting of 'the three councils of Leipzig' at which Bach was finally elected (by a unanimous vote) to the vacant post of Cantor, the presiding Council member declared that

> It was necessary to think in terms of a famous man, in order to inspire the *studiosi*.

instrumentalists from among' the large body of *externi* (Wolff 1998, p. 540) and, moreover, that he 'gave them lessons and was paid extra to do so' (Koopman 1998, p. 110). Neither statement, however, is attributed to a source. While the reader who follows Wolff's reference to *NBR* (p. 151) finds only an earlier formulation of the claim by the same author, a subsequent 'expanded version' (Wolff 1999) suggests that his thesis hangs on a single case, that of a 15-year-old *externus*, Gotthelf Engelbert Nietzsche. In a letter to the Thomasschule dated 11 November 1730 (see *BD II*, p. 207) Christoph Nietzsche seeks to have his son admitted to a full boarding place, 'especially as my son is very usable for music, as the Capellmeister will attest' ('zumahl da mein Sohn in *Musicis* wie der Herr *Capell* Mstr *attesti*ren wird, sehr wohl zu gebrauchen ist'). In this last – and rather ordinary – expression ('usable'/'zu gebrauchen') Wolff sees not just a parent's testimonial but 'a specific reference to Bach's top category of "usable" choral scholars' (as in the *Entwurff*). From this – and from this alone – he concludes not only that the young *externus* had been auditioned (and categorized) by Bach, but that he was already *functioning* as one of Bach's singers (and thus in the first choir?). Furthermore, on the premise that 'this guy Nietzsche can hardly have represented an isolated case', we are asked to accept that there were 'considerable alternative resources available to Bach' – and thence perhaps (ever more hypothetically) that concerted music performed by the first choir would routinely have made use of 'at least 12 singers' singing throughout all choruses.

[19] See *BD II*, p. 112.
[20] Bach 1773.

Es wäre nöthig auf einen berühmten Mann bedacht zu seyn, damit die Herren *Studiosi animir*et werden möchten.[21]

Doubtless the comment reflects an awareness of difficulties encountered by Bach's immediate predecessor. In his 1709 reminder ('Erinnerung') to the Town Council Kuhnau bemoans the fact that 'the principal *chorus musicus* is bereft of students'[22] as a result of defections to the opera and to (Telemann's) musical activities at the Neue Kirche,[23] and his later 'Proposal of the form in which church music in Leipzig can be improved' (1720) is still much concerned with the problem of attracting the *studiosi* back.[24] (In a subsequent controversy over the Cantor's rights at the university church, the Paulinerkirche, Bach was understandably sensitive to claims that he was not on good terms with the *studiosi*.[25])

The key issue was, of course, money. The Town Council traditionally put a certain number of Thomasschule pupils and municipal instrumentalists at the Cantor's disposal and was evidently unwilling to fund ever more elaborate music-making, at least on a regular basis; consequently, any extra performers the Cantor might wish to use were perhaps viewed as his personal responsibility.[26] Not surprisingly, Kuhnau was unhappy with this

---

[21] *BD II*, p. 95 = *NBR*, p. 103.

[22] 'Thus, supernumeraries of this sort would be very necessary indeed, especially now that the principal *chorus musicus* is bereft of students' ('Also wären dergleichen *Supernumerarii* sonderlich izo, da der Haupt *Chorus Musicus* von den Studenten entblöset ist, gar sehr nöthig'): Kuhnau (1709), ¶8 = Knick 1963, p. 125.

[23] 'The music for two or more choirs which ought to be heard on feast days is not even to be thought of; one can manage suchlike only if the students are not allowed to go to the Neue Kirche – as happened most recently, for example, at Dr Abicht's wedding at the Nikolaikirche' ('An die *Music* von zwey oder mehr *Chör*en, welche in großen Festtagen solte gehöret werden, darff man vollends nicht gedencken, und kan man dergleichen nur bewerckstelligen, wenn die Studenten nicht in die neüe Kirche kommen dürffen, wie zum *Exempel* neülichst bey Herrn D. Abichts Trauung in der Kirche zu *St. Nicolai* geschahe'). 'One cannot see where to take people from for . . . string-playing . . . as they have all gone over to the Neue Kirche' ('man [kann] nicht sehen . . ., wo zu der . . . Geigen*Music* . . . die Leüte herzunehmen seyn, da sie alle in die neüe Kirche gezogen werden'): Kuhnau (1709), ¶¶11, 12 = Knick 1963, p. 126. See also *ibid.*, ¶10 (p. 125); and Kuhnau (1720) = Knick 1963, pp. 128f.

[24] '*Project*, welcher Gestalt die Kirchen *Music* zu Leipzig könne verbeßert werden': Kuhnau (1720) = Knick, pp. 128f.

[25] *BD I*, pp. 35, 38 = *NBR*, pp. 120, 122f.

[26] Ironically, Bach was taken to task on one occasion by the 'Noble and Most Wise Council of the Town' for contravening regulations by bringing in a university student to act as stopgap First Prefect (*BD I*, pp. 99f). The school was sensitive to the possibility that valuable revenue would go to outsiders; for example, 'For weddings and other ceremonial banquets the pupils of the first *Cantorey* should always be given preference over the second; also, no *extraordinarii* should be permitted without the prior knowledge of the Rector and the Cantor' ('Bei Hochzeiten und andern Ehren-gelagen sollen die Schüler der ersten *Cantorey* denen andern allezeit vorgezogen, auch ohne Vorbewust des *Rectoris* und Cantoris keine *Extraordinarii* zugelassen'): *Ordnungen*, 1723 p. 74 (chap. 13 ¶10) = Knick 1963, p. 150.

arrangement and lobbied for *honoraria* to be made available in order to bring back students and others:

> The volunteers in our choir could also have a reward like all similar assistants in our Electoral and other lands.

> Die *Volontaires* unsers *Chori* könten auch, wie alle dergleichen *Adjuvan*ten in unsern Chur Fürstl. und andern Landen eine Ergözligkeit haben.[27]

For his part, Bach claims (in his *Entwurff*) that crucial *beneficia* which had at one time existed had now disappeared altogether (see above, pp. 98f):

> Indeed, it is acknowledged that even my predecessors Messrs Schelle and Kuhnau had to avail themselves of assistance from the *studiosi* if they wanted to produce a full and well-sounding musical ensemble – which they could actually do then, insofar as several vocalists (viz. a bass and tenor, and even an alto) as well as instrumentalists (particularly two violinists) were separately favoured with stipends by a Most Noble and Most Wise Council and were thereby moved to strengthen the church ensembles.

> Es ist ja *notorisch*, daß meine Herrn *Præanteceßores*, Schell und Kuhnau, sich schon der Beyhülffe derer Herrn *Studiosorum* bedienen müßen, wenn sie eine vollständige und wohllautende *Music* haben *produciren* wollen; welches sie dann auch in so weit haben *præstiren* können da so wohl einige *vocali*sten, als: *Baß*ist, u. *Tenori*st, ja auch *Alti*st, als auch *Instrumenti*sten, besonders 2 *Violi*sten von E. HochEdlen und Hochweisen Raht *a parte* sind mit *stipendiis* begnadiget, mithin zur Verstärckung derer Kirchen *Musiquen animiret* worden.(*Entwurff*, ¶16)

Although there is no evidence that any formal mechanism existed to provide the Cantor with extra funding, Bach does seem to have been able to attract outsiders with reasonable regularity; moreover, during Bach's tenure nine of 14 known additional performers did receive a financial reward (*Ergötzligkeit*) – see Table 7.[28] The amounts paid are fairly consistent – in most cases 12 thaler, with just 6 thaler going to Mittendorff for appearing 'from time to time' ('etliche mahl'). But while many more payments may well have been made (there is a substantial gap in the relevant documentation, between 1731 and 1745), only once (in 1728) does the number of known payments within a single year exceed two; see Table 8.

All those listed were students at the university (or recently had been). Amongst them is a future son-in-law of Bach's, then in his mid twenties:

[27] Kuhnau (1720) = Knick 1963, p. 128.

[28] Interestingly, when J. C. Lipsius was paid in 1727, it was 'with the intention that it will not be continued' ('mit der Bedeutung, daß man weiter nicht *continuiren* werde'): Schulze 1984, p. 46. The Council, while approving one such payment (to Altnickol in 1747), pointed out that 'the Cantor should, however, always indicate in advance whom he wished to employ' ('jedoch sollte es der Cantor allezeit vorhero melden, wen er darzu brauchen wollte'): *BD I*, p. 149.

Table 7. Known additional performers

date(s)	payment	name	voice/ instrument	source[a]
1723–7		F. G. Wild	fl, hps	*BD I*, pp. 127f
1724	12 thlr	G. F. Wagner *student*	?vn[b]	cf. *BD I*, p. 48
[1725]	10 thlr	"	?vn	
1726	12 thlr	"	vn	
1724–8		C. G. Wecker *student*	?fl +, voice	*BD I*, p. 129
1725	12 thlr	J. C. Lipsius *student*	?B	
1726	12 thlr	"	B	
1727	12 thlr	"	B	
1727	10 thlr	B. F. Völkner *student*	vn	
[1728]	12 thlr	J. F. Caroli *student*	?vn	
1728	12 thlr	C. G. Gerlach	?vn[c]	
1728	12 thlr	E. J. Otto *student*	?B	
1729	15 thlr	"	?B	
1730–4		J. C. Hoffmann *student*	B	*BD II*, p. 253
1731	12 thlr	J. F. Wachsmann *student*	?	
?1731–7		B. D. Ludewig (*student*)	instr., voice	*BD I*, pp. 141ff
1738–41		J. F. Agricola (*student*)	kbd	*BD III*, p. 76
1745	6 thlr	J. C. Mittendorff *student*	B	see also p. 108
1747	6 thlr	J. C. Altnickol (*student*)	B, vn, vc	see also pp. 14 and 109f

[a] For payments to students, see Schulze 1984.
[b] Wagner: also vc, org, hps; B
[c] Gerlach: also org, voice (?A)

It is hereby attested with my own hand that the bearer, Mr Johann Christoph Altnickol, has served in the *chorus musicus* continuously since Michaelmas 1745, appearing sometimes as violinist and sometimes as violoncellist, but mostly as vocal bass, and has thus supplied the want of bass voices to be found at the Thomasschule (because they cannot come to maturity as they depart all too soon). Leipzig, 25 May 1747.   Joh. Sebast. Bach

Daß Vorzeiger dieses Herr Johann Christoph Altnickol seit *Michaelis anno* 1745. dem *Choro Musico* unausgesetzet *assistiret*, indeme Er bald als *Violiste*, bald als *Violoncelliste*, meistens aber als *Vocal-Bassiste* sich *exhibiret*, und also dem Mangel derer auf der *Thomas*-Schule sich befindenden *Bass*-Stimmen (weiln sie wegen allzu frühzeitigen Abzugs nicht können zur Reiffe kommen) ersetzet; wird hiermit eigenhändig bezeüget. Leipzig. den 25. *Maji*. 1747.

Joh: Sebast: Bach.[29]

[29] *BD I*, pp. 148f; see also *BD II*, p. 434.

Table 8.   Annual numbers of additional performers

	1723	1724	1725	1726	1727	1728	1729	1730	1731	1732
no. of performers	1	3	4	4	4	4	1	1	3	2
no. of payments	–	1	2	2	2	3	1	–	1	–

	1733	1734	1735	1736	1737	1738	1739	1740	1741	1742
no. of performers	2	2	1	1	1	1	1	1	1	–
no. of payments	–	–	–	–	–	–	–	–	–	–

	1743	1744	1745	1746	1747	1748	1749	1750
no. of performers	–	–	1	–	1	–	–	–
no. of payments	–	–	1	–	1	–	–	–

Versatility such as Altnickol's – he was primarily an organist – was both commonplace (see above, pp. 14f) and necessary.[30] But his skills specifically as a string-player and bass singer will have made him especially valuable; indeed, it is violinists (?five) and bass singers (?five) who predominate in Table 7. The scarcity of bass voices amongst the Thomasschule pupils was nothing new: almost forty years earlier Kuhnau mentioned stipends that had previously existed for some singers,

> but especially for a strong bass (because low voices of this sort are not so readily to be expected from the school's youths . . .)

> vornehmlich aber auff einen starcken *Bassis*ten (denn von der Schul Jugend sind dergleichen tieffe Stimmen nicht so leichte zu gewarten . . .)[31]

None of this really supports the notion that numerous extra singers and instrumentalists were routinely drafted in simply in order to make the ensemble larger. A bass concertist and the occasional pair of flutes (or recorders)[32] will often have been needed, and good string-players would

---

[30] Koopman proposes that one of 'the many ways in which the number of players might have been increased' would be if a 'singer/instrumentalist' were to 'alternate between singing in the choir and playing his instrument to accompany an aria' (Koopman 1998, p. 113). The effect of this would of course be to reduce the size of the instrumental ensemble at exactly those moments when one might reasonably expect it to be at its fullest, i.e. in choruses. And although the parts occasionally indicate that a player switched instruments within a work (routinely between types of oboe; also violins/recorders in BWV244 and very probably flute/gamba in BWV245), there appears to be no such evidence for the same performer singing and playing an instrument within a single work. (I owe these examples to Joshua Rifkin.)

[31] Kuhnau (1709), ¶12 = Knick 1963, p. 126. Cf. Held 1894, p. 90.

[32] See *Entwurff*, ¶10.

always be useful. But if significantly larger numbers of additional 'usable' performers really were available on a reasonably regular basis, how could Bach possibly have imagined that their blatant omission from his *Entwurff* would escape the Town Council's attention?[33]

In any case, the crucial questions are not how many performers were *available* to Bach or where they came from, but how many he actually chose to use in concerted music and how he deployed them.[34] Even if we could establish with certainty the largest number of singers Bach had at his disposal, it would be wrong to conclude that that number constituted a vocal choir appropriate for concerted music.[35] As Rifkin has pointed out, 'the discontent so plainly vented in the *Entwurff* has less to do with the number of singers and players taking part in any actual performance than with their level of skill and the strain of pulling them together from disparate sources'.[36] If the only extra performers available were of limited ability, then extra performers as such would have been of little or no use in 'difficult and intricate' concerted music.[37]

This had been as true in the mid seventeenth century as it was in 1730. In the early 1660s Augustin Pfleger presented Duke Gustav Adolph of Mecklenburg with 'an account of the form in which a compendious but complete capella might most modestly and appropriately be maintained' at the Güstrow court.[38] His nine-strong ensemble comprises an organist, three other instrumentalists, two boy sopranos (plus a younger reserve) and three adult singers (of whom two serve also as instrumentalists, the third as Capellmeister). When the duke proposed enlisting an additional group of schoolboys, Pfleger responded as follows:

---

[33] One commentator turns this question round: 'what kind of a case would Bach have brought before the civic and school authorities if they knew that he, for the most part, was able to fare quite well with only a fraction of the forces he described?' (Wolff 1998, p. 541). Such a question implicitly misrepresents the arguments presented here and elsewhere but also ignores the fact that some pupils were needed as instrumentalists. For one suggestion of how a full complement of 12 pupils might have been deployed, see below, p. 144.

[34] Cf. the distinction between an available 'pool' and a team actually playing, described p. 94 above. In 1664 the number of boys maintained by Dresden's Kreuzkirche stood at 30, but special arrangements were made 'so that the church be provided with a pair of good trebles' ('damit aber die Kirche mit ein baar guten Discantisten . . . versehen werde') – presumably for concerted music: Held 1894, p. 70.

[35] Our own familiar world of amateur choral singing may tempt us to do just that, 'under the common-sense assumption that Bach, like most of us today, would have wanted to use any spare singers who happened to be around to bolster the choir for the chorales and choruses' (Butt 1998, p. 101).

[36] Rifkin 1982, p. 753.

[37] See *BD I*, p. 88.

[38] '. . . einen aufsatz, welcher gestalt eine *compendiose*, doch *complete* Capelle aufs geringst und füglichst zu unterhalten sey . . .': Nausch 1954, p. 10. (My thanks to Martin Geck and Joshua Rifkin for this reference.)

As regards the pupils whom Your Highness is graciously minded to use as part of the *chorus musicus*, [it] is indeed not unuseful for a full chorus, but to let the same sing in *Concerten* would give Your Highness little contentment. First, it is almost impossible to teach them the current idiom because of the bad habits they have already acquired. And secondly, assuming one or other of them were painstakingly taught something, it still would not have any lasting effect with them, as some, because of their continuing studies, would not make a proper profession of music, and some, [those who are] in the habit of drifting, [would] not be reliable; however, to obey Your Highness's most gracious wish, an exception can be made with some of the best, whom I will gladly instruct according to my ability and with whom I propose [to undertake] daily exercises, so that they can at least be used *pro ripienis* or *in pleno choro*.

Die schüler betreffend, welche Ihre D. *in Choro Musico* mit zu gebrauchen gnedigst gesinnt, ist zwar zu einem völligen Choro nicht undienlich, alleine dieselbe bei Concerten mit singen zu lassen, würde I. D. ein schlechtes contente geben. Und ist I^mo wegen ihrer schon bereits verderbten gewohnheit fast unmöglich den jetzigen modum, ihnen beizubringen. Und II^do gesetzt, es würde einem oder dem anderen etwas mit großer mühe beigebracht, kan es doch mit ihnen keine bestendigkeit haben, weilen etliche wegen Fortsetzung ihrer Studien keine rechtschaffene profession von der Musik machen würden, etliche aber so das vagiren gewohnt, keinen stand halten, doch aber, Ihro D. auf gnedigstes begehren zu gehorsamen, können etliche von den besten ausgelassen werden, welche ich gerne nach meinem Vermögen Instruiren Und ein tegliches Exercitium mit ihnen vornehmen will, damit sie wenigstens pro Ripienis oder in pleno Choro mit gebraucht werden können.[39]

Half a century or more later, 'the current idiom' (Bach's, at any rate) had become even more elaborate and complex, and it was perhaps correspondingly more important to differentiate between vocal concertists and ripienists (as Bach does right at the outset of his *Entwurff*) and between the requirements of different repertoires. Full vocal forces were never expected to be used at all times and in all repertoires, as a *Singordnung* prepared by the Darmstadt Cantor, Georg Philipp Zahn, in 1721 usefully reminds us:

¶11 . . . And, as not everyone can be used in *Kirchen Musiquen*, only those who are necessary each time in the *Music* [? the ensemble] should go up into the organ loft. The others should proceed to their proper places in order; those, however, who have taken part in the singing in the organ loft should, when it is ended, proceed to their seats below and not remain standing on the staircase or in the passage, let alone run off right out of the church.

¶11 . . . Und weil bey denen Kirchen Musiquen nicht alle können gebraucht werden, so sollen keine andere auf die Orgel gehen, als welche jedesmahl bey der

---

[39] Nausch 1954, pp. 10f.

Music nöthig sind, die andere sollen an ihren gehörigen Ort in ihre Ordnung sich begeben; diejenigen aber, so auf der Orgel mit gesungen, sollen nach dessen Endigung sich herunter in ihre Stühle begeben, nicht aber auf der Stiege und im Gang stehen bleiben, viel weniger gar aus der Kirche weglauffen.[40]

Darmstadt was far from exceptional. Osnabrück's 1731 *Chorordnung* echoes the same point:

¶7. Those who have been ordered by the Cantor or Prefect to serve in the musical ensemble in the organ loft should not run off out of the church just as they please either during the sermon or before the service has ended but [should] remain in the house of God until the service is fully over, [exactly] as the other students from the galleries must do . . .

¶7. Diejenigen, welche von dem Cantor oder Praefectis bey der Music auf der Orgel aufzuwarten befehligt worden, sollen weder unter der Predigt, noch vor geendigtem Gottesdienst nach ihren Gefallen aus der Kirche lauffen, sondern bis nach völlig geschlossenem Gottesdienst, wie die anderen Studenten aus den Priechen thun müssen, in dem Gotteshause verharren . . .

¶9. Whoever is not specifically required by the Cantor or Prefect for the musical ensemble in the organ loft – whether he is big or small – should never position himself in the organ loft but should attend service in the gallery, each in his appointed church.

¶9. Wer nicht zu der Musik auf der Orgel von dem Cantor oder Praefectis nahmentlich bestellet ist, der soll, er sey groß oder klein, auf der Orgel sich niemals finden lassen, sondern den Gottesdienst auf der Priechen, jeder in der ihm angewiesenen Kirche abwarten.[41]

With the 'astonishing' ('verwunderens-würdig') changes in musical fashions and consequent demands both for an expanded instrumental palette and for a higher technical standard of performance,[42] proper financial support was (Bach argues) all the more necessary:

so that individuals [*subjecta*] can be chosen and appointed who can assimilate current musical taste, get to grips with the new kinds of music, [and] thus be in a position to satisfy the composer and do justice to his work.

damit solche *subjecta choisiret* und bestellet werden können, so den itzigen *musica*lischen *gustum assequiren*, die neüen Arthen der *Music* bestreiten,

---

[40] Zahn 1721, quoted Noack 1967, p. 203; the *Singordnung* deals with such diverse matters as morning prayers, funerals, singing instruction, street singing, prefects and fines. For Telemann's evaluation of a proposed 24-strong street choir ('Gassen-Chor') in Hamburg, see Telemann [I], pp. 118f.

[41] Bösken 1937, p. 184 (*Chorordnung*, chap. 1). See also *ibid.*, p. 187 (chap. 4 ¶6).

[42] 'But as . . . artistry has progressed very much . . .' ('Da nun . . . die Kunst üm sehr viel gestiegen . . .') etc.: *Entwurff*, ¶17.

mithin im Stande seyn können, dem *Compositori* und deßen Arbeit *satisfaction* zu geben. (*Entwurff*, ¶17)

And with this key point Bach begins to wind up his *Entwurff*:

> The conclusion is accordingly easy to draw, that with the stopping of the *beneficia* my power to put the musical ensemble into a better state is removed.[43]

> Der Schluß ist demnach leicht zu finden, daß bey *ceßirenden beneficiis* mir die Kräffte benommen werden, die *Music* in beßeren Stand zu setzen. (*Entwurff*, ¶17)

Even if good instrumental resources were his main concern, for cantatas and other concerted works Bach still needed good singers, and good vocal concertists were inevitably harder to come by than adequate ripienists. By Kuhnau's own admission, the youths of the Thomasschule were better suited 'to capella parts and tuttis than to performing concerted music'.[44] The problem was, of course, not unique to Leipzig. When Johann Valentin Meder arrived in Danzig in the mid 1680s to take up a prestigious post there, he found that the two schoolboys allocated to the Marienkirche to supplement its five (rather unsatisfactory) salaried singers were usable only in the '*Ripieno Choro*' and not for '*Concertat-Music*'.[45] And of the six 'Music-Knaben' in Stuttgart's *Stiftsmusik* in 1715 we learn that only the two best were 'already capable of singing a concerted work'.[46] The situation would doubtless be well known to any cantor who relied mainly or entirely on young singers for all voice parts (SATB) – as distinct from a court establishment, for example. Interestingly, though, Bach himself never implies that his vocal concertists were unequal to the demands of his own exceptionally difficult music. And while C. P. E. Bach and J. F. Agricola do hint at shortcomings in J. S. Bach's performing forces, they certainly do not suggest that the shortcomings included inadequate *numbers* of singers.[47]

---

[43] Two decades earlier Kuhnau had found himself in a similar position: 'it has never been so very necessary as now that the stipends which were formerly used for some singers and two really good violinists be used for that [purpose] again' ('. . . niehmals so sehr alß izo nöthig gewesen, daß die vormahls auff einige Sänger . . . und zwei ordentliche gute *Violisten* angewendeten *Stipendia* wieder dazu angewendet würden'): Kuhnau (1709), ¶12 = Knick 1963, p. 126.

[44] 'zu denen Capellstimmen und denen *tutti*, alß zum *concertiren*': *ibid.*

[45] Rauschning 1931, p. 280.

[46] 'bereits ein Concert abzusingen capable': Owens (forthcoming).

[47] See Appendix 4, document 5. Only from the very end of Bach's life is there any recorded comment on the standard of singing under his supervision. When a visitor – perhaps Bach's eventual successor, Johann Gottlob Harrer – attended a rehearsal (probably in late 1749), it was reported that 'no usable *Discantist* could be found at the school' ('kein brauchbarer Discantist auf der Schule sich befand'): see Fröde 1984, p. 53. This could be interpreted to mean that standards of singing had declined so badly that there were no decent trebles at all, even for motets; but it seems more credible to surmise that at that particular moment no one soprano was 'usable' as a concertist.

In short, Bach may often have been on the lookout for a few good local musicians who might be persuaded – with or without payment – to take part in his technically demanding church music. (The collegium musicum directorship which he held, almost continuously, for well over a decade from 1729 will have kept him in contact with potentially useful outside players.) But there is very little reason to believe that he had any interest in adding vocal ripienists merely for the sake of greater numbers.

9

Instrument/singer ratios

Whatever difficulties may surround the size of Bach's vocal choir, the nature of his church *Instrumental Music* is reasonably clear-cut. The instrumentalists formed a single group (as against the four distinct vocal choirs), played a single repertoire (almost exclusively Bach's own concerted music), and had a single function (performance in one or other of the two principal city churches).

The *Entwurff*'s specified total of 'at least 18 persons for the instrumental group' (plus organ) is based on a string body of 11 – typically 3-3-2-2-1[1] – plus seven others (trumpets, kettledrums and woodwind), excluding the infrequent third oboe/second bassoon and the additional two flutes/recorders.[2] A full complement of 11 string-players, plus one musician for every additional instrument called for in a particular work, will thus produce the probable maximum needed. (Whether this full complement of strings was frequently achieved or not is, of course, a separate question.[3]) Thus, with 11 strings and one each for all other instrumental parts (including an unspecified bassoon), a richly scored work such as the Magnificat BWV243, for example, implies *c.*21 players.

Does the size of this instrumental ensemble tell us anything about the intended size of the vocal group? Does an ensemble as 'large' as *c.*21 players

---

[1] Or, in five-part writing with divided violas, 2-2-2-2-2-1 (see above, p. 99 note 26).

[2] See *Entwurff*, ¶10. Some writers have tacitly overridden Bach's own arithmetic: Koopman, for example, simply reads Bach's total as '20 or possibly 24 musicians' (instead of 18), plus organ (1998, p. 109).

[3] And the question has recently been addressed in detail in Rifkin 1996b and Rifkin 1998c. 'All in all, then, it seems overwhelmingly probable that Bach's "standard" violin section in his Leipzig vocal music – by which I mean the group of violins employed in church performances and larger secular productions – numbered 4 players. I see no reason to think that it ever went beneath this figure, and on the evidence of the parts, it seems only occasionally to have exceeded it' (1998c).

necessarily demand a correspondingly large number of singers? Specifically, does it – as is widely believed – require, at a minimum, all of the 12 (or 16) mentioned by Bach in the *Entwurff*?[4] Is there any evidence that Bach and his contemporaries would have shared this assumption?

Documentary information of a reasonably specific nature is quite sparse:

- At the Petrikirche in Hamburg (where Telemann was in charge from 1721) there seems to have been a 'pool' of 7 singers and 21 instrumentalists (including three trumpets and timpani). Two of the city's other four principal churches, for which Telemann was also responsible, had very similar resources: 7 plus 20 at the Nikolaikirche and 6 or 7 plus 21 at the Jacobikirche.[5]
- Mattheson (1728) dismisses as inadequate Johann Beer's 7-person *Kapelle* (four singers, two violins and organ) and advocates an ensemble of at least 23 (plus director).[6] Revealingly, however, the additions that Mattheson recommends seem to be exclusively instrumental; the vocal component thus remains just 4 voices.[7]
- Elsewhere Mattheson (1739) mentions in passing that a royal *Trauer-Music* might involve 7 singers and 17 instrumentalists.[8]
- A 'Specification of those persons who were present in the [Rudolstadt court] *Capelle* on His Highness's [Prince Friedrich Anthon's] birthday in Stadtilm 1742' lists a total of 43 performers, comprising 12 voices and

---

[4] See especially Smithers 1997, *passim*. As a corollary it is sometimes assumed, incorrectly, that 'small' vocal forces necessarily imply small numbers of instruments – and, specifically, that one-to-a-part voices imply single strings. See e.g. Knighton 1996 ('smaller-scale Bach, yes, but single strings, and one voice per part even in choruses?'); Schulze 1989, p. 14; Smithers 1997, p. 6; etc.

[5] Sittard 1890, p. 40. Mattheson puts the number of singers lower still: 'But here in Hamburg things are spread rather thin, especially with singers. Seventeen churches have five to six vocalists. In other large towns, such as Breslau, Berlin, Brunswick etc., almost every church has its own Cantor, plus assistants. And so several of the principal churches often have no [concerted] music for seven weeks at a time' ('Doch ist es hier in Hamburg, absonderlich mit Sängern, dünne bestellt. Siebzehn Kirchen haben fünff biß sechs Vocalisten. In andern grossen Städten, als da sind Breslau, Berlin, Braunschweig &c hat fast jede Kirche ihren eignen Cantorem, samt zugehörigen Adjuvanten. Hier soll es einer thun, mit einerley Leuten. Da denn manche Haupt-Kirche offt in sieben Wochen keine . . . Music haben'): Mattheson 1728, p. 64. C. P. E. Bach, Telemann's successor (from 1768), appears to have worked generally with 8 singers, and on occasion with 7, 9, 10 or even 12: see Rifkin 1985, pp. 162–5.

[6] For a partial quotation, see Koopman 1998, pp. 112f.

[7] Mattheson 1728, p. 64 (see Schulze 1989, pp. 13f). The additional instruments are two oboes, bassoon, three trumpets, timpani and violone, plus eight ripienists (even if their 'imprecise fingering and false blowing' would do 'more harm than good'). It should be remembered that Mattheson's figures refer to overall requirements – the 'pool' of performers – and do not necessarily relate to specific performing forces for individual works. (See also Mattheson 1739, p. 482.)

[8] Mattheson 1739, p. 480.

31 instruments – 21 strings, four woodwind, organ (26); two trumpets, timpani, two horns (5); singers arranged in three groups of four, the first labelled '1. Chor' (12).[9]

- The 'große *Concert*-Gesellschafft' in Leipzig, under the direction of two former pupils of Bach's (Gerlach and Schneider), had a membership of 26, which included six singers, five of whom doubled as string-players (1746–8);[10] see Illus. 17.

In each case ('pools' and performing 'teams' alike) the evidence shows instrumentalists easily outnumbering singers – which, of course, is the very opposite of today's common practice.[11]

Do the available iconographical sources point in the same direction? There are two pictures from early in the century which show roughly equal numbers of singers and instrumentalists. In the oft-reproduced frontispiece to the Leipzig hymn-book *Unfehlbare Engel-Freude* (Groschuff 1710) there are 12 singers and 11 instrumentalists: see Illus. 18 (and cf. pp. 54f above). Roughly equal numbers of each – 11? – are depicted in the engraving of the Freiberg Cathedral organ gallery from around the same time: see Illus. 19. The two ensembles are quite similar both in size (just over 20) and in composition (appearing to include vocal ripienists as well as trumpets and timpani). Yet neither suggests the new emphasis on woodwind instruments which characterizes Bach's Leipzig ensembles from a decade or so later.[12] Do they – with Beer (see above), who died as early as 1700 – perhaps reflect the taste and aesthetic of an earlier generation?

As part of the case he makes for proper financial support, Bach in his *Entwurff* compares his situation with that of his predecessors Schelle and Kuhnau:

> But as the current state of music is now quite different in nature from before, [and as] artistry has progressed very much [and] taste [has] changed astonishingly – such that music of the former kind no longer sounds [good] to our

[9] 'Specification Dererjehnigen Persohnen, so bey der Capell auf Serenissimo Geburthstag in Stadt Ilm 1742 seyend zugegen geweßen' (Stadtilm, 26 August 1742); see Engelke 1918–19, p. 604, and cf. above, p. 53. What work or works were performed on this occasion is not known, and it may of course be wrong to assume that the entire *Kapelle* was involved at any one time.

[10] See Schering 1941, p. 264. Similarly, Bernhard Dieterich Ludewig took part in Bach's collegium musicum as both instrumentalist and singer: see *BD I*, p. 141 = *NBR*, p. 196.

[11] Even the *dramma per musica Vereinigte Zwietracht der wechselnden Saiten* BWV207 has just the usual single copy for each voice part, although the original parts imply a string band larger than for any church piece (three copies for first violin, etc.): Rifkin 1995b, p. 127.

[12] The four violins/violas in the Freiberg illustration may at first glance suggest multiple strings – or at any rate two first violins – but are perhaps more likely to represent the upper four voices of a five-part instrumental line-up with divided violas.

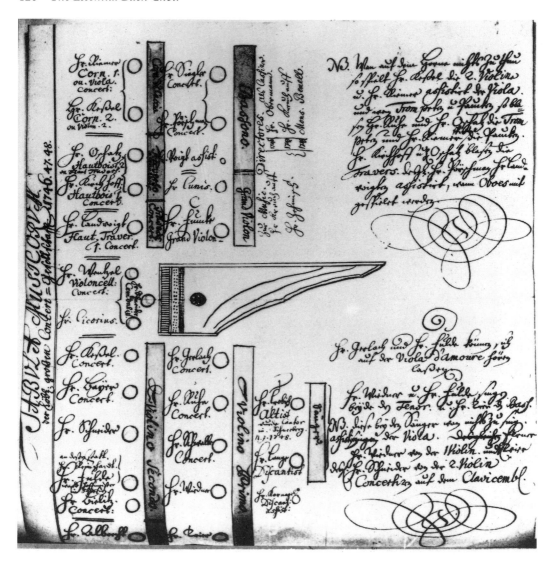

Illustration 17. 'Tabula Musicorum *der löbl. großen* Concert-Gesellschafft', *Leipzig, 1746–8: from J. S. Riemer's manuscript chronicle of events in Leipzig 1714–50, vol. ii*

ears and [such that] one is all the more in need of considerable assistance, so that *subjecta* can be chosen and appointed who can assimilate current musical taste, get to grips with the new kinds of music, [and] thus be in a position to satisfy the composer and do justice to his work – [now, despite all these changes,] the few *beneficia*, which should have been increased rather than reduced, have been completely withdrawn from the *chorus musicus*.

Da nun aber der itzige *status musices* gantz anders weder ehedem beschaffen, die Kunst üm sehr viel gestiegen, der *gusto* sich verwunderens-würdig geändert, dahero auch die ehemalige Arth von *Music* unseren Ohren nicht mehr klingen will, und mann üm so mehr einer erklecklichen Beyhülffe benöthiget

Illustration 18. F. Groschuff, Unfehlbare Engel-Freude *(Leipzig, 1710): frontispiece (engraving) and title-page (cf. detail, Illus. 12)*

ist, damit solche *subjecta choisiret* und bestellet werden können, so den itzigen *music*alischen gustum *assequiren,* die neüen Arthen der *Music* bestreiten, mithin im Stande seyn können, dem *Compositori* und deßen Arbeit *satisfaction* zu geben, hat man die wenigen *beneficia,* so ehe hätten sollen vermehret als veringert werden, dem *Choro Musico* gar entzogen. (*Entwurff,* §17)

In practical terms, these 'new kinds of music' not only made new stylistic and technical demands – upon both singers and players – but drew on a significantly expanded instrumental ensemble which included the newly

Illustration 19. Musicians in the organ gallery, Freiberg Cathedral, c.1710–14: engraving by J. G. Krügner after E. Lindner, showing the new G. Silbermann organ (cf. details, Illus. 13 and 14)

available woodwind instruments. There is no obvious sign of a corresponding expansion of vocal forces. Thus, when Telemann in the late 1720s observed that his ensemble ('Chor') in Hamburg was too small 'for the newer music',[13] we find that he was explicitly referring not to singers but to the number of instrumentalists at his disposal.

Six further iconographical sources better represent this new musical taste. Though none represents a church performance (and one may be rather late in date), they seem to be the nearest thing we have to relevant images of performing ensembles of the time.

- Illus. 20, Munich, *c.*1715: *c.*22–27 performers (excluding the director) – 6 singers (in the centre) and *c.*16–21 instrumentalists (including at least five trumpets and timpani)
- Illus. 21, Hamburg, 1719: 31 or more performers (excluding the director) – 4 singers (at the front) and at least 27 others[14]
- Illus. 22, ?Augsburg, *c.*1750: *c.*26–29 performers (excluding the two conductors) – 4 singers (see Illus. 23) and at least 22 instrumentalists (including two horns and over a dozen violins/violas)[15]
- Illus. 24, Jena, mid eighteenth century (outdoor): 38 performers – 4 singers (by the harpsichord) and 34 others (including one group of seven, who might also be singers)
- Illus. 25, Jena, mid eighteenth century (indoor): 33 performers – 4 singers (by the harpsichord) and 29 others (including one group of five, who might also be singers)
- Illus. 26, ?Nuremberg, *c.*1775: 15 performers – 4 singers[16] and 11 instrumentalists (two trumpets, four woodwind and four strings arranged around a harpsichord)[17]

How do the relative proportions of singers and instrumentalists found in these various documentary and iconographic sources compare with what we know of Bach's own practices in Leipzig? Table 9 (p. 128 below) brings together the most relevant sources and sets out the number of instruments for each voice indicated there.[18] The results are compared,

---

[13] 'für die neuere Music': Telemann [I], p. 32.

[14] It is of course possible that not all of the *c.*27 are instrumentalists.

[15] Two of the four singers appear to be sharing a single part, but a strictly literal reading of this detail would also dictate that the music being performed must be in no more than three vocal parts, rather than the usual four.

[16] The conductor, whose copy bears the words 'Lobet ihr Knechte des Herrn' but no music, is counted here as a singer.

[17] Reproduced in colour in *Early Music*, 24/4 (Nov 1996), pp. 620f.

[18] The data underlying Table 9 is, of course, the product of some unavoidable guesswork. I have assumed, for example, that in each case (except one) the entire ensemble is performing. (The exception is Illus. 22, in which the trumpeters and timpani-player are clearly not playing and are therefore not counted.)

Illustration 20. Musicians in the gallery of the Kongregationssaal, Munich, c.1715: engraving by J. A. Corvinus (detail)

Illustration 21.   Jubilee banquet (Jubelmahl) of the Hamburger Bürgerkapitäne, Drill-Haus, Hamburg, 1719: engraving by C. Fritzsch (detail) (cf. detail, Illus. 4)

Illustration 22. Concerted music-making at court, ?Augsburg, c.1750: engraving by G. B. Probst (cf. detail, Illus. 23)

Illustration 23. Vocal concertists, ?Augsburg, c.1750 (detail of Illus. 22)

Illustration 24. An outdoor performance by the collegium musicum, Jena, mid eighteenth century: water-colour (detail)

Illustration 25. A meeting of the collegium musicum, Jena, mid eighteenth century: water-colour

Illustration 26.   Concerted music-making, ?Nuremberg, c.1775: gouache (from a family album)

in Table 10, with some estimated figures for a variety of Bach's Leipzig compositions when sung either one to a part (by concertists alone) or two to a part (with the addition of ripienists, also singing one to a part, where copies for ripienists survive).[19] The table then shows the proportions produced with three and four singers to a part – i.e. with choirs of 12 and 16 respectively.[20] (The estimated numbers of instrumentalists for the Bach works are based on the 11-strong string group detailed in Bach's *Entwurff*.)[21]

[19] On the size of vocal ripieno groups, see above, pp. 40f. The number of singers given for the St John Passion excludes those who sang from the copies labelled 'Servus' and 'Pilatus' (see Table 5, p. 83 above).

[20] I have tried to ensure that in rounding off the proportions for ease of comparison I have not unduly favoured the point I am trying to demonstrate.

[21] *Entwurff*, ¶10; see above, p. 117 and note 1. Rifkin argues that in practice Bach's string group at Leipzig was most commonly somewhat smaller: see above, p. 117 note 3. With 7–9 strings there would obviously be correspondingly fewer instrumentalists per singer than is indicated in Table 10, column *a* – as few as 2¼ per singer for BWV110 – but the ratio of instruments to voices would still be, on average, discernibly higher than in column *b* or column *c*. In the cases of both BWV207 and the last version of the St John Passion (BWV245) there appear to have been more string-players than usual (perhaps 11 and 10 respectively), thus approximately 6 and 2 instruments per voice in BWV207 and BWV245 respectively. (In the St John Passion a smaller total of 9 strings would still imply almost 2 instruments per voice.)

Table 9.   Instruments per voice in contemporary sources

		singers	instruments	approx. number of instruments per voice
Hamburg, after 1721		7	21	3
Mattheson, 1728		4	23	6
Mattheson, 1739		7	17	2½
Stadtilm, 1742		12	31	2½
Leipzig, 1746–8 (Illus. 17)		6	20	3½
Jena, mid 18th cent. (Illus. 24)		4	34	8½
	or	11	27	2½
Jena, mid 18th cent. (Illus. 25)		4	29	7¼
	or	9	24	2¾
?Augsburg, *c.*1750 (Illus. 22)		4	*c.*20	5

Table 10.   Instruments per voice in selected works by Bach

BWV	title	singers	instrs.[a]	approx. number of instruments per voice		
				(a) with one singer per copy	(b) with 12 singers in all	(c) with 16 singers in all
22	*Jesus nahm zu sich die Zwölfe*	4	*c.*14 *(1)*	3½	1¼	1
117	*Sei Lob und Ehr dem höchsten Gut*	4	*c.*17 *(4)*	4	1⅓	1
207	*Vereinigte Zwietracht*	4	*c.*23 *(10)*	6	2	1½
245	St John Passion	8	*c.*17 *(4)*	2	1⅓	1
110	*Unser Mund sei voll Lachens*	8	*c.*22 *(9)*	2¾	1¾	1⅓

[a] italic number in brackets = the number of instruments (excluding special obbligato instruments) required in addition to (11) strings, organ and bassoon (see above, p. 99 note 26)

The approximate ratios of voices to instruments in the eight examples in Table 9 range from 2:5 to 1:7 – that is, for each singer there are from 2½ to 7¼ instrumentalists.[22] In all but one instance the estimates in column *a* of Table 10 fall perfectly within this same range. The exception, with the slightly

[22] Table 9 gives two possible interpretations for Illus. 24 and Illus. 25: under the more extreme reading of Illus. 24 (34 instrumentalists), the ratios of voices to instruments in Table 9 would range from 2:5 up to 2:17, so that for each singer there would be between 2½ and 8½ instrumentalists.

lower approximate relationship of two instrumentalists per singer, is the St John Passion, for which there is an unusual conjunction of large vocal forces and relatively modest instrumental ones. Its particular circumstances help explain why it may justly be regarded as atypical. On Good Friday in Leipzig Bach may have had rather more performers than usual at his disposal. On these occasions there was no concerted music-making by the second choir,[23] and consequently no pupils had to be seconded from choir I to serve as instrumentalists with choir II (see p. 99 above). In addition, one or more of the silent trumpeters would most probably have been reassigned to another instrument.[24] All this will have made a vocal ripieno group more feasible – and, of course, the chorus's role as the crowd in the telling of the Passion story naturally invited the use of extra voices. Yet at the same time the very subject matter of the Passion precluded the use of the fullest instrumental ensemble, as festive trumpets and timpani would have been wholly inappropriate. (For more on the distribution of voices in the St John Passion, see p. 83 above, and Appendix 6, pp. 204f below.)

Similar calculations based on 16 singers – often considered to be 'Bach's preferred number' in concerted music[25] – produce, by contrast, ratios tellingly lower than even the lowest in Table 9. As Table 10 column *c* shows, with 16 singers the vocal group is nearly as large as the instrumental ensemble – or, more often, the two groups are roughly equal in size. Table 10 column *b* shows that with 12 singers, too, there are consistently fewer instruments per singer than in the historical examples listed in Table 9; while even the highest figure in column *b* (2 instruments per singer) has no counterpart in column *a* except for the atypical St John Passion.

In short, the correlation between Table 9 (distilling the available archival and pictorial evidence) and Table 10 column *a* (illustrating the ratios achieved with a chorus of single voices) confirms what the musical and theoretical sources have already suggested: that, however numerous the instruments, a small group of concertists singing one to a part (with or without the occasional addition of a similar group of ripienists) was the essential vehicle of concerted choral music in Bach's time.

---

[23] At the other church only 'Lieder' (i.e. Passion chorales) were sung: Schering 1936, p. 166.

[24] For example, the second trumpeter listed in the *Entwurff*, Johann Cornelius Gentzmer (Genßmar), had been a *Kunstgeiger* before becoming a *Stadtpfeifer*: see *BD I*, p. 65. In Illus. 4 (p. 14 above: a detail of Illus. 21), a horn hangs from the music desk next to a string-player in the last row of the band, on the extreme left.

[25] Koopman 1997, p. 542.

10

Balance

There remains one further barrier to accepting a chorus made up of concertists only: namely, the conviction that a chorus of four young singers would inevitably be drowned out by most instrumental ensembles – that for Bach's chorus movements a satisfactory and 'natural' balance between concertists and instruments is 'in reality impossible'.[1]

Much of our thinking about the church music of the past may be subconsciously coloured by the quintessentially 'ethereal', soft-edged, floated tones of Anglican trebles. But sopranos and (boy) altos in eighteenth-century Germany were significantly older than their counterparts today (see above, pp. 12f) and may have sounded very different: when selecting pupils for the Thomasschule, Bach seems to have been particularly interested in voices which he called 'strong' or 'quite strong'.[2]

Conversely, it is now widely understood that most Baroque instruments are intrinsically more transparent in sound, and quite a bit softer, than their modern counterparts.[3] Trumpet-playing, however, is still often unduly forceful, lacking 'the gentler, richer, and less strident' tone which Bach is most likely to have known.[4] Especially in its clarino register, the natural trumpet was certainly capable of sounding magically delicate:

[1] Koopman 1998, p. 118. The danger of holding preconceived ideas on such matters is graphically demonstrated in the February 1989 issue of *Early Music*: on p. 9 an eminent scholar concludes that 'it does not seem logical that a work with two horns and three oboes [i.e. the First Brandenburg Concerto] should be performed with only single strings', while reproduced on the front cover is an early-eighteenth-century painting of a Venetian ensemble consisting of two horns, two oboes, 6 strings and harpsichord. See Schulze 1989 (and Rifkin 1991).

[2] See Appendix 2, below; see also *BD I*, p. 48. Cf. Scheibel 1721, p. 58.

[3] Notwithstanding arguments put forward in Kroesbergen/Wentz 1994, pp. 482–95.

[4] Barclay 1998, p. 4. Barclay describes the vented trumpet (a valveless trumpet with finger holes), in general use for natural-trumpet parts today, as a twentieth-century invention which 'resembles its Baroque counterpart only superficially' (*ibid.*, p. 1).

an Instrument heretofore chiefly practis'd in yᵉ rough Consorts of yᵉ Field; but now instructed in gentler Notes, it has learnt to accompany yᵉ softest Flutes [i.e. recorders], and can joyn with the most charming Voices.[5]

Even 'unpractised masters' ('nicht geübte Meister'), Mattheson tells us (1713), should be able to bring the instrument 'to such sweetness that even a recorder or some other gentle instrument may play in concert with it and be heard quite distinctly'.[6] (Any significant problems of balance between recorder and trumpet in the Second Brandenburg Concerto are presumably of our own making.)

Positioning (and dynamics[7]) always required careful handling, as Scheibe reminds us:

> If there happen to be trumpets and kettledrums in the musical ensemble, one should hide them as much as possible and place them behind all the other intruments if one does not wish their rattling sounds to obscure harmony and melody as well as singers and instruments; in particular, one should always set them at a distance from the voices, as it is to these that they are most detrimental.

> Wenn etwa Trompeten and Pauken bey der Musik sind: so soll man sie, so viel wie möglich, verstecken, und hinter alle übrige Instrumente stellen, wenn man nicht durch ihr prasselndes Geräusche so wohl Harmonie und Melodie, als Sänger und Instrumente, unvernehmlich machen will; insonderheit aber soll man sie von den Singestimmen allemal entfernen, weil sie diesen am schädlichsten sind.[8]

In music involving trumpets and kettledrums, Scheibe recommends both a string body based on four or five violins per part (as opposed to the *Entwurff*'s two or three) and – 'where possible' – more than one singer per part:

> The vocal parts should also, where possible, have more than one to a part, because the choruses otherwise make no impact.

> Die Singestimmen sollen auch, wo möglich, mehr, als einmal, bestellet seyn, weil sich die Chöre sonst gar nicht ausnehmen.[9]

It follows from this that, for choruses *without* trumpets and kettledrums, one singer per part represented a norm requiring no comment. We should

---

[5] Keller ?1699, dedication; see also Caspar Hentzschel (1620), quoted Downey 1996, p. 275 and n. 47.

[6] 'zu solcher *douceur . . ./* daß auch eine *flute douce* oder anderes gelindes *Instrument* mit demselben *concerti*ren und gar vernehmlich gehöret werden mag': Mattheson 1713, p. 265.

[7] J. S. Petri advised a trumpeter thus: 'It is best for him to ask the musical director to write in his *piano* or *forte* for him, against each note' ('Er thut am besten, wenn er den Musikdirector bittet, ihm sein *piano* oder *forte* bey jeder Note vor zu schreiben'): Petri 1767, p. 46, quoted Butt 1994, pp. 103, 206.

[8] Scheibe 1745, p. 713 (first published 1740).

[9] *Ibid.*

also note that Scheibe advocates not 'several' voices per part (as he does for motets)[10] but merely 'more than one'. In any case, as one of those in the forefront of the Enlightenment, Scheibe – who also says that oboes should double violins – may be presumed to have had a simpler idiom than Bach's in mind (less 'turgid and confused'[11]), one closer perhaps to that of Telemann, Hasse or Graun.

From the earliest days of concerted music-making in Germany, vocal concertists were accorded special attention:

> But above everything this must be taken into consideration: that the instrumental choirs truly be placed not too near the *concertato* voices associated with them, which causes the *cantores* with their voices (which are the most important thing) to be obscured and not to be heard well. Instead one can place the instrumental choir either away to the side or even right opposite, so that one can perceive and observe one above the other that much more exactly and clearly – and especially the *concertato* vocal parts.

> Vor allen dingen aber ist diese in acht zu nehmen/ daß ja die *Chori Instrumentales* nicht zu nahe bey ihre zugehörige *Concertat*-Stimmen gestellet/ und dadurch die *Cantores* mit ihren Stimmen (daran zum allermeisten gelegen) *obscuriret* unnd nicht wol gehöret werden. Sondern man kan die *InstrumentalChor* entweder auff die Seiten abwerts/ oder aber gar gegenuber stellen/ damit man eins vorm andern/ unnd sonderlich die *Concertat- Vocal*-Stimmen desto eigentlicher und deutlicher vernemen unnd *observiren* könne.[12]

More directly relevant to performance practices of Bach's time is the advice of Mattheson (1739):

> Singers must, in all places, stand at the front . . .

> Die Sänger müssen allenthalben voran stehen . . .[13]

and that of Scheibe (1745):

> With vocal music one should see in particular that the vocal parts are allowed to be heard best and most clearly, and that they are not obscured by the instruments. To that end it will be best if he [the director] places the vocalists on their own [or 'in the open'], so that they are facing the listeners, with the instrumentalists standing either sideways on or, best of all, behind the singers.

> Man soll bey Vocalmusiken darauf insonderheit sehen, daß sich die Singestimmen am besten und am deutlichsten hören lassen, und daß sie nicht

---

[10] See above, p. 29 and note 3.

[11] 'schwülstig', 'verworren': Scheibe 1745, p. 62 (first published 1737). See *BD II*, p. 286 = *NBR*, p. 338.

[12] Praetorius 1619, p. 197.

[13] Mattheson 1739, p. 484, §30.

durch die Instrumente unvernehmlich gemachet werden. Zu dem Ende wird es am besten seyn, wenn er die singenden Personen ganz frey stellet, daß sie das Gesichte gegen die Zuhörer kehren, die Instrumentalisten aber entweder seitwärts, oder, welches am besten ist, hinter den Sängern stehen.[14]

Questions of vocal/instrumental balance already present themselves in two of Bach's earliest works. In the *Actus tragicus* (?1707), *Gottes Zeit ist die allerbeste Zeit* BWV106, sheer practicality suggests that a choir in the modern sense is unwarranted.[15] Here the 'orchestra' is a delicate, funereally muted 'chamber' ensemble comprising just five instruments (two recorders, two gambas and organ),[16] giving (in David Schulenberg's words) 'every indication [that the work] was conceived for an ensemble of four singers balancing the four melody instruments'.[17] Florid, 'soloistic' moments in the vocal writing confirm the impression that any ripieno group would prove a mere encumbrance: see Ex. 14.

By contrast, another cantata of the Mühlhausen period, *Gott ist mein König* BWV71 (1708), calls for a large instrumental ensemble of a fairly familiar kind, with three trumpets and timpani. It is easy to assume that such a work demands large vocal forces; and, sure enough, the (largely autograph) performance materials include not only the usual set of four vocal parts for concertists but also a further four for ripienists, who are deployed in a variety of ways as shown in Table 4A (p. 68 above). Indeed, Bach's clear if old-fashioned designation of the whole cantata (with its four vocal parts and 14 independent instrumental parts) as 'âb 18. è se piace 22' (see Illus. 8, p. 37 above) indicates that the four ripieno voices are (as we may now expect) optional,[18] and that the work may be performed, in all its instrumental opulence, with just four singers.[19] (This interpretation would seem to be confirmed by the contemporary set of printed parts, which neither includes ripieno parts nor hints that any were to be added.)

From the start of his career, Bach simply followed long-standing convention in adopting a one-per-part chorus (with or without an optional ripieno group) as the essential medium of concerted vocal music. Four (good) singers, standing well forward,[20] were evidently considered perfectly capable of achieving a satisfactory balance with even a large instrumental group. If we also accept[21] that the choruses of the early hunting cantata *Was mir*

[14] Scheibe 1745, pp. 712f.
[15] The *Neue Bach-Ausgabe* (1/34) gives 'tutti'/'solo' rubrics which have no basis in the sources. Cf. Schulenberg in Boyd 1999, p. 198.
[16] No further continuo instruments seem to have been intended.
[17] Boyd 1999, p. 198.
[18] See above, pp. 36 and 38.
[19] Cf. also Ex. 8, p. 76 above.
[20] See above, p. 130.
[21] With, for example, Boyd (1990, p. 115) and Neumann (1971, p. 224).

Ex. 14. J. S. Bach, *Gottes Zeit ist die allerbeste Zeit* (*Actus tragicus*) BWV106/2d, bars 180–185

behagt, ist nur die muntre Jagd BWV208 (?1713, repeated ?1716) – with its two horns and oboe band – are intended for just the four characters (Diana, Pales, Endymion and Pan),[22] we must surely pause to consider whether or not the Weimar church cantatas too might function in this way. In any event, it seems that during Bach's time at Weimar (1708–17) the ducal chapel never comprised more than eight singers;[23] as Butt notes, 'most scholars agree that Bach had neither the room nor the resources to perform the Weimar [church] cantatas with ripienists'.[24]

Were conditions and musical fashions so very different a decade later at Leipzig? In the early part of the century, the collegium musicum which

[22] See Rifkin 1996a, p. 593 and n. 58. Cf. also Illus. 26, showing a comparable ratio of wind instruments to voices.

[23] *BD II*, pp. 48, 55, 62f = *NBR*, pp. 71f; see also Appendix 6 Table VII, below, and Rifkin 1997a, p. 306.

[24] In Boyd 1999, p. 98.

performed concerted music at the Neue Kirche (see Illus. 27) was said to number 'perhaps 40'. How precise this figure is meant to be[25] and how frequently the entire group performed together may be open to debate, but one thing is reasonably clear: the 'Singechor' within it consisted of just four singers, all of them university students.[26] And there is no suggestion that Gottfried Heinrich Stölzel was other than impressed by what he had heard in Leipzig in the early years of the century:

> The collegium musicum which he [Melchior Hoffmann] directed was not only very strong in numbers but also excellent to hear. For the vocal choir consisted of . . . Herr Langmasius as bass; . . . *Magister* Marckgraf as soprano; the late Herr Helbig . . . as tenor; and, if I'm right, the late Herr Krone . . . as alto. Similarly the instrumental choir, which the aforementioned also graced, was crowned by . . . Herr Pisendel . . . In all it consisted of probably 40 persons. At that time such a choir [i.e. ensemble] could be heard only in the Neue Kirche in Leipzig on high feasts and during Fair-time; is it any wonder that, animated by Hoffmann's fine taste, it attracted many listeners?

> Das *Collegium musicum,* welches er [Melchior Hoffmann] dirigirte, . . . war nicht allein sehr starck besetzt, sondern ließ sich auch vortreflich wohl hören. Denn das Singechor machten . . . Herr Langmasius, als Basso; . . . Hr. *M.* Marckgraf, als Sopran; der seel. Hr. Helbig . . ., als Tenore; und, wo mir recht, der seel. Hr. Krone . . ., als Contralto aus. Das Instrumenten-Chor, welches zwar die obigen auch zierten, krönte gleichsam . . . Herr Pisendel . . . In allen bestunds wohl aus 40. Personen. Ein solcher Chor ließ sich damahls zwar nur an hohen Festen, und zur Meßzeit, in der neuen Kirche zu Leipzig hören: was Wunder, wenn solches, durch den feinen hofmannischen Geschmack belebet, viele Hörer nach sich zoge?[27]

Underlying a widespread tendency to overlook the implications of such evidence is the simple preconception noted at the head of this chapter: that a satisfactory balance between four (or even eight) voices and one of Bach's larger instrumental ensembles is just not possible. Bach's day-to-day

[25] See Rifkin 1995a, pp. 227ff, for a discussion of the significance (or otherwise) of the number 40 and of the evidence of J. M. Gesner (1738) and J. C. Trömer (1745). See also Appendix 4, document 3 and note 1.

[26] See Richter 1907, p. 59, and Glöckner 1990, pp. 136f, 156ff. In 1736 Gerlach pointed out that at the Neue Kirche he was responsible 'for just as large a musical ensemble as happens in other churches' ('vor eine eben so starcke Music, als wie in andern Kirchen geschiehet'): Glöckner 1990, pp. 136, 155. The comment carries no implication that a greater number of singers were to be heard in concerted music elsewhere.

[27] As quoted by Mattheson (1740, pp. 117f) in a biographical note on Melchior Hoffmann; Hoffmann was director of this student collegium musicum from 1707 to 1710. Telemann, who had founded it in 1702, also thought highly of it; see his autobiographical note of 1718 in Telemann [II], pp. 95f.

Illustration 27. Neue Kirche, Leipzig, after 1710: engraving by J. C. Oberdörffer (detail)

experience, however, presumably told him otherwise[28] – unless we wish to question his practical competence as a composer. In BWV21, for instance, the lone soprano and alto concertists are explicitly pitted not only against 'tutti' tenors and basses (i.e. concertists plus ripienists) but also against the full orchestra, trumpets and all: see Ex. 8, p. 76 above.

It is a fundamental, if counter-intuitive, principle of acoustics that two identical sounds heard simultaneously are scarcely any louder than one.[29] For perceived loudness to be doubled, the number of such sounds must in fact be doubled three times over (i.e. multiplied by eight); thus, in order to achieve twice the volume produced by a quartet of vocal concertists, a total of 32 or so equally strong singers would be needed.[30] A 16-strong choir thus sounds nowhere near twice as loud as four singers; indeed, its volume would normally be matched by four solo voices singing several degrees louder. Ironically, it is precisely this acoustical fact – the very modest difference in volume between a vocal quartet and a 12- or 16-strong choir – that helps prevent the modern superabundance of singers in Bach's music from always overbalancing its instrumental support.

[28] My own experience tells me the same. Not one of the many reviews of performances I gave of the St Matthew Passion in Germany in 1995 – even those unashamedly hostile to the use of 'minimalist' forces – mentions any problem of balance between voices and instruments. Following an earlier performance I had conducted of the Mass in B Minor, also in Germany, a satisfied customer whose view had been obscured by a church pillar was incredulous when told afterwards that there had been, variously, only one or two voices per part.

[29] Sound can be measured objectively in terms of its intensity (the rate of energy output per square metre), and the combined intensity of two or more sound-sources is found by simple arithmetical addition. However, the human ear, which is sensitive to a very wide range of intensities, responds not so much to the actual increase in intensity of a sound but rather to the incremental increase; i.e., the ear senses roughly the same increase in sound-level between 1 and 10 units of intensity as between 10 and 100, or indeed between 1000 and 10,000 units. For this reason a logarithmic scale based on the bel (= 10 decibels) is used to represent sound-levels on a linear scale. (0 is the level just perceptible to the human ear, and 14 bels (140dB) the level at which sound is painful.) On this scale a doubling of intensity produces an increase in sound-level of just 3dB, another doubling a further 3dB, and so on. Thus, a 20dB sound and an additional 20dB sound together produce 23dB, while two of 50dB produce 53dB together, etc.

The increase in perceived loudness for a given rise in decibel level depends on a number of factors (including frequency, actual sound-level and complexity of sound). For the frequency range covered by the human voice and by the majority of orchestral instruments, an increase of 8–10dB is judged as a doubling in loudness. Thus a rise in sound-level of 3dB increases the loudness in the ratio 5 to 4 (i.e. only a quarter again as loud), and 5dB in the ratio 3 to 2 (i.e. half again as loud). (See also *New Grove*, 'Sound', §5, and Tennent 1971, §7 'Acoustical units and definitions'.) But if two unequal sound sources are added and one is 5dB or more below the other, then the quieter sound makes a negligible contribution to the total.

[30] These numbers assume a theoretically perfect accord amongst the multiple singers of each part; discrepancies in, for example, tuning and vibrato could tend to reduce any increase in volume.

This may help us recognize that the function of a ripieno group has much less to do with volume or balance than with sonority: while a choir with two or more voices on each part is not necessarily significantly louder than a group of (one-to-a-part) concertists, it does produce a different colour and texture. In some contexts the sonority and character of the larger group may be welcome – in crowd scenes, chorales, dignified and slow-moving *stile antico* movements; in others it may not – when agility and athleticism are called for, or in affective and chromatic writing. But Bach does not depend on additional singers to create the fuller texture; he can achieve comparable extra weight whenever he wishes, simply by using his instruments to reinforce the vocal lines.[31] Ripieno singers, in other words, may enhance the differentiation between solo and tutti passages but are rarely indispensable to achieve it. And in many a movement the modern practice of using multiple voices from start to finish merely serves to weaken an intended (and structurally fundamental) contrast of sonorities – an interplay of solo voices and tutti ensemble wholly analogous to the dialoguing of the instrumental concertino group and full ensemble within a *concerto grosso*.

More important, the blanket substitution of multiple voices for single voices is more than a marginal change to Bach's vocal scoring: it hands his music over to an essentially different medium.

---

[31] For a discussion of the ripieno parts added to BWV21, see Rifkin 1996a, pp. 584f, 594.

11

Conclusions

If we are prepared to follow where the evidence leads, we must surely conclude that nearly all of Bach's concerted 'chorus' writing was designed to be performed with just one good singer on each part.

To test the soundness of this conclusion, let us take a final look at one of Bach's earliest large-scale cantatas, *Gott ist mein König* BWV71, written for Mühlhausen's annual *Ratwechsel* (changing of the council) and performed on 4 February 1708 at the town's Marienkirche. Uniquely, the work survives in two independent sets of parts, each associated with the work's first performance: the actual performance material (in manuscript) and a set of printed parts issued by the Town Council shortly afterwards.[1] Let us suppose that only the printed set had survived. Faced with its four vocal copies, we should by now understand that a total of four singers is implied for the entire work – though we might also recognize from the nature of the writing that some ripieno doubling, selective and optional, could be appropriate. Orthodox thinking, by contrast, would unhesitatingly dictate that there be several voices on each part throughout all four choruses – a 'common-sense' interpretation bolstered by the presence of trumpets and drums in the work's outer movements.

Which of these two very different possibilities did Bach have in mind? As it happens, his intentions are made perfectly clear in the other surviving set of parts (the manuscript set), which includes not only the usual concertists' material but also – exceptionally – a further four parts for ripienists.[2] As some Leipzig works would lead us to expect, the Mühlhausen ripienists turn out to have a limited role: in two movements (1, 7) they participate only spo-

---

[1] This cantata – or 'Mottetto', as Bach calls it (see Melamed 1995, pp. 29f) – is one of only two vocal works by Bach to appear in print during the composer's lifetime.

[2] See Table 3A (p. 61 above), and Appendix 5 below.

radically, in another (3) they remain silent, and in only one (6) do they sing from start to finish.[3] A further significant detail is added by the composer's autograph score, which also survives: its superscription 'âb 18. è se piace 22' leaves no doubt that any participation by ripienists is explicitly optional (see above, p. 36 and Illus. 8).

In other words, it is the four concertists who carry all the chorus writing; the occasional doubling by ripienists is clearly inessential.[4]

This arrangement of forces – a team of four vocal concertists performing all solo movements and all choruses, with an optional four ripienists used selectively in some of the chorus movements – is exactly the reverse of the one to which we have long been accustomed, where multiple ripienists carry all the chorus writing, and concertists are supernumerary in the choruses. And, indeed, conventional thinking would have imposed the latter arrangement on BWV71 if the printed parts alone had survived. Yet the actual vocal configuration of the cantata agrees perfectly with the very considerable evidence for Bach's other concerted works, and lies squarely within the documented traditions to which Bach belonged. It is clear that in Bach's Leipzig, as in many other centres, a group of vocal concertists sang choruses and solo movements alike; occasionally a second vocal quartet, standing elsewhere and singing from a separate set of copies, might be added as a ripieno group in some (though rarely all) of the choral writing. With up to 20 or more instrumentalists, an ensemble of this sort was wholly typical of its time.

Most of us have studied Bach's *Entwurff* only in search of clues to the way in which Bach performed his own cantatas, Passions and masses: in our haste, we have fallen into the trap of reading the document, with its rationale for choirs of 12 or 16 singers, as a simple prescription for the performance of his concerted choruses. Choirs of this sort were the norm in eighteenth-century English cathedrals and royal establishments, whence they were naturally borrowed to sing in (for example) Handel's oratorios. But if choirs of 12–16 did exist at Leipzig, Bach would have used them only for the relatively simple 'motet' repertoire, and not for his own concerted music. What we have inadvertently created is a hybrid, a veritable hippogriff in which a plausibly Bachian orchestral body is grafted on to an alien, perhaps Handelian, vocal group.[5] This hybrid can no longer be presumed to reflect either Bach's actual practice or his 'ideal'. The smaller vocal medium used by Bach may well seem extraordinary today, but only because it tends to be viewed against

---

[3] See Exx 5a and 5b (pp. 66f above), and Table 4A (p. 68 above).

[4] To characterize this as Bach's '*introducing* a vocal quartet *in place of* a chorus' is to view a fundamental principle through the wrong end of a telescope (Wolff 1998, p. 541; emphases added).

[5] Such cross-breeding passes unnoticed because recent 'historically informed' performance has seemingly adopted the 'small' chorus of 12–20 voices as a paradigm for almost all Baroque choral music.

the reassuringly familiar background of the nineteenth- and twentieth-century choral tradition – a tradition which makes it easy to assume that a choir must (by definition) have multiple voices on each part.

Loyalty to the conventional image of Bach's choir rests on a series of further assumptions which turn out to be equally questionable:

- that cantatas demand the same type of vocal ensemble as the traditional motet repertoire;
- that ripienists are essential in all chorus movements;
- that concertists are inessential in all chorus movements;
- that copy-sharing between vocal concertists and ripienists was perfectly feasible and happened routinely;
- that large instrumental ensembles always imply large numbers of singers;
- that the *Entwurff* describes a 'line-up' of singers for a performance, rather than a 'pool' from which Bach would draw both singers and instrumentalists.

And behind all this may lurk the notion that great music demands great forces. Certainly, the special emphasis which has frequently been placed on the role of 'extra musicians'[6] seems to spring largely from the simple preconception that Bach could not possibly have chosen to use the medium of a one-to-a-part choir unless circumstances allowed him no alternative.[7]

The consequence of these various misunderstandings is that a pool of singers large enough to ensure the year-round performance of a conservative repertoire of simple motets has been assigned in its entirety to an incomparably more complex repertoire, that of Bach's own concerted works. This 'difficult' ('schwer') and 'intricate' vocal music was not written for *all* the singers available to Bach but primarily and predominantly for

---

[6] See, for example, Koopman 1998, pp. 110–13; Smithers 1997, pp. 36f, 46, 48, 56 etc.; and Wolff 1998, p. 540.

[7] '. . . it is nonsense to think that the situation was always as problematic as in the smallest provincial town': Koopman 1998, p. 118. While a 'shortage' of resources undoubtedly created administrative problems for Bach, the use of a group of concertists – functioning (quite conventionally) both as soloists and as chorus – had nothing *per se* to do with any shortage and involved no compromise: it was the very medium of concerted vocal music, both in church and elsewhere. To be sure, a group of capable vocal ripienists would probably have been considered a desirable *additional* resource (albeit one to be used selectively) in certain contexts, but Bach would only rarely have planned on using such an additional ripieno group and made it an integral part of his strategy when composing. It is true that a lack of qualified singers may have put performance standards at risk, and may on occasion have influenced compositional decisions such as scoring and the allocation of vocal solos. But if that did ever happen – if those decisions did in fact represent 'compromises' forced upon him by 'inadequate' resources – those would still have been the choices that he made, and they would still have formed part of the work that he wrote.

a very select handful – for what Walther calls 'a selection of the best singers',[8] i.e. those chosen as concertists.

My guess is that Bach may have thought of a 12-strong first choir in roughly the following terms:

- *chorales & chant:*   12 singers
- *motets:*   8 singers + 4 additional voices/reserves
- *cantatas:*   3–4 concertists + 8–9 others, serving variously as string players (especially for viola, cello and violone) or as singers (ripienists or reserve/additional concertists)

In Chapter 1 I drew attention to a fundamental distinction between the *chorus pro capella* and *coro favorito* of Schütz's time and asked which of these two types of choir was destined to become the essential vehicle for the concerted music of J. S. Bach. The answer should now be clear. The underlying principles of Lutheran vocal music were unchanged: elaborate concerted writing remained the province of groups of solo voices, while simpler and more conservative idioms might be choral (in the modern sense). 'Bach truly brought the legacy of the seventeenth century into the eighteenth', Wolff tells us;[9] and, indeed, Bach stood right in the mainstream of Lutheran tradition in viewing concertists as the essence of the concerted choir. Telemann and Graupner – to name but two of the other candidates for the Leipzig post in 1723 – evidently took the same conventions for granted.[10]

It would of course be foolish to exaggerate the importance of any single aspect of musical performance practice. But neither should we underestimate the potential of a redefined Bach choir to shed new light on some of

[8] See above, p. 35 and note 21. As Scheibel says, 'quantity is not always the issue; rather, it is to be regarded as a waste if a chorus has more people in it than are needed' ('es liegt nicht allemahl an der Menge; Es ist vielmehr eine Verschwendung zu nennen/ wenn ein Chor stärcker besetzt ist als es vonnöthen thut'): Scheibel 1721, p. 54.

[9] Wolff 1995, p. 201. Yet Wolff also believes that it would have been an 'historical aberration' for Bach to have adopted this particular seventeenth-century principle: Wolff 1998, p. 541.

[10] The surviving performing parts to Graupner's two 1723 Leipzig test pieces, for example, 'expressly feature, with all desirable clarity, separate solo and ripieno parts for the singers': *ibid.*, p. 540. (There is, of course, nothing in the least exceptional in such original performing parts possessing 'all desirable clarity' in these matters – hence their enormous but still underestimated value as evidence.) A single set of vocal ripieno parts survives for each piece (the set of parts belonging to *Lobet den Herrn* is incomplete, lacking a bass part: see Wolff 1996, p. 133). But Wolff's description, while seeming to hint at some special significance in this circumstance, fails to convey just how Graupner's vocal scoring works: as always, concertists – Wolff's 'solo' voices – sing all the choral writing; as often, ripienists sing only intermittently. For the considerable body of corroborative evidence from Telemann's practice, see Swack 1999.

Western civilization's most highly regarded treasures.[11] In particular, we stand to regain an otherwise lost dimension of Bach's musical thinking – an interplay between solo voices and full ensemble which serves to clarify words and sonorities and also to elucidate the musical structures.

In any case, the venerable image of an 'ideal' 12- (or 16-)strong Bach choir singing continuously throughout each and every chorus may now be laid to rest. It is high time to rehabilitate the choir of concertists.

---

[11] It has proved tempting to play down the importance of the issue: 'One-to-a-part performances today may tell us much about Bach's choral music but they might not come any nearer to the actual sound of Bach's performances' (Butt 1998, p. 100). (Does a string quartet playing a Haydn quartet not come rather nearer to the 'actual sound' – and sense – of Haydn's performances than a string orchestra?) And it is surprising to find more attention being devoted to justifying prevalent practice – including, by implication, a hybrid of recent origin ('period' band with modern-size choir) – than to clarifying Bach's own: 'being part of our existing culture', performing Bach's choral works with a vocal group of 16 or so 'carries with it a spark of "authenticity" (in the sense of immediacy, familiarity and performer identity; and, one might add, the conductor's belief that he is right!) that would parallel that of the original performers' (*ibid.*). Even if the redefining of 'authenticity' in this Taruskinian sense does reflect 'a fundamental change in the attitude towards historically informed performance and its relation to scholarship', I see no justification for believing that it produces 'a more critical stance towards whatever evidence emerges' (*ibid.*). Like it or not, period-instrument orchestras are also now 'part of our existing culture' – and so, for that matter, are vocal ensembles which sing one to a part.

Epilogue

> Let us hope it is not true, but if it is, let us hope it will not be
> generally known.
>
> (A contemporary response to Darwin's theory of evolution)

The purpose of this book has been to show that, in at least one respect, Bach's own choral practice differed significantly from our own, and from what we have always taken on trust. We now have, I believe, a far more detailed and accurate picture of his chosen medium than the one handed down to students such as myself in the late 1960s, when the idea that the Leipzig church works had been intended for a chorus of as few as 12 or 16 voices still seemed quite radical.[1]

In fact, the conventional view has probably been around in some form since 1837 or so, when the *Entwurff* was first published.[2] But only in the early 1980s was it first subjected to serious critical inspection, when Joshua Rifkin, on the basis of a thorough re-examination of surviving vocal copies, concluded that 'Bach normally presented his cantatas with concertists alone, one reading from each part in the materials'.[3] This proposition was greeted – perhaps predictably – with instant disbelief. It was self-evidently non-sensical to suggest that Johann Sebastian Bach could have intended any of his choral masterpieces to be sung by a mere quartet of voices.

But have we all been mesmerized by the idea that a 'choir' must always be larger than a 'mere quartet' of voices? and that a larger group of (less expert) singers is inherently more desirable than a skilled 'consort' in any movement labelled 'chorus'?

Let us for a moment contemplate a fanciful analogy with the classical string quartet repertoire. Imagine that, through changes in fashion and

---

[1] It was also assumed that all choral movements were, as a matter of course, sung from start to finish by the full vocal choir, without differentiation.

[2] *Neue Zeitschrift für Musik*, 7/38 (10 Nov 1837), pp. 149ff. The more focused image of three singers – a concertist and two ripienists – sharing a single copy emerged only much later; see above, p. 51 and note 28, and Rifkin 1999b.

[3] Rifkin 1982, p. 753.

accidents of history, the string quartet as a performance medium had become obsolete by the middle of the nineteenth century, but that its literature was then rediscovered several generations later, in a very different musical climate. Imagine, too, that in a culture uninterested in historical performance styles this repertoire came to be played by a related but different medium, the string orchestra. In this scenario, quartet music would soon become indelibly associated with the string orchestra, its original manner of performance a matter of no practical relevance. In such circumstances, it would be easy to assume that the true home of these works had *always* been the string orchestra – albeit originally a surprisingly small one, with only 12 to 16 string-players. Historical data would tend to be interpreted in that light, or perhaps put quietly to one side in mild puzzlement.[4]

Against such a background, any proposal that the quartet repertoire belonged to an hypothetical 'original' four-person ensemble would be sure to cause dismay and to be branded as a simplistic and over-literal interpretation of the evidence. A 'minimal' string orchestra of this sort would be a manifestly inadequate vehicle for the spiritual greatness of the music; only in the direst of circumstances would Haydn, Mozart, Beethoven and Schubert ever have had to compromise to this degree. Why would anyone possibly wish to re-create such a group?

At Boston in 1981 Joshua Rifkin met with an instantly hostile reception, led by a colleague in what *The New Yorker* described as 'a stinging reply, heavy with sarcasm'.[5] One might have expected Rifkin's peers to react, after due deliberation, with a scrupulous re-appraisal of familiar sources and a painstaking search for new data to support or rebut his thesis. Instead, it seems that his audience – and, in due course, the wider musicological world – reached a hasty consensus that this absurd new 'hypothesis' was best allowed to die an early death.

This scholarly verdict soon filtered through to critics, performers and thence to the musical public. All were left in little doubt that an impudent assault on an innocent tradition had been successfully rebuffed; Rifkin's 'theory' lacked substance and could therefore safely be ignored. This, of course, was exactly what most people wanted to hear; the practical implica-

[4] Even if extant performing parts gave no hint that more than one player had read from them, pictures of string orchestras would demonstrate that such copy-sharing had been universal practice. It would be taken for granted that hundreds of duplicate copies had disappeared. Conductors would learn to make certain simple adjustments in line with 'period' practice (assigning the occasional 'soloistic' passage to a solo instrument, or extrapolating double-bass parts from cello parts). The occasional document reporting or depicting a mere four musicians in a performance setting would be cited as a warning against taking such evidence too literally, or would be explained away as showing just the nucleus of a string orchestra which in actual performance must have been supplemented by numerous unnamed and perhaps unpaid extra players.

[5] Kenyon 1981, p. 189; see also introductory comments to Appendix 6.

tions of the new approach – in institutional, commercial, political, professional, personal and emotional terms – were all too unsettling to contemplate.[6] The familiar fiction thus resumed its charmed existence.

Five years elapsed before any extensive rejoinder to Rifkin's ideas appeared in print[7] and a further ten before the first of my own contributions to *Early Music*, in which I asked rhetorically: 'should the issue really be allowed to disappear so conveniently from public view?'[8]

Whether or not Rifkin's conclusions were accepted wholesale, it is hard to understand how anyone who became acquainted with his arguments could have undervalued the quality of his research or the importance of the subject. Is it not axiomatic that to understand a musical work fully we must first understand its intended medium? Yet few scholars appear to have had their curiosity sufficiently aroused to engage with the subject in depth.[9] Some profess to be 'Still waiting for the book' from Rifkin;[10] others, noticing that Rifkin has published numerous articles developing his earlier findings in new depth, seem to regard this activity as adequate proof 'that the premise and the reasoning supporting it defy common sense'.[11] Even the very fact that the thesis 'has not taken hold' has been held up (with distinctly dubious logic) as justification for disregarding it.[12] For the most part, though, the issue has been viewed as a faintly amusing (or irritating) sideshow,[13] or as a matter of no consequence at all.[14]

There are signs, however, that the tide of opinion may finally have begun to turn. The 1999 volume on Bach in the 'Oxford Composer Companions'

---

[6] Future generations will doubtless be bemused at – or amused by – the resistance which these ideas first encountered and the vehemence with which they were sometimes rejected; see Appendix 7 (especially Koopman, Smithers, Stauffer and Wolff).

[7] See Wagner 1986. Robert Marshall had earlier floated a couple of hypothetical ideas as alternatives to Rifkin's conclusions; see Marshall 1983.

[8] Parrott 1996, p. 551. In due course, my comments drew two lengthy responses: Koopman 1998 (of which Parrott 1998 is a critique) and Smithers 1997.

[9] The scholarly advisor to one leading performer still has the avowed 'intention of not getting entangled in the dispute': Wolff 1999.

[10] Wolff 1998.

[11] Stauffer 1995.

[12] See *ibid.*, and Koopman 1997, p. 542; see also Rifkin 1997b, p. 731.

[13] Thus, with commercial recordings of the Mass in B Minor 'the temptation for conductors entering the lists to "do something different" must be very great, and there have been instances in recent times of performances in which a new approach has been attempted by, for example, . . . assigning some (or in one famous case, all) the choral writing to soloists': Boyd 1995.

[14] As a friend succinctly put it, 'The ploy is familiar: if you don't like it, it's not true; and if it turns out to be true, it's not important.' One writer claims that 'silence in many distinguished quarters is less one of subjugation at the feet of this long-running theory than a refusal to let the matter exude an importance beyond its station': Freeman-Attwood 1998, p. 83. This sidesteps the question of whether the thesis has any historical merit, while quietly endorsing the wish that it should attract as little attention as possible (cf. the epigraph, p. 147 above).

series, for example, allows that 'the vocal parts of cantata choruses are conceptually solo – often virtuoso – lines that may or may not have been reinforced'.[15] Younger Bach scholars in general, notably in North America, appear to have espoused the new thinking (privately, at least) with relative ease. John Butt observes that there has been 'a considerable shift in favour of Rifkin's position among the younger scholars within the community of American Bach scholars over the last few years, and even some of the more vociferous opponents have become remarkably more muted in their criticism'.[16] The recent confirmation that Telemann's practice was substantially the same as Bach's[17] may signal the start of a broader scholarly appreciation of the whole subject. 'There are even rumours of Bach scholars in Germany paying more attention to Rifkin's theory',[18] and the conservative periodical *Musik und Kirche* has chosen this moment to reopen discussion of the subject.[19] Meanwhile, at least three London-based period ensembles (besides my own) have recently begun to dip their toes into these fresh waters, both in concert and with recordings.

Bach's choral output stands at the very pinnacle of Western musical achievement, and it would be unjust, if not unmusical, to dismiss the essential nature of his chorus as a mere side issue. Taking stock of (and facing up to) the mass of pertinent historical data on Bach's choir may seem unduly onerous to some, but – for all those seriously involved with his music, whether as amateurs or professionals – it holds the possibility of bringing Bach's creativity into sharper focus. How – or indeed whether – we wish to reflect any new historical understanding in our performances is, of course, a quite separate issue, a legitimately subjective matter; it is not the purpose of this book to promulgate a new orthodoxy for today's performances of Bach's music.[20] I would never argue that there is only one 'acceptable' or 'permissible' way of performing this or any other repertoire; but it is regrettable that this potentially revelatory approach to Bach's concerted works has been resolutely

[15] Boyd 1999, p. 99 (Butt, 'Chorus').
[16] Butt 1998, p. 100.
[17] See Swack 1999.
[18] Butt 1998, p. 100.
[19] See Appendix 7, p. 211 below.
[20] The one-to-a-part chorus, we are told, 'should hardly become a norm for the entire field of Bach performance without more familiarity with the practice and more available and willing performers' (Butt 1998, p. 100). To my knowledge, no one (certainly neither I nor Rifkin) has argued that performers are under any binding obligation to follow one practice rather than another; but I do believe that performers of Bach's music should not espouse any one stylistic model until they have understood the other plausible options. And how can performers attain 'more familiarity' with a now-unfamiliar practice – making themselves 'more available and willing' to swim against the tide – unless scholars and critics have the courage to pursue historical arguments even if they undercut conventional practice?

ignored by almost everyone in positions of influence (as scholars, critics, conductors, promoters).[21] The effect has been to shield others (not least the musical public) from the mode of performance which (as this book argues) best reflects Bach's own practice.

What do we stand to discover in such performances? In elaborate concerted music such as Bach's, a quartet of 'the best' singers (i.e. concertists) can effortlessly bring to bear both the verbal subtlety and freedom of solo singing and the flexibility, clarity and expressivity of chamber music. And the smaller ensemble – with concertists positioned to achieve the best projection (of text as well as tone) – is able to assume a more compact layout, with improved contact among its key members. Rather than placing an emphasis on the communal effort of many performers, such an ensemble exploits the skills of the best singers and instrumentalists 'concerting' with each other.[22]

In suitable buildings,[23] with good singers, refined trumpet-playing and sensitive placement of performers, there are handsome dividends: Bach's glorious music acquires an ever sharper focus. Fulness of sound is still there when needed, achieved not by multiple voices but by Bach's skilful scoring. As Joshua Rifkin observed back in 1982,

> the music itself creates something of an aural illusion in fully scored passages: solo voices in ensemble, especially when doubled or intricately accompanied by instruments, become all but indistinguishable from a larger chorus . . . the music sheds some weight, perhaps, but takes on new flexibility and incisiveness.[24]

We learnt several decades ago that the pianoforte is not intrinsically superior to the harpsichord as a vehicle for Bach's keyboard music, merely different from it. But while those who play Bach's harpsichord music on the pianoforte may still sometimes claim that the composer would have preferred it thus, they know better than to say that he *wrote* it for the modern pianoforte. Is it too much to demand that equal frankness apply to the matter of Bach's chorus?

Rifkin's insights deserve to take their place (however belatedly) amongst the landmarks of twentieth-century Bach scholarship – and performance. What better musical offering to Bach, 250 years after his death, than to explore his music more thoroughly in its essential medium?

---

[21] Philippe Herreweghe candidly admits: 'I'm not a musicologist, and [Rifkin] probably can make better arguments, though I haven't studied them': Sherman 1997, p. 283.

[22] For theological perspectives on such performing forces, see Butt 1998, *passim*.

[23] Bach's music is never heard to advantage in over-resonant acoustics, whatever the forces; it is simply too 'intricate'.

[24] Rifkin 1982, p. 754.

Acknowledgements

My active engagement with the present subject began in 1982, but it was not until the turn of 1998/9 that the idea of producing a book first occurred to me. Along the way numerous friends and colleagues – amongst them Lisa Agate, Aloysia Assenbaum, Malcolm Bruno, John Butt, Geraldine Frank, Christian Hilz, John Holloway, Richard D. P. Jones, Michael Lowe, Graham Nicholson, Samantha Owens, Eva Pfarrwaller, Julian Podger, Peter Amadeus Schneider, Jeanne Swack, Pippa Thynne, John Toll, Jane Van Tassel, Jeremy White and Richard Wistreich – have given me invaluable assistance, whether by debating ideas, supplying information, reading early drafts, or advising on details of translation and presentation; I wish to thank them all. Jill Shiu assisted me with a question of acoustics, Peter G. McC. Brown (Trinity College, Oxford) prepared translations of Latin passages, and Francis Lamport (Worcester College, Oxford) gave detailed advice on the many German texts; all have been generous with their expertise. The staff of the Bodleian Library (Oxford), the University of Oxford Faculty of Music Library, and the British Library (London) quietly expedited my research on numerous occasions, and various German institutions (see pp. ix–xi) helpfully and efficiently made material available to me. Bruce Phillips, Eirian Griffiths and (again) Pippa Thynne all played vital roles in ensuring that publication did not remain merely a distant goal; my sincere thanks to each of them.

The excellent work of my own Taverner Consort and Players and its administrative team, Malcolm Bruno and Victoria Newbert, has always been an important stimulus, as have my collaborations with various other ensembles in Europe and north America; my thanks in particular to Hans Georg Schäfer for invitations to perform before German audiences.

To three people above all I owe a particular debt of gratitude. Emily Van Evera (my wife) has perhaps suffered more than most from my dogged determination to get this book out within an exceptionally short space of time, and of course she has also contributed greatly to the result, not least through her own keen appreciation of the subject and sensitive understanding of Bach's music. Eric Van Tassel's critical role has extended considerably beyond that of copy-editor; from the time of the book's genesis (in article form) through to the final stages of its publication, he has not only given me the full benefit of his finely honed editorial skills but also, in countless detailed and stimulating discussions, contributed valuable new thinking whilst seeking to help me clarify and improve my own.

Joshua Rifkin's groundbreaking work was the sole catalyst for my own involvement with the subject and the prime inspiration for the present endeavour. But I have benefited also, during what has often seemed a lonely pursuit, from Rifkin's personal supportiveness – answering innumerable queries, sharing fresh information and insight, and steering me around various pitfalls of Bach scholarship. It remains to be seen whether Rifkin will receive the public recognition that is his due, but if this book helps dispel the general confusion that has for too long obscured the significance of his findings, it will perhaps go some way towards repaying my own personal debt.

1 January 2000

Appendices

Illustration 28. A meeting of the Leipzig Town Council, 1713: engraving by J. C. Lünig. The Bürgermeister sits at the head of the table with his deputy and the town clerk; to his left are 11 councillors, to his right two minute-takers

Appendix 1

Bach's written undertakings to the Leipzig Town Council (1723)

1.
Bach's initial undertaking to the Town Council
Source: *BD I*, p. 175 (cf. *NBR*, p. 102)

Demnach bey E:E. Hochw.-Rathe der Stadt Leipzigk ich endesbenanter zu dem bey der *Thomas*-Schule daselbst *vacant*en *Cantor* Dienste mich gemeldet, und dißfalls auf meine Persohn zu *reflectiren* geziemend gebeten, Als verspreche ich krafft dieses, daß daferne mein suchen statt finden und mir solcher Dienst aufgetragen werden solte, ich nicht nur binnen *dato* und 3 oder höchstens vier Wochen von der bey dem HochFürstlich Anhalt-Cöthischen Hoffe auf mir habenden Bestallung mich losmachen und dieserwegen wohlgedachtem Rathe den *Dimißion*-Schein ein-händigen, sondern auch, wenn ich solchen *Cantor*-Dienst würcklich antrete, mich der Schul-Ordnung, so bereits vorhanden, oder noch aufgerichtet werden möchte, mich gemäs verhalten, absonderlich aber die Knaben, so auf die Schule *recipir*et worden nicht alleine in denen darzu gehörigen ordentlichen Stunden, sondern auch *privatißime* im Singen ohne Entgeld *informir*en, und was mir sonst darbey zu thun oblieget, allenthalben gebührend verrichten, nicht weniger, daferne, iedoch mit vorbewust und Bewilligung E. E: Hochweisen Raths, zu meiner *sublevation* beym *informir*en in der Lateinischen Sprache jemand erfordert werden solte, denselben aus meinen eigenen Mitteln ohne von E. E. Hochweisen Rathe, oder sonst etwas zu begehren, davor vergnügen will, Treülich und ohne Gefehrde; Urkundlich habe ich darüber diesen *Revers* unter meiner Hand und Petschafft von mir gestellet. Geschehen Leipzigk den 19ten *Aprill*, 1723.

> Johann Sebastian Bach
> p.t: Hochfürstlich Anhalt-
> Cöthenscher Capellmeister.

Whereas I, the undersigned, have applied to you, the Noble and Most Wise Council of the Town of Leipzig, for the vacant post of Cantor at the Thomasschule there, and have duly asked to be considered in this regard, I do hereby faithfully and unre-servedly promise – if my quest succeeds and the said post is offered to me – that within three or at most four weeks from today's date I shall not only release myself from the position I have at the princely court of Anhalt-Cöthen and hand over the certificate of dismissal to the respected Council, but also, when I actually take up the said post of Cantor, conduct myself in accordance with the already existing School Regulations or any which may yet be drawn up; [and] especially, however, [that I shall] instruct the boys who are admitted to the school not only in the usual classes associated [with the post] but also privately (without remuneration) in singing, and attend to whatever else is incumbent upon me, [and that] equally, in case – but [only] with the Noble and Most Wise Council's prior knowledge and permission – someone should be required to relieve me with Latin instruction, [I shall] reward the same out of my own pocket, without demanding anything from the Noble and Most Wise Council or otherwise. In witness whereof I have given this undertaking under my own hand and seal. Done at Leipzig, 19 April 1723.

Johann Sebastian Bach
pro tempore Capellmeister to the Prince of Anhalt-Cöthen

2.
Bach's final undertaking to the Town Council
Source: *BD I*, pp. 177f (cf. *NBR*, pp. 104f)

Cantoris bey der Thomas-
Schule
Revers.

Demnach E. E. Hochweiser Rath dieser Stadt Leipzig mich zum *Cantor*n der Schulen zu *St. Thomas* angenommen und einen *Revers*, in nachgesezten Puncten von mir zuvollziehen begehret, nemlich:

1.) Daß ich denen Knaben, in einem erbarn eingezogenen Leben und Wandel, mit gutem Exempel vorleuchten, der Schulen fleißig abwarten, und die Knaben treulich *informir*en,

2.) Die *Music* in beyden Haupt-Kirchen dieser Stadt, nach meinem besten Vermögen, in gutes Aufnehmen bringen,

3.) E. E. Hochweisen Rathe allen schuldigen *respect* und Gehorsam erweisen und deßen Ehre und *reputatio*n aller Orthen bester maßen beobachten und befördern, auch so ein Herr des Raths die Knaben zu einer *Music* begehret, ihme dieselben ohnweigerlich folgen laßen, außer diesen aber denenselben auf das Land, zu Begräbnüßen oder Hochzeiten, ohne des regierenden Herrn Bürgermeisters und der Herren Vorsteher der Schulen Vorbewust und Einwilligung zureisen keinesweges verstatten.

4.) Denen Herren *Inspector*en und Vorstehern der Schulen in allen und ieden, was im Nahmen E. E. hochweisen Raths dieselbige anordnen werden, gebührende Folge leisten,

5.) Keine Knaben, welche nicht bereits in der *Music* ein *fundament* geleget, oder sich doch darzu schicken, daß sie darinnen *informir*et werden können, auf die Schule nehmen, auch solches, ohne derer Herren *Inspector*en und Vorsteher Vorwißen und Einwilligung, nicht thun.

6.) Damit die Kirchen nicht mit unnöthigen Unkosten beleget werden mögen, die Knaben nicht allein in der *Vocal-* sondern auch in der *Instrumental-Music* fleißig unterweisen.

7.) Zu Beybehaltung guter Ordnung in denen Kirchen die *Music* dergestalt einrichten, daß sie nicht zulang währen, auch also beschaffen seyn möge, damit sie nicht *opern*hafftig herauskommen, sondern die Zuhörer vielmehr zur Andacht aufmuntere.

8.) Die neue Kirche mit guten Schülern versehen,

9.) Die Knaben freundlich und mit Behutsamkeit *tractir*en, daferne sie aber nicht folgen wollen, solche *moderat* züchtigen, oder gehöriges Orts melden;

10.) Die *Information* in der Schule und was mir sonsten zuthun gebühret, treulich besorgen,

11.) Und da ich solche selbst zuverrichten nicht vermöchte, daß es durch ein ander tüchtiges *Subjectum*, ohne E. E. Hochweisen Raths, oder der Schule, Beytrag, geschehe, veranstalten,

12.) Ohne des regierenden Herrn Bürgermeisters Erlaubnüß mich nicht aus der Stadt begeben,

13.) In LeichBegängnüßen iederzeit, wie gebräuchlich, so viel möglich, bey und neben denen Knaben hergehen,

14.) Und bey der *Universität* kein *officium*, ohne E. E. Hochweisen Raths *Consens* annehmen solle und wolle;

Alß ver*reversir*e und verpflichte ich mich hiermit und in Krafft dieses, daß ich diesen allen, wie obstehet, treulich nachkommen und, bey Verlust meines Dienstes, darwieder nicht handeln wolle.

Zu Uhrkund habe ich diesen *Revers* eigenhändig unterschrieben und mit meinem Petschafft bekräfftiget. So geschehen in Leipzig, den 5. *Maii*, 1723.

Johann Sebastian Bach.

Undertaking by the Cantor at the Thomasschule

Whereas the Noble and Most Wise Council of this Town of Leipzig has engaged me as Cantor of the Thomasschule and has requested of me a written undertaking in respect of the following points, namely:

(1) That I set the boys a shining example with a respectable, retiring life style, serve the school diligently, and instruct the boys conscientiously;

(2) Put the music in both the principal churches of this town into good order, to the best of my ability;

(3) Show the Noble and Most Wise Council all due respect and obedience and uphold and promote its honour and reputation everywhere as best I may; also, if a member of the Council requests the boys for a musical performance, let them do his bidding without fail, but otherwise on no account permit them to travel to the country, for funerals or weddings, without the prior knowledge and consent of the serving Bürgermeister and of the school's Governors;

(4) Duly comply with the school's Inspectors and Governors in each and every instruction that the same shall issue in the name of the Noble and Most Wise Council;

(5) Admit into the school no boys who have not already acquired a grounding in music or who are not suited to being instructed therein, nor do so without the prior knowledge and consent of the Inspectors and Governors;

(6) Diligently instruct the boys not only in vocal but also in instrumental music, so that the churches may not be put to unnecessary expense;

(7) For the maintenance of good order in church, arrange that the music not last too long, and take care that it not appear operatic in nature but, much rather, that it rouse the listeners to devotion;

(8) Supply the Neue Kirche with good pupils;

(9) Treat the boys in a friendly manner and with discretion but, if they refuse to obey, castigate them moderately or report them to the appropriate authority;

(10) Conscientiously attend to the instruction in the school and to whatever else it behoves me to do;

(11) And, if I am unable to undertake this myself, organize for it to be done by another proficient person, without further cost to the Noble and Most Wise Council or to the school;

(12) Not leave the town without permission from the serving Bürgermeister;

(13) So far as possible, always walk in funeral processions alongside the boys, as is customary;

(14) And not take up or seek to take up any appointment at the university, without the Noble and Most Wise Council's approval;

Therefore I do hereby undertake and pledge myself firmly to observe all of the above points conscientiously and, on pain of forfeiting my post, not to act contrary to them.

In witness whereof I have set my own hand to this undertaking and ratified it with my seal. Done thus in Leipzig, 5 May 1723.

Johann Sebastian Bach.

Appendix 2

Bach's audition reports (1729)

In 1729 nine places for *alumni* (resident pupils) became vacant at the Thomasschule. In a letter of 18 May 1729 to the Town Council, the chairman of the school's governors, Dr C. L. Stieglitz, noted that Bach required a total of 44 singers to serve the five churches. Submitted with the letter from Stieglitz were two documents drawn up by the Cantor (together with two from the Rector): the first is reproduced in the text (see above, pp. 94f); the second comprised succinct musical assessments of various applicants (document 3 below). Similar reports on four further candidates (numbered *[i]–[iv]* below) were written around the same time (documents 1–2, 4–6 below). In place of translations of the original documents, the summary on pp. 161f tabulates Bach's assessments.

1.

Before 9 May 1729
Source: *BD I*, p. 130

Vorzeiger dieses *[i]* Erdmann Gottwald Pezold von Auerbach, *æt:* 14. Jahr, hat eine feine Stimme und ziemliche *Profectus*. So hiermit eigenhändig *attestiret* wird

von

Joh: Seb: Bach.

2.

Before 9 May 1729
Source: *BD I*, p. 130

Vorzeiger dieses *[iv]* Johann Christoph Schmied von Bendleben aus Thüringen *æt:* 19. Jahr, hat eine feine *Tenor* Stimme und singt vom Blat fertig.

Joh: Seb: Bach
Direct: Musices

3.
Before 18 May 1729

Source: *BD I*, pp. 131f (cf. *NBR*, pp. 140f)

Die jenigen Knaben zu bey itziger *vacanz* auf die Schule zu *S. Thomæ* als *Alumni recipiret* zu werden verlangen, sind folgende: als.

(1) Zur Music zu gebrauchende, u. zwar *Soprani*sten.

1   Christoph Friedrich Meißner von Weißenfels, *æt:* 13 Jahr, hat eine gute Stimme u. feine *profectus*

2   Johann Tobias Krebs von Buttstädt, *æt:* 13. Jahr, hat eine gute starcke Stimme u. feine *profectus*.

3   Samuel Kittler von Bellgern, *æt:* 13 Jahr hat ein ziemlich starcke Stimme u. hübsche *profectus*.

4   Johann Heinrich Hillmeyer von GehringsWalde *æt:* 13 Jahr, hat eine starcke Stimme wie auch feine *profectus*.

5   Johann August Landvoigt von Geschwitz *æt:* 13 Jahr, hat eine *passable* Stimme; die *profectus* sind ziemlich

6   Johann Andreas Köpping von Großboden; *æt:* 14 Jahr, hat eine ziemlich starcke Stimme; die *profectus* sind *mediocre*.

7   Johann Gottlob Krause von GroßDeuben, *æt:* 14 Jahr, deßen Stimme etwas schwach und die *profectus* mittelmäßig

8   Johann Georg Leg aus Leipzig, *æt:* 13 Jahr, deßen Stimme etwas schwach, und die *profectus* geringe

*Alti*sten.[1]

9   Johann Gottfried Neucke von Grima, *æt:* 14 Jahr, hat eine starcke Stimme, u. ziemlich feine *profectus*.

10   Gottfried Christoph Hoffmann von Nebra, *æt:* 16 Jahr, hat eine *passable* *Alt*stimme, die *profectus* sind aber noch ziemlich schlecht.

(2) Die, so nichts in *Musicis præstiren*

(1)   Johann Tobias Dieze.

(2)   *[ii]* Gottlob Michael Wintzer.

(3)   Johann David Bauer.

(4)   Johannen Margarethen Pfeilin Sohn.

(5)   Gottlob Ernst *Hausius*.

(6)   Wilhelm Ludewigs Sohn Friedrich Wilhelm.

(7)   Johann Gottlob Zeymer.

(8)   Johann Gottfried Berger.

(9)   Johann Gottfried Eschner.

(10)   *Salomon* Gottfried Greülich.

(11)   Michael Heinrich Kittler von Prettin. etc.

> *Joh: Sebast: Bach*
> *Direct: Musices*
> *v[nd] Cantor zu S.*
> *Thomæ.*

---

[1] Bach's style of numbering for these two altos has been emended for clarity.

4.
Before 18 May 1729
Source: *BD I*, p. 134

[i] Gottwald Pezold von Aurich, *æt:* 14. Jahr, hat eine feine Stimme und die *profectus* sind *passable.*
[iv] Johann Christoph Schmid von Bendleben *æt:* 19 Jahr, hat eine ziemlich starcke *Tenor* Stimme, und trifft gar hübsch. etc.

5.
Before 21 May 1729?
Source: *BD I*, p. 134

[iii] Carolus Heinrich Scharff, *æt:* 14 Jahr, hat eine ziemliche *Alt* Stimme, und mittelmäßige *Profectus in Musicis.*

J S Bach.
Cantor etc.

6.
3 June 1729
Source: *BD I*, p. 135

[ii] Obig benandter Wünzer hat eine etwas schwache Stimme und noch wenige *profectus,* dörffte aber wohl (so ein *privat exercitium* fleißig getrieben würde) mit der Zeit zu gebrauchen seyn.
Leipzig. den 3 *Jun:* 1729

Joh: Seb: Bach.
Cantor etc.

In document **3** Bach categorizes candidates as 'those usable in music', subdivided into sopranos (nos. 1–8) and altos (nos. 9–10), and 'those who have no musical ability' (nos. (1)–(11)). Bach's observations in the above six documents may be summarized as follows:

	name	*birthplace*	*age*	*type*	*voice*	*proficiency*
1.	C. F. Meißner	Weißenfels	13	s	good	fine
2.	J. T. Krebs (jun.)	Buttelstedt b.Weimar	13	s	good, strong	fine
3.	S. Kittler	Belgern	13	s	quite strong	nice[a]
4.	J. H. Hillmeyer	Gehringswalde	13	s	strong	fine
5.	J. A. Landvoigt	Gaschwitz	13	s	passable	fair
6.	J. A. Köpping	Großbothen	14	s	quite strong	mediocre

	name	birthplace	age	type	voice	proficiency
7.	J. G. Krause	Großdeuben	14	S	somewhat weak	moderate
8.	J. G. Leg	Leipzig	13	S	somewhat weak	slight
[i]	E. G. Petzold	Auerbach	14	?	fine	fair/ passable
(2)[ii]	G. M. Wintzer	Leipzig	14	?	somewhat weak	still limited[b]
[iii]	C. H. Scharff	Mügeln	14	A	fair	moderate
9.	J. G. Neicke	Grimma	14	A	strong	quite fine
10.	G. C. Hoffmann	Nebra	16	A	passable	still quite poor
[iv]	J. C. Schmied	Bendeleben	19	T	fine/fairly strong	'sings fluently at sight'/ 'performs very nicely'[c]

[a]   'a pleasant treble voice' ('eine annehmliche Stimme zum Discante') (*BD I*, p. 133)
[b]   'but with time [he] probably ought to be usable – if a course of private exercise is diligently undertaken' (document 6).
[c]   documents 2, 4

Appendix 3

The *Entwurff* (1730): text and translation

Source: *BD I*, pp. 60–4 (cf. *NBR*, pp. 145–51); facsimile edn, Kassel, 1955 (Paragraph numbers, added for ease of reference, do not appear in the original document.)

Kurtzer, iedoch höchstnöthiger Entwurff einer wohlbestallten Kirchen *Music*; nebst einigem unvorgreiflichen Bedencken von dem Verfall derselben.

¶1 Zu einer wohlbestellten Kirchen *Music* gehören *Vocali*sten und *Instrumenti*sten.

¶2 Die *Vocali*sten werden hiesiges Ohrts von denen *Thomas* Schülern *formiret*, und zwar von vier Sorten, als *Discanti*sten, *Alti*sten, *Tenori*sten, und *Baß*isten.

¶3 So nun die *Chöre* derer Kirchen Stücken recht, wie es sich gebühret, bestellt werden sollen, müßen die *Vocali*sten wiederum in 2erley *Sorten* eingetheilet werden, als: *Concerti*sten und *Ripieni*sten.

¶4 Derer *Concerti*sten sind *ordinaire* 4; auch wohl 5, 6, 7 biß 8; so mann nemlich *per Choros musiciren* will.

¶5 Derer *Ripieni*sten müßen wenigstens auch achte seyn, nemlich zu ieder Stimme zwey.

¶6 Die *Instrumenti*sten werden auch in verschiedene Arthen eingetheilet, als: *Violi*sten, *Hautboi*sten, *Fleuteni*sten, *Trompetter* und Paucker. *NB.* Zu denen *Violi*sten gehören auch die, so die *Violen*, *Violoncelli* und *Violons* spielen.

¶7 Die Anzahl derer *Alumnorum Thomanæ Scholæ* ist 55. Diese 55 werden eingetheilet in 4 *Chöre*, nach denen 4 Kirchen, worinne sie theils *musicir*en, theils *motetten* und theils *Chorale* singen müßen. In denen 3 Kirchen, als zu S. *Thomæ*, S. *Nicolai* und der Neüen Kirche müßen die Schüler alle *musicalisch* seyn. In die Peters-Kirche kömmt der Ausschuß, nemlich die, so keine *music* verstehen, sondern nur nothdörfftig einen *Choral* singen können.

¶8 Zu iedweden *musicalischen Chor* gehören wenigsten 3 *Soprani*sten, 3 *Alti*sten, 3 *Tenori*sten, und eben so viel *Baß*isten, damit, so etwa einer unpaß wird (wie denn sehr offte geschiehet, und besonders bey itziger Jahres Zeit, da die *recepte*, so von dem Schul *Medico* in die Apothecke verschrieben werden, es ausweisen müßen) wenigstens eine 2 *Chörig*te *Motette* gesungen werden kan. (*NB.* Wiewohln es noch beßer, wenn der *Coetus* so beschaffen wäre, daß mann zu ieder Stimme 4 *subjecta* nehmen, und also ieden *Chor* mit 16. Persohnen bestellen könte.)

§9   Machet demnach der *numerus*, so *Musicam* verstehen müßen, 36 Persohnen aus.

§10   Die *Instrumental Music* bestehet aus folgenden Stimmen; als:

2 auch wohl 3 zur		—	*Violino* 1.
2 biß 3 zur		—	*Violino* 2.
2 zur	—	—	*Viola* 1.
2 zur	—	—	*Viola* 2.
2 zum	—	—	*Violoncello.*
1 zum	—	—	*Violon.*
2 auch wohl nach Beschaffenheit 3 zu denen			*Hautbois.*
1 auch 2 zum —		—	*Basson.*
3 zu denen	—	—	*Trompetten*
1 zu denen	—	—	Paucken.

summa 18. Persohnen wenigstens zur *Instrumental-Music*. *NB* füget sichs, daß das KirchenStück auch mit Flöten, (sie seynd nun *à bec* oder *Traversieri*), *componiret* ist (wie denn sehr offt zur Abwechselung geschiehet) sind wenigstens auch 2 Persohnen darzu nöthig. Thun zusammen 20 *Instrumenti*sten.

§11   Der *Numerus* derer zur Kirchen *Music* bestellten Persohnen bestehet aus 8 Persohnen, als 4. StadtPfeifern, 3 KunstGeigern und einem Gesellen. Von deren *qualität*en und *musical*ischen Wißenschafften aber etwas nach der Warheit zu erwehnen, verbietet mir die Bescheidenheit. Jedoch ist zu *consideriren*, daß Sie theils *emeriti*, theils auch in keinem solchen *exercitio* sind, wie es wohl seyn solte.

§12   Der *Plan* davon ist dieser:

Herr Reiche	zur	1 *Trompette.*
Herr Genßmar	—	2 *Trompette.*
vacat	—	3 *Trompette.*
vacat	—	Paucken.
Herr Rother	—	1 *Violine.*
Herr Beyer	—	2 *Violine.*
vacat	—	*Viola.*
vacat	—	*Violoncello.*
vacat	—	*Violon.*
Herr Gleditsch	—	1 *Hautbois.*
Herr Kornagel	—	2 *Hautbois.*
vacat	—	3 *Hautbois* oder *Taille*
Der Geselle	—	*Basson.*

§13   Und also fehlen folgende höchstnöthige *subjecta* theils zur Verstärckung, theils zu ohnentbehrlichen Stimmen, nemlich:

2 *Violi*sten zur 1 *Violin.*
2 *Violi*sten zur 2 *Violin.*
2 so die *Viola* spielen.
2 *Violoncelli*sten.
1 *Violoni*st.
2 zu denen *Flöten.*

¶14   Dieser sich zeigende Mangel hat bißhero zum Theil von denen *Studiosis*, meistens aber von denen *Alumnis* müßen ersetzet werden. Die Herrn *Studiosi* haben sich auch darzu willig finden laßen, in Hoffnung, daß ein oder anderer mit der Zeit einige Ergötzligkeit bekommen, und etwa mit einem *stipendio* oder *honorario* (wie vor diesem gewöhnlich gewesen) würde begnadiget werden. Da nun aber solches nicht geschehen, sondern die etwanigen wenigen *beneficia*, so ehedem an den *Chorum musicum* verwendet worden, *succeßive* gar entzogen worden, so hat hiemit sich auch die Willfährigkeit der *Studiosorum* verlohren; Denn wer wird ümsonst arbeiten, oder Dienste thun? Fernerhin zu gedencken, daß da die 2de *Violin* meistens, die *Viola*, *Violoncello* und *Violon* aber allezeit (in Ermangelung tüchtiger *subjectorum*) mit Schülern habe bestellen müßen: So ist leicht zu erachten was dadurch dem *Vocal Chore* ist entgangen. Dieses ist nur von Sontäglichen *Musiquen* berühret worden. Soll ich aber die Fest-Tages *Musiquen*, (als an welchen in denen beeden HauptKirchen die *Music* zugleich besorgen muß) erwehnen, so wird erstlich der Mangel derer benöthigten *subject*en noch deütlicher in die Augen fallen, sindemahln so dann ins andere *Chor* die jenigen Schüler, so noch ein und andres *Instrument* spielen, vollends abgeben, u. mich völlig dern beyhülffe begeben muß.

¶15   Hiernechst kan nicht unberühret bleiben, daß durch bißherige *reception* so vieler untüchtigen und zur *music* sich gar nicht schickenden Knaben, die *Music* nothwendig sich hat vergeringern und ins abnehmen gerathen müßen. Denn es gar wohl zu begreiffen, daß ein Knabe, so gar nichts von der *Music* weiß, ja nicht ein mahl eine *secundam* im Halse *formiren* kan, auch kein *musica*lisch *naturel* haben könne; *consequenter* niemahln zur *Music* zu gebrauchen sey. Und die jenigen, so zwar einige *principia* mit auf die Schule bringen, doch nicht so gleich, als es wohl erfordert wird, zu gebrauchen seyn. Denn da es keine Zeit leiden will, solche erstlich Jährlich zu *informiren*, biß sie geschickt sind zum Gebrauch, sondern so bald sie zur *reception* gelangen, werden sie mit in die *Chöre* vertheilet, und müßen wenigstens *tact* und *ton*feste seyn üm beym Gottesdienste gebraucht werden zu können. Wenn nun alljährlich einige von denen, so *in musicis* was gethan haben, von der Schule ziehen, und deren Stellen mit andern ersetzet werden, so einestheils noch nicht zu gebrauchen sind, mehrentheils aber gar nichts können, so ist leicht zu schließen, daß der *Chorus musicus* sich vergeringern müße.

¶16   Es ist ja *notorisch*, daß meine Herrn *Præanteceßores*, Schell und Kuhnau, sich schon der Beyhülffe derer Herrn *Studiosorum* bedienen müßen, wenn sie eine vollständige und wohllautende *Music* haben *produciren* wollen; welches sie dann auch in so weit haben *præstiren* können da so wohl einige *vocalisten*, als: *Baßist*, u. *Tenorist*, ja auch *Altist*, als auch *Instrumentist*en, besonders 2 *Violist*en von E. HochEdlen und Hochweisen Raht *a parte* sind mit *stipendiis* begnadiget, mithin zur Verstärckung derer Kirchen *Musiquen animiret* worden.

¶17   Da nun aber der itzige *status musices* gantz anders weder ehedem beschaffen, die Kunst üm sehr viel gestiegen, der *gusto* sich verwunderens-würdig geändert, dahero auch die ehemalige Arth von *Music* unseren Ohren nicht mehr klingen will, und mann üm so mehr einer erklecklichen Beyhülffe benöthiget ist, damit solche *subjecta choisiret* und bestellet werden können, so den itzigen *musica*lischen gustum *assequiren*, die neüen Arthen der *Music* bestreiten, mithin im Stande seyn können, dem *Compositori* und deßen Arbeit *satisfaction* zu geben, hat man die wenigen *beneficia*, so ehe hätten sollen vermehret als veringert werden, dem *Choro Musico* gar entzogen. Es ist ohne dem etwas Wunderliches, da man von denen teütschen

Musicis prætendiret, Sie sollen *capable* seyn, allerhand Arthen von *Music,* sie komme nun aus *Italien* oder *Franckreich, Engeland* oder Pohlen, so fort *ex tempore* zu *musiciren,* wie es etwa die jenigen *Virtuosen,* vor die es gesetzet ist, und welche es lange vorhero *studiret* ja fast auswendig können, überdem auch *quod notandum* in schweren Solde stehen, deren Müh und Fleiß mithin reichlich belohnet wird, *præstiren* können; man solches doch nicht *consideriren* will, sondern läßet Sie ihrer eigenen Sorge über, da denn mancher vor Sorgen der Nahrung nicht dahin dencken kan, üm sich zu *perfectioniren,* noch weniger zu *distinguiren.* Mit einem *exempel* diesen Satz zu erweisen, darff man nur nach Dreßden gehen, und sehen, wie daselbst von Königlicher Majestät die *Musici salariret* werden; Es kan nicht fehlen, da denen *Musicis* die Sorge der Nahrung benommen wird, der *chagrin* nachbleibet, auch überdem iede Persohn nur ein eintziges *Instrument* zu *excoliren* hat, es muß was trefliches und *excellentes* zu hören seyn. Der Schluß ist demnach leicht zu finden, daß bey *ceßirenden beneficiis* mir die Kräffte benommen werden, die *Music* in beßeren Stand zu setzen.

§18   Zum Beschluß finde mich genöthiget den *numerum* derer itzigen *alumnorum* mit anzuhängen, iedes seine *profectus in Musicis* zu eröffnen, und so dann zu reiferer Überlegung es zu überlaßen, ob bey so bewandten Ümständten die *Music* könne fernerhin bestehen, oder ob deren mehrerer Verfall zu besorgen sey. Es ist aber nothwendig den gantzen *coetum* in drey *Claßes* abzutheilen.

§19   Sind demnach die brauchbaren folgende:

(1)   Pezold, Lange, Stoll, *Praefecti.* Frick, Krause, Kittler, Pohlreüter, Stein, Burckhard, Siegler, Nitzer, Reichhard, Krebs *major* u. *minor,* Schöneman, Heder und Dietel.

§20   Die *Motetten* Singer, so sich noch erstlich mehr *perfectioniren* müßen, üm mit der Zeit zur *Figural Music* gebrauchet werden zu können, heißen wie folget:

(2)   Jänigke, Ludewig *major* und *minor,* Meißner, Neücke *major* und *minor,* Hillmeyer, Steidel, Heße, Haupt, *Suppius,* Segnitz, Thieme, Keller, Röder, Oßan, Berger, Lösch, Hauptman und Sachse.

§21   Die von lezterer *sorte* sind gar keine *Musici,* und heißen also:

(3)   Bauer, Graß, Eberhard, Braune, Seyman, Tietze, Hebenstreit, Wintzer, Ößer, Leppert, Haußius, Feller, Crell, Zeymer, Guffer, Eichel und Zwicker.

§22   *Summa.* 17 zu gebrauchende, 20. noch nicht zu gebrauchende, und 17 untüchtige. Leipzig, den 23. *Aug.* 1730.

Joh: Seb: Bach.
Director Musices.

Brief yet highly necessary outline of a properly constituted church musical establishment, with some sober reflections on the decline of the same.

§1   A properly constituted church musical establishment must have vocalists and instrumentalists.

§2   The vocalists in the present locality are made up of pupils from the Thomasschule, and are specifically of four sorts, viz. trebles, altos, tenors, and basses.

§3   Now, in order that the choirs for [concerted] church pieces be correctly constituted, as is befitting, the vocalists must be divided further into two sorts, viz. concertists and ripienists.

§4   Concertists are ordinarily four [in number], indeed even five, six, seven [and] up to eight – if one wishes, that is, to perform music *per choros* [i.e. for more than one choir].

§5   Ripienists must also be at least eight [in number], namely, two for each voice.

§6   The instrumentalists are also divided into various kinds, viz. violinists, oboists, flute/recorder-players, trumpeters, and drummers. NB 'Violinists' also include those who play violas, cellos and violones.

§7   The total number of Thomasschule *alumni* [resident pupils] is 55. These 55 are divided into four choirs, for four churches in which they have partly to perform [concerted] music, partly to sing motets, and partly to sing chorales. In three churches (the Thomaskirche, the Nikolaikirche and the Neue Kirche) the pupils must all be 'musical' [i.e. capable at least of performing the traditional motet repertoire]. Those left over go to the Petrikirche, namely, those who do not understand music at all but, rather, can just barely sing a chorale.

§8   Each 'musical' choir must have at least three sopranos, three altos, three tenors, and as many basses, so that even if one person falls ill (as very often happens, and particularly at this time of year [late August], as the prescriptions written by the school doctor for the apothecary must show), at least a two-choir motet can be sung. (NB though it would be better still if the student body were composed in such a way that one could take four individuals [*subjecta*] for each voice and thus set up each choir with sixteen persons.)

§9   Accordingly, the number of those who must understand *musica* works out at 36 persons.

§10   The instrumental group consists of the following parts, viz.:

2 or even 3 for	violin 1
2 to 3 for	violin 2
2 for	viola 1
2 for	viola 2
2 for	violoncello
1 for	violone
2 or even – if required – 3 for	oboes
1 or 2 for	bassoon
3 for	trumpets
1 for	kettledrums

total: at least 18 persons for the instrumental group. NB in the event of the [concerted] church piece being also composed for recorders or transverse flutes, as very often happens for variety, at least two more persons are needed in addition, making 20 instrumentalists in all.

¶11   The number of persons appointed to the church musical establishment consists of eight persons, viz. four *Stadtpfeifer*, three string-players [*Kunstgeiger*] and one apprentice. Discretion forbids me to make any truthful mention of their qualities and musical knowledge. However, it must be borne in mind that they are partly *emeriti* [and] also partly not at all in practice to the proper extent.

¶12   Here is a table of this:

Herr Reiche [aged 63]	trumpet 1
Herr Genßmar [45]	trumpet 2
vacant	trumpet 3
vacant	kettledrums
Herr Rother [65]	violin 1
Herr Beyer [49]	violin 2
vacant	viola
vacant	violoncello
vacant	violone
Herr Gleditsch [46]	oboe 1
Herr Kornagel [41]	oboe 2
vacant	oboe 3 or *taille*
The apprentice	bassoon

¶13   And so the following highly necessary *subjecta* are lacking, partly as reinforcements and partly for essential parts, namely:

2 violinists for violin 1
2 violinists for violin 2
2 who play viola
2 violoncellists
1 violone player
2 for flutes/recorders

¶14   The shortage evident here has hitherto had to be made up partly by *studiosi* [from the university] but mostly by the school's own *alumni*. The *studiosi* have also shown themselves willing to do this in the hope that one or other of them would in time receive some sort of reward and perhaps be granted a *stipendium* or *honorarium* (as was formerly the custom). But now, as this has not come about, and as instead whatever few *beneficia* were formerly accorded to the *chorus musicus* have been completely withdrawn one after the other, cooperation from the *studiosi* has disappeared too; for who will work or render services for nothing? Furthermore it should be borne in mind that, because the second violin has mostly had to be taken by pupils, and the viola, violoncello and violone always so (for want of more capable *subjecta*), it is easy to imagine what the vocal choir has thereby lost. Only Sunday performances have been touched on here. But if I mention feast-day performances (viz. those on which I have to look after the music in both principal churches at the same time), the shortage of required *subjecta* will immediately be even more apparent, since I must then let the other choir have all those pupils who also play one instrument or another and must completely forgo their assistance.

¶15   Besides, it cannot remain unmentioned that, as a result of the admission hitherto of so many unproficient and musically quite untalented boys, music has necessarily had to deteriorate and decline. For it is very easy to see that a boy who knows nothing at all of music, and who can never even form [the interval of] a second in his throat, cannot have any natural musical talent either – and is consequently never going to be usable in music-making; and [that] those who do bring a few precepts with them to the school are not going to be usable as quickly as is required. For, as there is no time to instruct them first thing each year until [such time as] they are fit to be used, they are instead distributed among the [various] choirs as soon as they are admitted, and must at least be secure in metre and pitch [if they are] to be used in church services. Now, if each year several of those who have achieved something in *musica* leave the school and their places are taken by others who are in some cases not yet ready to be used but for the most part have no ability whatsoever, it is easy to conclude that the *chorus musicus* must deteriorate.

¶16   Indeed, it is acknowledged that even my predecessors Messrs Schelle and Kuhnau had to avail themselves of assistance from the *studiosi* if they wanted to produce a full and well-sounding musical ensemble – which they could actually do then, insofar as several vocalists (viz. a bass and tenor, and even an alto) as well as instrumentalists (particularly two violinists) were separately favoured with stipends by a Most Noble and Most Wise Council and were thereby moved to strengthen the church *Musiquen.*

¶17   But as the current state of music is now quite different in nature from before, [and as] artistry has progressed very much [and] taste [has] changed astonishingly – such that music of the former kind no longer sounds [good] to our ears and [such that] one is all the more in need of considerable assistance, so that *subjecta* can be chosen and appointed who can assimilate current musical taste, get to grips with the new kinds of music, [and] thus be in a position to satisfy the composer and do justice to his work – [now, despite all these changes,] the few *beneficia*, which should have been increased rather than reduced, have been completely withdrawn from the *chorus musicus*. It is, anyhow, rather odd that German musicians are expected to be capable of immediately performing at sight music of all kinds, whether from Italy or France, England or Poland, just as, perhaps, can those virtuosi for whom it is written and who have studied it long beforehand, [who] indeed know it almost from memory, [and] who moreover, it should be noted, are also in receipt of solid wages, with which their pains and diligence are richly rewarded. These things, though, are not given any consideration; rather, they [i.e. German musicians] are left to fend for themselves, so that many a one, out of [sheer] concern for his livelihood, cannot think of improving – let alone distinguishing – himself. To illustrate this point one only has to go to Dresden and see what sort of salaries the musicians there receive from His Royal Majesty. It cannot fail, since the musicians are relieved of concern for their livelihood, *chagrin* is left behind, [and] moreover each person also has to master only a single instrument; it must be [an] exquisite and excellent [thing] to hear. The conclusion is accordingly easy to draw, that with the stopping of the *beneficia* my power to put the musical ensemble into a better state is removed.

¶18   In conclusion, I find myself compelled to append herewith a reckoning of the number of current *alumni*, to make known the skill of each one in *musica*, and thus to leave it to more mature reflection whether music can survive in such circumstances, or whether its still greater decline is to be feared. It is necessary to classify the whole student body in three categories.

¶19   Accordingly, the following are those who are usable:

(1) Pezold, Lange, Stoll, *prefects*. Frick, Krause, Kittler, Pohlreüter, Stein, Burckhard, Siegler, Nitzer, Reichhard, Krebs *major* and *minor*, Schöneman, Heder, and Dietel.

¶20   The names of the motet singers, who first have still to perfect themselves further, so that in time they can be used for figural music, are as follows:

(2) Jänigke, Ludewig *major* and *minor*, Meißner, Neücke *major* and *minor*, Hillmeyer, Steidel, Heße, Haupt, Suppius, Segnitz, Thieme, Keller, Röder, Oßan, Berger, Lösch, Hauptman, and Sachse.

¶21   The last sort are not *musici* at all, and their names are:

(3) Bauer, Graß, Eberhard, Braune, Seyman, Tietze, Hebenstreit, Wintzer, Ößer, Leppert, Haußius, Feller, Crell, Zeymer, Guffer, Eichel, and Zwicker.

¶22   Total: 17 usable, 20 not yet usable, and 17 unproficient. Leipzig, 23 August 1730.

Joh. Seb. Bach
Director Musices

Appendix 4

Some contemporary accounts of concerted music-making

This Appendix brings together the only known contemporary accounts of J. S. Bach as a director (1, 3–5), to which is added a further description of concerted music-making sometimes – mistakenly, it seems – associated with him (2). All five extracts have on occasion been cited to demonstrate that Bach's usual church ensemble in Leipzig was 'large' and thus included large numbers of singers.[1]

In practice, although two accounts (1, 2) describe performances in church, only one of them (2) relates to liturgical practice; the remaining three (3–5), which are quite general in tone, would seem to be at least equally evocative of performance by a collegium musicum. Also, while from one document (2) we learn the size of a string section, in only one instance (3) is a total number of performers given – and then in a highly rhetorical context.[2] Attention is variously drawn to the variety of instruments (1, 2), to their abundance (2) or more generally to the largeness of an ensemble (3, 5). But in each case specific information about singers – whose very presence must be inferred – is conspicuous by its absence.

[1] See for example Smithers 1997, who specifically claims that all these sources actually 'contradict' the idea of 'choirs of only four (or five) singers' (pp. 12f). Smithers also manages to find evidence of a modern 'choir' (p. 37) in a single line of a poem by Johann Christian Trömer, alluding to an outdoor performance in Leipzig in 1727: 'Die *Musicant* war mehr als 40 an die Szhahl' ('There were more than 40 musicians in total'): Trömer 1745, p. 30.

[2] See above, p. 136 note 25.

1.
Christoph Ernst Sicul, *Das Thränende Leipzig Oder* SOLENNIA LIPSIENSIA ([Leipzig], 1727), p. 22
Source: *BD II*, p. 175 (cf. *NBR*, pp. 136f)

On 17 October 1727 a memorial service for Christiane Eberhardine, Electress of Saxony, was held in the Paulinerkirche (the university church), Leipzig. It was for this event that Bach was commissioned to write the *Trauer Ode* BWV198 (*Laß, Fürstin! laß noch einen Strahl*).

§25. Wie nun, bis alle ihren Sitz eingenommen, mit der Orgel *præambulir*et, und die von Herrn *M.* Johann Christoph Gottscheden, *Collegii Mariani Collegiato*, gefertigte Trauer-Ode unter die Anwesenden durch die Pedelle ausgetheilet war; also ließ sich auch darauf die Trauer-Music, so dießmahl der Herr Capellmeister, Johann Sebastian Bach, nach Italiänischer Art *componir*et hatte, mit *Clave di Cembalo*, welches Herr Bach selbst spielete, Orgel, *Violes di Gamba*, Lauten, Violinen, *Fleutes douces* und *Fleutes traverses &c.* und zwar die Helffte davon vor- die andere Helffte aber nach der Lob- und Trauer-Rede hören.

§25. When a preamble had been played on the organ (until everyone was seated) and [copies of] the Ode of Mourning written by Magister Johann Christoph Gottsched, member of the *Collegium Marianum*, had been distributed among those present by the Beadles, there followed the Music of Mourning, which this time Capellmeister Johann Sebastian Bach had composed in the Italian style, with harpsichord, which Herr Bach himself played, organ, violas da gamba, lutes, violins, recorders and flutes etc., half being heard before the oration of praise and mourning, the other half after it.

2.
Christian Gerber, *Geschichte der Kirchen-Ceremonien in Sachsen* (Leipzig, 1732), p. 283
Source: Smend [1951], p. 135 (cf. *NBR*, pp. 326f)

Leipzig heard its first 'oratorio' Passion – at the Neue Kirche – as early as 1717. Johann Kuhnau responded in 1721 with his own St Mark Passion (at the Thomaskirche), and Bach's St John Passion BWV245 followed in 1724. The following account of the introduction of this genre in an unidentified town points in any case not to Leipzig, centre of commerce and learning, but to courtly Dresden.

Vor funfzig und mehr Jahren war der Gebrauch, dass am Palm-Sonntage die Orgel in der Kirche schweigen musste, es ward auch an solchem Tage, weil nun die Char- und Marterwoche anfange, keine Music gemacht. Bisher aber hat man gar angefangen, die Passions-Historia, die sonst so fein de simplici et plano, schlecht und andächtig abgesungen wurde, mit vielerlei Instrumenten auf das künstlichste zu musiciren ... Als in einer vornehmen Stadt diese Passions-Music, mit 12 Violinen, vielen Hautbois, Fagots und anderen Instrumenten mehr, zum ersten mal gemacht ward, erstaunten viel Leute darüber und wussten nicht, was sie daraus machen sollten.

Fifty and more years ago it was the custom that on Palm Sunday the organ in church should remain silent; there was also no music on that day because Holy Week was beginning. But since then the Passion story, which formerly was so finely sung, simply and plainly, modestly and devoutly, has begun to be performed with great artifice, with divers instruments . . . When Passion music of this sort was done for the first time in a leading town, with 12 violins [i.e. strings], many oboes, bassoons, and other instruments besides, many people were astonished and did not know what to make of it.

3.
Johann Matthias Gesner, *M. Fabii Qvinctiliani De Institutione Oratoria Libri Dvodecim . . .* [an edition of Quintilian's *Institutio oratoria*] (Göttingen, 1738), p. 61
Source: *BD II*, pp. 331f (cf. *NBR*, pp. 328f)

Before becoming professor of philology at the University of Göttingen, Gesner spent four years as Rector of the Thomasschule in Leipzig (1730–4), in renewed friendship with Bach, whom he had first known in Weimar. (During this spell his wife stood godmother to one of Bach's children.) His famous editorial footnote occurs at a point in the text (1.12.3) where Quintilian 'is speaking of the capacity possessed by man of comprehending and doing several things at once; adducing as an example a player on the lyre, who can at the same time utter both words and tones and besides play on the instrument and mark time with his foot'.[3]

Haec omnia, Fabi, paucissima esse diceres, si videre tibi ab inferis excitato contingeret, Bachium, vt hoc potissimum vtar, quod meus non ita pridem in Thomano Lipsiensi collega fuit: manu vtraque & digitis omnibus tractantem vel polychordum nostrum, multas vnum citharas complexum, vel organon illud organorum, cuius infinitae numero tibiae follibus animantur, hinc manu vtraque, illic velocissimo pedum ministerio percurrentem, solumque elicientem plura diuersissimorum, sed eorundem consentientium inter se sonorum quasi agmina: hunc, inquam si videres, dum illud agit, quod plures citharistae vestri, & sexcenti tibicines non agerent, non vna forte voce canentem citharoedi instar, suasque peragentem partes, sed omnibus eundem intentum, & de xxx vel xxxx adeo symphoniacis, hunc nutu, alterum supplosione pedis, tertium digito minaci reuocantem ad rhythmos & ictus; huic summa voce, ima alii, tertio media praeeuntem tonum, quo vtendum sit, vnumque adeo hominem, in maximo concinentium strepitu, cum difficillimis omnium partibus fungatur, tamen eadem statim animaduertere, si quid & vbi discrepet, & in ordine continere omnes, & occurrere vbique, & si quid titubetur restituere,

---

[3] Spitta 1889, p. 259.

membris omnibus rhythmicum, harmonias vnum omnes arguta aure metientem, voces vnum omnes, angustis vnis faucibus edentem. Maximus alioquin antiquitatis fautor, multos vnum Orpheas & viginti Arionas complexum Bachium meum, & si quis illi similis sit forte, arbitror.

You would say that all this amounted to very little, my dear Fabius [= Quintilian], if you could be brought back from the dead and see Bach (I single him out, because not so long ago he was my colleague at St Thomas's in Leipzig) using both hands and all his fingers as he plays either our *polychordum* (which combines a number of *citharae* in one instrument) or that instrument of instruments which has an infinite number of pipes filled with air by bellows, running over it here with both hands, there by manoeuvring with his feet at great speed, one man bringing out several serried ranks (as it were) of sounds that are utterly different but nonetheless in harmony with one another – if, as I say, you were to see him achieving what several of your *cithara* players and any number of *tibia* players could not achieve, not just singing with one voice like a man who sings to the *cithara* and performing his own part, but attending to everything at the same time and, out of a group of thirty or even forty musicians [*symphoniaci*], reminding one of the rhythm and the beat by nodding his head, another by stamping with his foot, a third by wagging his finger; giving the correct note to one with the top range of his voice, another with the bottom, a third with the middle; furthermore, although he is but one man with the hardest role of all to play, while the performers combine to make a great deal of noise, nevertheless at the same time noticing immediately if anything sounds wrong, and what is wrong, and holding them all together in due order, and stepping in at any point and putting right any unsteadiness, carrying the rhythm in every limb, one man testing every harmony with his sharp ear, one man producing every voice from the confines of his one throat. In other respects I am a keen supporter of antiquity; but I think that my dear Bach, and anyone else who may happen to be like him, contains in his one person many an Orpheus and a score of Arions.[4]

4.

[Johann Abraham Birnbaum], *Unpartheyische Anmerckungen über eine bedenckliche stelle in dem sechsten stück des Critischen Musicus* ('Impartial observations on a questionable passage in Part 6 of *Der Critische Musikus*') ([Leipzig], n.d. [1738]), pp. 23f

Source: *BD II*, pp. 303f (cf. *NBR*, p. 346)

Birnbaum's anonymously published pamphlet, dedicated to and in defence of J. S. Bach, was a response to J. A. Scheibe's well-known criticism of Bach's music as 'turgid' and 'confused' (see above, p. 133). Its author, a good keyboard player, taught rhetoric at the University of Leipzig. (The term 'Chor' as used in this passage carries no specific connotation of a *vocal* choir and so is

---

[4] Translation by Peter G. McC. Brown.

here translated simply as 'ensemble' ('. . . impossible for a whole ensemble'/ 'for a musical ensemble').)

Ist es dem Herrn Hof-Compositeur nichts unmögliches, mit zwey händen sachen auf dem clavier vollkommen wohl und ohne den geringsten fehler zu spielen, da sowohl haupt- als mittelstimmen das ihrige rechtschaffen zu thun haben: wie sollte das einem gantzen Chore, welches aus so viel persohnen besteht, davon jede nur auf eine stimme achtung zu geben hat, unmöglich seyn? Der einwurf, daß die hierzu nöthige accuratesse, und ein durchgängig beobachtetes gleiches tempo bey vielen unmöglich zu erhalten sey, ist von keiner erheblichkeit. Es hat dieses allerdings seine schwierigkeiten, die aber doch deßwegen nicht unüberwindlich sind. Kann eine gantzes kriegs-heer dahin gebracht werden, daß auf ein gegebenes zeichen, man vieler tausend menschen bewegungen erblickt, als wenn es nur eine wäre: so muß dergleichen accuratesse bey einem musicalischen Chor, das aus ungleich wenigern persohnen besteht desto sicherer möglich seyn. Den deutlichsten beweis von dieser möglichkeit, selbst bey musicalischen Chören, sehen wir an wohl ein-gerichteten Königl. und Fürstl. Capellen. Wer das glück gehabt hat die so berühmte Capelle des grösten hofs in Sachsen, einmahl concert halten zu sehen; wird an der wahrheit dieser sache nicht mehr zweifeln können.

If it is not an impossibility for the Court Composer [i.e. Bach] to play things on the keyboard with two hands completely satisfactorily and without the slightest error, where both principal and inner voices have to work properly, how should it be impossible for a whole ensemble, which consists of so many persons each of whom has to pay attention only to one part? The objection that with large numbers it is impossible to achieve the necessary accuracy for this, and an even tempo through-out, is not sustainable. This admittedly has its difficulties, but they are not therefore insurmountable. If an entire army can be trained so that at a given signal the move-ments of many thousands of men are seen as a single movement, similar accuracy must be all the more surely possible for a musical ensemble, which consists of incomparably fewer persons. The clearest proof of this possibility, even for musical ensembles, we see in well-ordered royal and princely capellas. Whoever has had the good fortune to see the famous capella of the greatest court in Saxony perform will no longer be able to doubt the truth of this matter.

5.

Anon. [Carl Philipp Emanuel Bach and Johann Friedrich Agricola], Obituary of J. S. Bach, in Mizler 1754, p. 171

Source: *BD III*, p. 87 (cf. *NBR*, pp. 305f)

J. S. Bach's second eldest son, just nine years old when his family moved to Leipzig in 1723, was first an *externus* at the Thomasschule, then (from 1731 to 1734) a student of law at its university. Agricola too studied at the university (1738–41), before moving to Berlin, and at the same time was a pupil of J. S. Bach's (see above, Table 7, p. 109).

In 1775 C. P. E. Bach reported to Forkel that 'The account of my late father's life in Mizler . . . was pieced together by the late Agricola and me in Berlin . . .

It is not worth much. The deceased, like myself and all true musicians, was no lover of dry, mathematical stuff.'[5]

Die beständige Uebung in Ausarbeitung vollstimmiger Stücke, hatte seinen Augen eine solche Fertigkeit zu Wege gebracht, daß er in die stärksten Partituren, alle zugleich lautende Stimmen, mit einem Blicke, übersehen konnte. Sein Gehör war so fein, daß er bey den vollstimmigsten Musiken, auch den geringsten Fehler zu entdecken vermögend war. Nur Schade, daß er selten das Glück gehabt, lauter solche Ausführer seiner Arbeit zu finden, die ihm diese verdrießlichen Bemerkungen ersparet hätten. Im Dirigiren war er sehr accurat, und im Zeitmaaße, welches er gemeiniglich sehr lebhaft nahm, überaus sicher.

His constant practice in working out full-voiced pieces had given his eye such fluency that even in the biggest scores he could take in all the simultaneously sounding parts at a glance. His hearing was so fine that even in the largest ensembles he was capable of detecting the slightest mistake. It is just a pity that he seldom had the good fortune of finding exclusively such performers of his work as would have spared him disagreeable observations of this sort. In directing he was very accurate, and in matters of tempo, which he generally took very lively, [he was] exceedingly sure.

[5] Clark 1997, p. 72.

Appendix 5

Sources of Bach's concerted vocal music

This table lists works (a) for which one or more original vocal copies survive and (b) which are scored for three or more voices (thus BWV51, for example, is omitted).

BWV	title	liturgical occasion	first (subsequent) performance(s)	vocal scorings	extant vocal copies	extant score?	NBA
1	*Wie schön leuchtet der Morgenstern*	Annunciation	1725	S, T, B, SATB	SATB ǀ —	–	I/28
2	*Ach Gott, vom Himmel sieh darein*	Trinity II	1724	A, T, B, SATB	SATB ǀ —	√	I/16
3	*Ach Gott, wie manches Herzeleid*	Epiphany II	1725	T, B, SA, SATB	SATB ǀ —	√	I/5
4	*Christ lag in Todes Banden*	Easter	c.1707–8 (1724, 1725?)	A, T, B, SA, ST, SATB	SATB ǀ —	–	I/9
5	*Wo soll ich fliehen hin*	Trinity XIX	1724 (c.1732–5)	S, A, T, B, SATB	SATB ǀ —	√	I/24
6	*Bleib bei uns, denn es will Abend werden*	Easter Monday	1725 (c.1735–9)	S, A, T, B, SATB	SATB ǀ —	√	I/10
7	*Christ unser Herr zum Jordan kam*	St John the Baptist	1724	A, T, B, SATB	SATB ǀ —	–	I/29
8	*Liebster Gott, wenn werd ich sterben*	Trinity XVI	1724 (c.1735–9; in D, c.1746–7)	S, A, T, B, SATB	SATB ǀ —[1]	–	I/23
9	*Es ist das Heil uns kommen her*	Trinity VI	c.1732–5 (c.1740–7)	T, B, SA, SATB	SATB ǀ —	√	I/17.2

[1] BWV8: There are two sets of concertists' parts, one for each version of the work.

BWV	title	liturgical occasion	first (subsequent) performance(s)	vocal scorings	extant vocal copies	extant score?	NBA
10	*Meine Seel erhebt den Herren*	Visitation	1724 (*c.*1740–7)	S, T, B, AT, SATB	SATB ǀ —	√	I/28.2
11	*Lobet Gott in seinen Reichen (Ascension Oratorio)*	Ascension	(?)1735	S, A, T, B, TB, SATB	SATB ǀ —	√	II/8
12	*Weinen, Klagen, Sorgen, Zagen*	Easter III	1714 (1724)	A, T, B, SATB	SATB ǀ —	√	I/11.2
13	*Meine Seufzer, meine Tränen*	Epiphany II	1726	S, A, T, B, SATB	SATB ǀ —	√	I/5
14	*Wär Gott nicht mit uns diese Zeit*	Epiphany IV	1735	S, T, B, SATB	SATB ǀ —	√	I/6
16	*Herr Gott, dich loben wir*	New Year (Circumcision)	1726 (*c.*1728–31, 1749)	A, T, B, SATB	SATB ǀ —	√	I/4
17	*Wer Dank opfert, der preiset mich*	Trinity XIV	1726	S, A, T, B, SATB	SATB ǀ —	√	I/21
18	*Gleichwie der Regen und Schnee vom Himmel fällt*	Sexagesima	*c.*1713–15 (1724)	S, B, TB, SATB	SATB ǀ —	–	I/7
19	*Es erhub sich ein Streit*	St Michael	1726	S, T, B, SATB	SATB ǀ —	√	I/30
20	*O Ewigkeit, du Donnerwort*	Trinity I	1724	A, T, B, SATB	SATB ǀ —	√	I/15
21	*Ich hatte viel Bekümmernis*	Trinity III	1714 (*c.*1717–22; 1723)	S, T, SB, SATB	SATB ǀ SATB[2]	–	I/16
23	*Du wahrer Gott und Davids Sohn*	Quinquagesima	1723 (1724; *c.*1728–31)	T, SA, SATB	SATB ǀ —[3]	√	I/8.1
24	*Ein ungefärbt Gemüte*	Trinity IV	1723	A, T, B, SATB	SATB ǀ —	√	I/17.1
25	*Es ist nichts Gesundes an meinem Leibe*	Trinity XIV	1723	S, T, B, SATB	SATB ǀ —	–	I/21
26	*Ach wie flüchtig, ach wie nichtig*	Trinity XXIV	1724	S, A, T, B, SATB	SATB ǀ —	√	I/27
27	*Wer weiß, wie nahe mir mein Ende*	Trinity XVI	1726	S, A, T, B, SATB	SATB ǀ —	√	I/23
28	*Gottlob! nun geht das Jahr zu Ende*	Christmas I	1725	S, T, B, AT, SATB	SATB ǀ —	√	I/3
29	*Wir danken dir, Gott, wir danken dir*	(Inauguration of Leipzig Town Council)	1731 (1739, 1749)	S, A, T, B, SATB	SATB ǀ SATB	√	I/32.2

[2]   BWV21: See Rifkin 1996a.
[3]   BWV23: Also, four inserts containing the revised version of the final chorale.

BWV	title	liturgical occasion	first (subsequent) performance(s)	vocal scorings	extant vocal copies	extant score?	NBA
30a	*Angenehmes Wiederau*	(*Dramma per musica*: for Johann Christian von Hennicke)	1737	S, A, T, B, SAB, SATB	SATB	√	I/29
31	*Der Himmel lacht! die Erde jubilieret*	Easter	1715 (1724; 1731)	S, T, B, SATB, SSATB	SSATB | —	–	I/9
32	*Liebster Jesu, mein Verlangen*	Epiphany I	1726	S, B, SB, SATB	SATB | —	√	I/5
33	*Allein zu dir, Herr Jesu Christ*	Trinity XIII	1724	A, T, B, TB, SATB	SATB | —	√	I/21
34a	*O ewiges Feuer, O Ursprung der Liebe*	Wedding	1726	S, A, B, SB, AT, SATB	SATB | —	–	I/33
36	*Schwingt freudig euch empor*	Advent I	1731 (earlier *Fassung* c.1726–30)	S, T, B, SA, SATB	SATB | —	√	I/1
36b	*Die Freude reget sich*	(Congratulatory cantata for a member of the Rivinus family of Leipzig)	c.1735	S, A, T, SATB	SATB | —	–	I/38
37	*Wer da gläubet und getauft wird*	Ascension	1724 (1731)	T, B, SA, SATB	SATB | —	–	I/12
38	*Aus tiefer Not schrei ich zu dir*	Trinity XXI	1724	S, A, T, SAB, SATB	SATB | —	–	I/25
39	*Brich dem Hungrigen dein Brot*	Trinity I	1726	S, A, B, SATB	SATB | —	√	I/15
40	*Dazu ist erschienen der Sohn Gottes*	Second Day of Christmas (26 Dec)	1723 (c.1746–9)	A, T, B, SATB	SATB | —	√	I/3
41	*Jesu, nun sei gepreiset*	New Year (Circumcision)	1725 (c.1732–5)	S, A, T, B, SATB	SATB | —	√	I/4
42	*Am Abend aber desselbigen Sabbats*	Easter I	1725 (1731; c.1742)	A, T, B, ST, SATB	SATB | —	√	I/11.1
43	*Gott fähret auf mit Jauchzen!*	Ascension	1726	S, A, T, B, SATB	SATB | —	√	I/12
44	*Sie werden euch in den Bann tun*	Ascension I	1724	S, A, T, B, TB, SATB	SATB | —	√	I/12
45	*Es ist dir gesagt, Mensch, was gut ist*	Trinity VIII	1726	A, T, B, SATB	SATB | —	√	I/18

BWV	title	liturgical occasion	first (subsequent) performance(s)	vocal scorings	extant vocal copies	extant score?	NBA
46	*Schauet doch und sehet*	Trinity X	1723	A, T, B, SATB	SATB | —	–	I/19
47	*Wer sich selbst erhöhet, der soll erniedriget werden*	Trinity XVII	1726 (*c*.1735–9; *c*.1742)	S, B, SATB	SATB | —	√	I/23
48	*Ich elender Mensch, wer wird mich erlösen*	Trinity XIX	1723	A, T, SATB	SATB | —	√	I/24
52	*Falsche Welt, dir trau ich nicht*	Trinity XXIII	1726	S, SATB	SATB | —	√	I/26
55	*Ich armer Mensch, ich Sündenknecht*	Trinity XXII	1726	T, SATB	SATB | —	√	I/26
56	*Ich will den Kreuzstab gerne tragen*	Trinity XIX	1726	B, SATB	SATB | —	√	I/24
57	*Selig ist der Mann*	Second Day of Christmas (26 Dec)	1725	S, B, SB, SATB	SATB | —	√	I/3
59	*Wer mich liebet, der wird mein Wort halten*	Whit Sunday	by 1723 (?1724)	S, B, SB, SATB	ATB | —	√	I/13
60	*O Ewigkeit, du Donnerwort*	Trinity XXIV	1723	AT, AB, SATB	SATB | —	–	I/27
62	*Nun komm, der Heiden Heiland*	Advent I	1724 (*c*.1732–5)	T, B, SA, SATB	SATB | —	√	I/1
63	*Christen, ätzet diesen Tag*	Christmas Day	1714 (1723; 1729(?))	A, T, B, SB, AT, SATB	SATB | AT[4]	–	I/2
64	*Sehet, welch eine Liebe hat uns der Vater erzeiget*	Third Day of Christmas (27 Dec)	1723 (*c*.1742)	S, A, B, SATB	SATB | —	√	I/3
67	*Halt im Gedächtnis Jesum Christ*	Easter I	1724	A, T, SATB	SATB | —	√	I/11.1
68	*Also hat Gott die Welt geliebt*	Whit Monday	1725 (1735–9)	S, B, SATB	SATB | —	–	I/14
69a	*Lobe den Herrn, meine Seele*	Trinity XII	1723 (1727)	S, A, T, B, SATB	SATB | —	–	I/20
70	*Wachet! betet! betet! wachet!*	Trinity XXVI	1723 (1731)	S, A, T, B, SATB	SATB | —	–	I/27

[4] BWV63: The two ripienists' parts are not designated as such and are merely labelled 'Alto'/'Tenore'; on other anomalous features of these parts, see Rifkin 1996a, p. 599 n. 33.

BWV	title	liturgical occasion	first (subsequent) performance(s)	vocal scorings	extant vocal copies	extant score?	NBA
71	*Gott ist mein König*	(Inauguration of Mühlhausen Town Council)	1708	A, B, ST, SATB	SATB	SATB[5]	√	I/32.1
72	*Alles nur nach Gottes Willen*	Epiphany III	1726	S, A, B, SATB	SATB	—	√	I/6
73	*Herr, wie du willt, so schicks mit mir*	Epiphany III	1724 (*c.*1732–5)	T, B, SATB	SATB	—	–	I/6
74	*Wer mich liebet, der wird mein Wort halten*	Whit Sunday	1725	S, A, T, B, SATB	SATB	—	–	I/13
76	*Die Himmel erzählen die Ehre Gottes*	Trinity II	1723 (1724–5; 1740s)	S, A, T, B, SATB	SATB	S(×2)A[6]	√	I/16
78	*Jesu, der du meine Seele*	Trinity XIV	1724 (1735–9?)	T, B, SA, SATB	SATB	—	–	I/21
79	*Gott der Herr ist Sonn und Schild*	Reformation Festival	1725 (1730)	A, B, SB, SATB	SATB	—	√	I/31
81	*Jesus schläft, was soll ich hoffen*	Epiphany IV	1724	A, T, B, SATB	SATB	—	√	I/6
83	*Erfreute Zeit im neuen Bunde*	Purification	1724 (1727)	A, T, B, SATB	SATB	—	–	I/28.1
84	*Ich bin vergnügt mit meinem Glücke*	Septuagesima	(?)1727	S, SATB	SATB	—	√	I/7
85	*Ich bin ein guter Hirt*	Easter II	1725	S, A, T, B, SATB	SATB	—	√	I/11.1
87	*Bisher habt ihr nichts gebeten in meinem Namen*	Easter V	1725	A, T, B, SATB	SATB	—	√	I/12
88	*Siehe, ich will viel Fischer aussenden*	Trinity V	1726	S, T, B, SA, TB, SATB	SATB	—	√	I/17.2
89	*Was soll ich aus dir machen, Ephraim*	Trinity XXII	1723	S, A, B, SATB	SATB	—	–	I/26
91	*Gelobet seist du, Jesu Christ*	Christmas Day	1724 (1731 or 1732; rev. 1746–7)	S, T, B, SA, SATB	SATB	—	√	I/2

[5] BWV71: The designation on the autograph score, 'âb 18. è se piace 22', indicates that the ripienists' parts are optional, while the published set of parts makes no provision for ripienists.

[6] BWV76: While one soprano ripienist's part contains all three choral movements (1, 7 and 14), the other has only no. 1. (No. 14 – a repeat, to different words, of no. 7 – is also lacking in the alto ripienist's part.)

BWV	title	liturgical occasion	first (subsequent) performance(s)	vocal scorings	extant vocal copies	extant score?	NBA
2	*Ich hab in Gottes Herz und Sinn*	Septuagesima	1725	S, A, T, B, SATB	SATB ǀ —	√	I/7
93	*Wer nur den lieben Gott läßt walten*	Trinity V	1724 (*c.*1732–3)	S, T, B, SA, SATB	SATB ǀ —	–	I/17.2
94	*Was frag ich nach der Welt*	Trinity IX	1724 (?*c.*1732–5)	S, A, T, B, SATB	SATB ǀ —	√	I/19
95	*Christus, der ist mein Leben*	Trinity XVI	1723	S, T, B, SATB	SATB ǀ —	√	I/23
96	*Herr Christ, der einge Gottessohn*	Trinity XVIII	1724 (?1734; 1747)	S, A, T, B, SATB	SATB ǀ —	√	I/24
97	*In allen meinen Taten*	[?]	(?)1734 (*c.*1735–9, *c.*1740–7)	S, A, T, B, SB, SATB	SATB ǀ —	√	I/34
98	*Was Gott tut, das ist wohlgetan*	Trinity XXI	1726	S, A, T, B, SATB	SATB ǀ —	√	I/25
99	*Was Gott tut, das ist wohlgetan*	Trinity XV	1724	A, T, B, SA, SATB	SATB ǀ —	√	I/22
100	*Was Gott tut, das ist wohlgetan*	[?]	*c.*1734–5 (*c.*1737(?), *c.*1742)	S, A, B, AT, SATB	SATB ǀ —	√	I/34
101	*Nimm von uns, Herr, du treuer Gott*	Trinity X	1724	S, T, B, SA, SATB	SATB ǀ —	–	I/19
102	*Herr, deine Augen sehen nach dem Glauben*	Trinity X	1726 (*c.*1737?)	A, T, B, SATB	S ǀ —	√	I/19
103	*Ihr werdet weinen und heulen*	Easter III	1725 (1731)	A, T, SATB	SATB ǀ —	√	I/11.2
104	*Du Hirte Israel, höre*	Easter II	1724	T, B, SATB	SATB ǀ —	–	I/11.1
107	*Was willst du dich betrüben*	Trinity VII	1724	S, T, B, SATB	SATB ǀ —	–	I/18
108	*Es ist euch gut, daß ich hingehe*	Easter IV	1725	A, T, B, SATB	SATB ǀ —	√	I/12
109	*Ich glaube, lieber Herr*	Trinity XXI	1723	A, T, SATB	SATB ǀ —	√	I/25
110	*Unser Mund sei voll Lachens*	Christmas Day	1725 (*c.*1728–31)	A, T, B, ST, SATB	SATB ǀ SAT	√	I/2
112	*Der Herr ist mein getreuer Hirt*	Easter II	1731	A, B, ST, SATB	SATB ǀ —	√	I/11.1
114	*Ach, lieben Christen, seid getrost*	Trinity XVII	1724 (*c.*1740–7)	S, A, T, B, SATB	SATB ǀ —	√	I/23

BWV	title	liturgical occasion	first (subsequent) performance(s)	vocal scorings	extant vocal copies	extant score?	NBA
116	*Du Friedefürst, Herr Jesu Christ*	Trinity XXV	1724	A, T, STB, SATB	SATB ǀ —	√	I/27
120a	*Herr Gott, Beherrscher aller Dinge*	Wedding	1729	S, B, AT, SATB	SATB ǀ —	√	I/33
121	*Christum wir sollen loben schon*	Second Day of Christmas (26 Dec)	1724	S, A, T, B, SATB	S(×2)ATB ǀ —[7]	√	I/3
122	*Das neugeborne Kindelein*	Christmas I	1724	S, B, SAT, SATB	SATB ǀ —	√	I/3
123	*Liebster Immanuel, Herzog der Frommen*	Epiphany	1725	A, T, B, SATB	SATB ǀ —	–	I/5
124	*Meinen Jesum laß ich nicht*	Epiphany I	1725	T, B, SA, SATB	SATB ǀ —	√	I/5
125	*Mit Fried und Freud ich fahr dahin*	Purification	1725 (*c.*1735–9)	A, B, TB, SATB	SATB ǀ —	–	I/28.1
126	*Erhalt uns, Herr, bei deinem Wort*	Sexagesima	1725	T, B, AT, SATB	SATB ǀ —	–	I/7
127	*Herr Jesu Christ, wahr' Mensch und Gott*	Quinquagesima	1725	S, T, B, SATB	SATB ǀ —	√	I/8.1
128	*Auf Christi Himmelfahrt allein*	Ascension	1725	T, B, AT, SATB	SATB ǀ —	√	I/12
129	*Gelobet sei der Herr, mein Gott*	Trinity	(?)1726 (1732–5, *c.*1743–7)	S, A, B, SATB	SATB ǀ —	–	I/15
130	*Herr Gott, dich loben alle wir*	St Michael	1724	A, T, B, ST, SATB	SAT ǀ —	√	I/30
133	*Ich freue mich in dir*	Third Day of Christmas (27 Dec)	1724	S, A, T, B, SATB	SATB ǀ —	√	I/3
134	*Ein Herz, das seinen Jesum lebend weiß*	Easter Tuesday	1724 (1st version) (1731 (2nd); ?1735 (3rd))	T, AT, SATB	S(×2)ATB ǀ —	√	I/10
136	*Erforsche mich, Gott, und erfahre mein Herz*	Trinity VIII	1723	A, T, B, TB, SATB	SATB ǀ —	√	I/18

[7] BWV121: Both soprano copies are concertist's copies (i.e. both include movement 5 – a recit. – as well as the two complete choral movements).

BWV	title	liturgical occasion	first (subsequent) performance(s)	vocal scorings	extant vocal copies	extant score?	NBA
137	*Lobe den Herren, den mächtigen König der Ehren*	Trinity XII	(?)1725 (c.1746–7)	A, T, SB, SATB	SATB | —	–	I/20
139	*Wohl dem, der sich auf seinen Gott*	Trinity XXIII	1724 (c.1744–7)	S, A, T, B, SATB	SATB | —	–	I/26
140	*Wachet auf, ruft uns die Stimme*	Trinity XXVII	1731	T, B, SB, SATB	SATB | —	–	I/27
147	*Herz und Mund und Tat und Leben*	Visitation	1723 (c.1728–31; c.1735–9)	S, A, T, B, SATB	SATB | —	√	I/28.2
151	*Süßer Trost, mein Jesus kömmt*	Third Day of Christmas (27 Dec)	1725 (c.1728–31)	S, A, T, B, SATB	SATB | —	√	I/3
153	*Schau, lieber Gott, wie meine Feind*	New Year I	1724	A, T, B, SATB	SATB | —	–	I/4
154	*Mein liebster Jesus ist verloren*	Epiphany I	1724 (c.1736–7)	A, T, B, AT, SATB	SATB | —	√	I/5
162	*Ach! ich sehe, itzt, da ich zur Hochzeit gehe*	Trinity XX	1716 or 1715 (1723)	S, A, T, B, AT, SATB	SATB | —	–	I/25
164	*Ihr, die ihr euch von Christo nennet*	Trinity XIII	1725	A, T, B, SB, SATB	SATB | —	√	I/21
166	*Wo gehest du hin*	Easter IV	1724	S, A, T, B, SATB	SATB | —	–	I/12
167	*Ihr Menschen, rühmet Gottes Liebe*	St John the Baptist	1724	A, T, B, SA, SATB	SATB | —	–	I/29
168	*Tue Rechnung! Donnerwort*	Trinity IX	1725 (c.1746–9)	T, B, SA, SATB	SAT | —	√	I/19
169	*Gott soll allein mein Herze haben*	Trinity XVIII	1726	A, SATB	SATB | —	√	I/24
172	*Erschallet, ihr Lieder*	Whit Sunday	1714 (1717–23; 1724; 1731; after 1731)	T, B, SA, SATB	SATB | —	–	I/13
174	*Ich liebe den Höchsten von ganzem Gemüte*	Whit Monday	1729	A, T, B, SATB	SATB | —	√	I/14
175	*Er rufet seinen Schafen mit Namen*	Whit Tuesday	1725 (after 1725)	A, T, B, AB, SATB	SATB | —	√	I/14

BWV	title	liturgical occasion	first (subsequent) performance(s)	vocal scorings	extant vocal copies	extant score?	NBA
176	Es ist ein trotzig und verzagt Ding	Trinity	1725	S, A, B, SATB	SATB | —	√	I/15
177	Ich ruf zu dir, Herr Jesu Christ	Trinity IV	1732 (c.1742)	S, A, T, SATB	SATB | —	√	I/17.1
178	Wo Gott der Herr nicht bei uns hält	Trinity VIII	1724	A, T, B, SATB	SATB | —	–	I/18
181	Leichtgesinnte Flattergeister	Sexagesima	1724 (c.1743–6)	S, A, T, B, SATB	SATB | —	–	I/7
182	Himmelskönig, sei willkommen	Palm Sunday or Annunciation	1714 (1724, c.1728–31 (1728?))	A, T, B, SATB	SATB | —[8]	√	I/8.2
183	Sie werden euch in den Bann tun	Ascension I	1725	S, A, T, B, SATB	SATB | —	√	I/12
184	Erwünschtes Freudenlicht	Whit Tuesday	1724 (1731)	T, SA, SATB	SATB | —	√	I/14
185	Barmherziges Herze der ewigen Liebe	Trinity IV	1715 (1723, c.1746–7)	A, B, ST, SATB	SATB | —	√	I/17.1
187	Es wartet alles auf dich	Trinity VII	1726 (c.1735–9, 1749(?))	S, A, B, SATB	SATB | —	√	I/18
190	Singet dem Herrn ein neues Lied	New Year (Circumcision)	1724 (c.1735–9)	A, T, B, TB, SATB	SATB | —	√	I/4
192	Nun danket alle Gott	[?]	c.1730	SB, SATB	SAB | —	–	I/37
193	Ihr Tore zu Zion	(Inauguration of Leipzig Town Council)	1727	S, A, SA	SA | —	–	I/32.1
194	Höchsterwünschtes Freudenfest	Consecration of Störmthal church and organ; Trinity	1723 (1724, 1726(?), 1731)	S, T, B, SB, SATB	SATB | —	√	I/31
195	Dem Gerechten muß das Licht	Wedding	1742 (previous version c.1727–32?; rev. version c.1748–9)	S, B, SATB	SATB | SATB	√	I/33

[8] BWV182: There are two separate sets of concertists' parts, each belonging to its own set of instrumental parts.

BWV	title	liturgical occasion	first (subsequent) performance(s)	vocal scorings	extant vocal copies	extant score?	NBA
201	*Geschwinde, geschwinde, ihr wirbelnden Winde*	—	1729 (c.1735–9, 1749)	S, A, T, B, SB, AT, TB, SBB, ABB, SATTBB	SATTBB | SA[9]	√	I/40
206	*Schleicht, spielende Wellen*	(Birthday and name day of August III)	planned for 1734, perf. 1736 (1740)	S, A, T, B, SATB	SATB | —	√	I/36
207	*Vereinigte Zwietracht der wechselnden Saiten*	(Installation of Professor Gottlieb Kortte)	1726	A, T, SB, SATB	SATB | —[10]	√	I/38
211	*Schweigt stille, plaudert nicht*	—	1734	S, T, B, SB, STB	STB | —	√	I/40
213	*Laßt uns sorgen, laßt uns wachen*	(Birthday of Crown Prince Friedrich Christian of Saxony)	1733	S, A, T, B, ST, AA, AT, SATB	SATB | [A][11]	√	I/36
214	*Tönet, ihr Pauken! Erschallet, Trompeten*	(Birthday of Queen/Electress Maria Josepha)	1733	S, A, T, B, SATB	SATB | —	√	I/36
215	*Preise dein Glücke, gesegnetes Sachsen*	(Anniversary of election of August III as King of Poland)	1734	S, T, B, STB, SATB, SATB+SATB,	SATB+SATB | —	√	I/37
226	*Der Geist hilft unser Schwachheit auf*	Funeral of Rector J. H. Ernesti	1729	SATB+SATB	SATB+SB | —	√	III/1
232[I]	Missa = Kyrie, Gloria (Mass in B Minor)		dedicated 1733	S, A, B, SS, SA, ST, SATB, SSATB	SSATB | —	√	II/1
232[III]	Sanctus in D (Mass in B Minor)		1725 (1726 or 1727; c.1743–8)	SSSATB	SSSATB | —	√	II/1
234	Missa in A		c.1738 (1743–6, 1748–9)	S, A, B, SATB	SAT | —	√	II/2
237	Sanctus in C		1723	SATB	SATB | —	√	II/2

[9] BWV201: See p. 61 above (Table 3A note *d*).

[10] BWV207: There is one set of concertists' parts for BWV207, another for BWV207a (*Auf, schmetternde Töne der muntern Trompeten*).

[11] BWV213: An additional vocal copy, marked 'Echo', contains solely the echo alto part for movement 5.

BWV	title	liturgical occasion	first (subsequent) performance(s)	vocal scorings	extant vocal copies	extant score?	NBA
240	Sanctus in G		c.1742	SATB	SATB ǀ —	√	II/9
244	St Matthew Passion	Good Friday	?1727; by 1729 (1736, c.1742, perhaps c.1743–6)	S^I, S^{II}, A^I, A^{II}, T^I, T^{II}, B^I, B^{II}, AT^{II},[12] A^I+$SATB^{II}$, T^I+$SATB^{II}$, SA^I+$SATB^{II}$, $SATB^I$, $SATB^{II}$, $SATB^{I+II}$, $SATB^I$+II+S, $SATB^I$+$SATB^{II}$, $SATB^I$+$SATB^{II}$+S	SATB+SATB ǀ S^{13}	√	II/5
245	St John Passion	Good Friday	1725 (2nd version)	S, A, T, B, B+ SATB, SATB	SATB ǀ $SATB^{14}$	√	II/4
248^I	Christmas Oratorio, Part I	Christmas Day	1734	A, T, B, SB, SATB	SATB ǀ —	√	II/6
248^{II}	Christmas Oratorio, Part II	Second Day of Christmas (26 Dec)	1734	A, T, B, ST, SATB	SATB ǀ —	√	II/6
248^{III}	Christmas Oratorio, Part III	Third Day of Christmas (27 Dec)	1734	A, T, B, SB, SATB	SATB ǀ —	√	II/6
248^{IV}	Christmas Oratorio, Part IV	New Year (Circumcision)	1735	T, SS, SB, SATB	SATB ǀ $[S]^{15}$	√	II/6
248^V	Christmas Oratorio, Part V	New Year I	1735	A, T, B, AT, SAT, SATB	SATB ǀ —	√	II/6
248^{VI}	Christmas Oratorio, Part VI	Epiphany	1735	S, T, TB, SATB	SATB ǀ —	√	II/6
249	Easter Oratorio	Easter	1725 (c.1738, c.1743–6, 1749)	S, A, T, B, SA, SATB	SATB ǀ —	√	II/7
250– 252	Three Chorales	Weddings	composed c.1729?	SATB	SATB ǀ —	–	III/2.1

[12] BWV244: There is also a brief duet passage for two basses (Pontifex I and II), with the continuo of Choir I: see p. 83 above (Table 5).

[13] BWV244: There are two copies of the 'Soprano in ripieno' part (by different scribes); it is unclear whether the two were ever used together. See also Table 5.

[14] BWV245: See Table 5, and Appendix 6, pp. 204f below.

[15] BWV248(IV): An additional vocal copy for soprano contains solely the echo part for movement 39.

Appendix 6

Bach's chorus

by Joshua Rifkin

[This essay was written for presentation at the annual meeting of the American Musicological Society in Boston, Mass., in November 1981. Owing to unforeseen problems, barely half of the paper was delivered on that occasion. It is here published for the first time.

The lecture script is here partly adapted to the 'house style' of this book, and a few references to lecture 'handouts' and recorded extracts are omitted. Four tables and the music examples in the original handouts are replaced by cross-references to the text of this book; the remainder have been relabelled.]

Scholars, performers, and even the broader public have long shared certain basic assumptions about the size and disposition of the chorus with which J. S. Bach presented his cantatas and other concerted vocal works. The most explicit statement of these assumptions – and the evident foundation for their restatement in subsequent literature – appears in a classic study by Arnold Schering on the performance of the Leipzig sacred music. According to Schering, the forces normally available to Bach for this repertory included a total of twelve singers, divided into equal numbers of sopranos, altos, tenors, and basses. Each section, in turn, consisted of a *Concertist*, or principal singer, and two supporting *Ripienisten*. The concertist sang alone in recitatives and arias, and led the entire section in choruses and chorales; in these movements, Schering suggested, the ripienists stood on either side of him, reading from the music that he held.

At first sight, this image of three singers clustered around a single part may seem like merely an incidental detail in Schering's carefully wrought tableau. In closer focus, however, we can see that it in fact constitutes the linchpin on which our whole conception of Bach's choral practice depends. Almost without exception, the original performing materials to his vocal works – sacred or secular, whenever or wherever composed – contain only one copy of each voice line present in the score. The arrangement envisioned by Schering, therefore, offers just about the only possible way of reconciling even the very small chorus that we believe Bach to have had with the number of parts that he would have provided for it.

Given the weight thus resting on the idea of their use by three singers at once, it may come as a surprise to find that the parts themselves appear at best oddly suited to this purpose. A look at a typical representative – the tenor of the cantata BWV 172 – reveals the nature of the problem. The part contains all the movements of the cantata in continuous sequence, with 'tacet' indications for those in which the tenor remains silent; the only real difference between it and its modern equivalent lies in the absence of such niceties as bar numbers and the fact that movements do not invariably begin at the left-hand margin nor measures end at that on the right. It takes little effort to imagine a concertist reading from this music, as he would have sung everything that it contains. But it becomes harder to imagine a pair of ripienists reading from the part as well, since it seems to furnish no indication of where they should and should not sing.

Schering did not ignore this matter entirely. In his own description of the parts, he obliquely proposed that the ripienists would have oriented themselves in accordance with the headings of individual numbers, singing in those marked 'Chorus' or 'Choral' and resting in those designated 'Recitativo' and 'Aria'. Yet even this attractive suggestion breaks down when confronted with the actual sources. To begin with, the headings scarcely occur with sufficient regularity to have served as much of a guide to ripienists. In particular, those very pieces that we most readily interpret as choruses – extended opening movements with a four-part or larger vocal complement – rarely carry any designation at all; the part from BWV 172 already examined provides a typical case in point. At the same time, however, we cannot read the absence of a heading as a kind of shorthand for choral performance, since many numbers clearly meant for soloists also lack a generic description. The first movement of BWV 59, for example, calls for soprano and bass alone. 'Tacet' markings in the original alto and tenor parts refer to the piece as 'Duetto', confirming Bach's expectation of having it sung by soloists; yet the bass part – the soprano does not survive – presents the music without this, or any other, accompanying title.

The problems encountered in single movements increase in those not-infrequent cases when Bach links two movements of contrasted vocal scoring and furnishes a generic heading for only one or neither of them. The Gloria of the Mass in B Minor BWV 232 provides a good illustration. The 'Domine Deus', scored for tenor and the first of the two sopranos required in the Mass, leads directly into the 'Qui tollis', a four-part movement written for the second soprano and the three lower voices. In virtually every performance known to me, the shift from the two- to the four-part texture brings with it a shift from solo to choral forces. The original parts leave no doubt about the solo interpretation of the 'Domine Deus', as the tenor bears the inscription 'Duetto' at the start of this movement. But as we see from Table I, the tenor has no further marking at the start of the 'Qui tollis', nor do any of the other parts. How a group of ripienists reading from this material could have known to sing at this point would seem a mystery indeed – especially if we recall that Bach evidently prepared these parts not for his own musicians but for members of the electoral chapel in Dresden, who may never even have sung the piece under his direction.

Adding to the difficulties posed by missing headings, many of the headings that do appear in Bach's materials conflict either with others in the same set of parts or with what the musical substance itself seems to imply. For example, the *Christmas*

Table I   Missa BWV 232(I), 'Domine Deus' and 'Qui tollis': headings in parts (— =
no heading)

	Domine Deus	Qui tollis
Soprano I	Domine fili	—, 50 bars rest
Soprano II	—, 95 bars rest	—
Alto	Domine Deus, 95 bars rest	—
Tenore	Duetto	—
Basso	Domine Deus, 95 bars rest	—

Oratorio BWV 248 contains three movements – Nos. 7, 38, and 40 – that combine or
alternate a recitative in the bass with a chorale in the soprano. All three would presumably have received a similar performance. Yet as Table II reveals, the labels in
the parts show a lack of consistency that renders them senseless if treated as indications of vocal scoring: Nos. 7 and 38 have headings that point in diametrically opposite directions; that in the bass of No. 7 goes counter to the nature of the music; and
that in the soprano to No. 40 conveys two mutually contradictory messages.

Table II   *Christmas Oratorio* BWV 248, Nos. 7, 38, and 40: headings in parts

	No. 7	No. 38	No. 40
Soprano	Choral.	Recit.	Recit: con Chorale
Basso	Choral.	Recit: accomp:	Recit:

A second example – the double-choral movement 'So ist mein Jesus nun gefangen' from the St Matthew Passion BWV 244 – exhibits both contradictory and missing headings in a musical situation so complex as to make Schering's interpretation
of these markings all but collapse under its own weight. The vocal portion of the
movement starts with the soprano and alto of the first chorus singing against a
series of violent interjections from all four voices of Chorus II. At the words 'Sind
Blitze, sind Donner in Wolken verschwunden', the meter and tempo change, the
remaining voices of Chorus I join the texture, and both choirs sing together, in unison or antiphony, until the end of the movement. Even the most resolutely 'authen-
tic' modern performances give the first section of the piece with two soloists from
Chorus I pitted against massed voices in Chorus II, then have the first chorus
become a full choir at 'Sind Blitze, sind Donner'. The parts, however, show no such
differentiation. The soprano of Chorus II does have the heading 'Chorus' at the
start; but as we see from Table III, all the other parts in both groups read Aria at this
spot, and no member of the set has any supplemental indication at the change of
meter.

If Bach's materials as we have examined them so far have not revealed any char-
acteristics that would facilitate the sort of performance described at the outset, we
might ask if they do not perhaps show other features – such as divided passages or

Table III   St Matthew Passion, BWV 244, Nos. 27a ('So ist mein Jesus nun gefangen') and 27b ('Sind Blitze, sind Donner'): headings in parts (— = no heading)

	No. 27a	No. 27b
Soprano. Chori 1^mi	Aria	—
Alto 1. Chori	Aria. Duetto	—
Tenore 1. Chori	Aria	—
Basso 1. Chori	Aria	—
Soprano Chori II	Chorus	—
Alto Chori II	Aria	—
Tenore Chori II	Aria	—
Basso Chori II	Aria	—

verbal directives presupposing more than one executant – that would testify to their use in this fashion nevertheless. The answer proves negative. Admittedly, we have seen that the parts contain the rubrics 'chorus' and 'chorale', and even 'tutti' makes an occasional appearance. But none of these terms necessarily implies the presence of a second or third singer reading from the same music. I shall discuss some of the most important 'tutti' markings in greater detail subsequently. For now, we might simply recall that the appearance of this word within a part frequently served as nothing more than a sign of orientation for a single performer. For example, in the original oboe and bassoon parts to the Suite in C Major BWV 1066, the inscription 'Tutti' alternates with 'Trio', clearly to help the three woodwind players distinguish between those passages in which they appear as a concerted group and those in which they proceed in unison with the rest of the ensemble.

As for 'chorus' and 'chorale', the examples from the *Christmas Oratorio* and the St Matthew Passion should already have made us wary of reading any binding performance implications into the words themselves. For reasons of time, I shall say nothing more about 'chorale'; but 'chorus' merits some further comment. Unlike us, musicians of Bach's day did not invariably associate this term with the idea of having each line in a musical texture sung by several voices. A recollection of Gottfried Heinrich Stölzel's, for instance, shows that the so-called *Singechor* at the Neue Kirche in Leipzig consisted of exactly four members in the first decade of the eighteenth century, and later documents indicate that the group retained both the same name and the same size in the 1730s and 1740s as well. Opera composers, moreover, regularly used the heading 'coro' to designate a number – usually the final one – uniting most or all the individual participants in the action; the ensemble for eight soloists that closes Alessandro Scarlatti's *La caduta de' decemviri* offers just one of many readily accessible examples. Bach himself clearly knew this terminological practice well enough to follow it in his own rather operatic *Coffee Cantata* BWV 211. The little drama unfolded in the piece involves two characters: Ließgen, a soprano; and her father, Schlendrian, a bass. In addition, a tenor introduces and comments on the story. It would seem a foregone conclusion that Bach designed the music for these three singers alone – especially since the original soprano and bass parts, both copied entirely in his hand, carry not only the usual voice designations but the names of their respective characters as well. Yet in all three parts, the trio with which the cantata ends bears the heading 'Chorus'.

Inevitably, the failure of Bach's parts to match the expectations inherent in Schering's paradigm for their use raises some question about that side of the paradigm which we have not yet considered: the number and distribution of singers in the chorus itself. Schering does not refer directly to any specific sources for most of his assertions on this matter; but an examination of the relevant documentary material shows that his case rests almost entirely on a single piece of evidence – Bach's well-known *Entwurff . . .*, a memorandum submitted to the Leipzig town council on 23 August 1730. A careful reading of this document thus seems in order.

To understand the *Entwurff*, we must understand something of the circumstances in which it originated. As music director to the city of Leipzig and cantor of the boarding school attached to St Thomas's church, Bach had direct or indirect responsibility for almost all the vocal music performed at services in four different houses of worship: St Thomas's, commonly known as the Thomaskirche; St Nicholas's, or the Nikolaikirche; the Neue Kirche; and St Peter's, the Petrikirche. The liturgy at St Peter's required no music beyond simple chorales. That at the Neue Kirche, on the other hand, included not only chorales but also a motet and, on high feasts, a cantata; this last, however, lay not in Bach's hands but in those of the church organist together with a group of student instrumentalists and the *Singechor* referred to earlier. St Thomas's and St Nicholas's, the two principal churches, arranged their music [as shown in Table 2, p. 19 above]. On Sundays throughout the year, the service at one church included a motet and a cantata, while the other had a motet alone; St Thomas's housed the ceremony with the cantata one week, St Nicholas's the next. On feast days, each church had two services with music – a more elaborate one in the morning, a simpler one for the afternoon Vespers, or vice versa. On these occasions, the less elaborate service also included a cantata, although one not so complex as that in the other ceremony. Finally, one or the other church, again in alternation, housed a concerted Passion on Good Friday.

With the exception of the cantatas at the Neue Kirche, Bach had to provide singers for all the music in the four churches, as well as deputy conductors – called prefects – to lead them in the motets and in the cantatas presented as part of the lesser services at St Thomas's or St Nicholas's on feast days. Singers and prefects alike came from the ranks of the fifty-five or so *alumni*, or resident pupils, of the Thomasschule, who ranged in age from their early teens to the early twenties. In accordance with both custom and the differing demands of the churches, Bach divided this body into four separate choirs. The first of these sang at the more elaborate of the services held in St Thomas's or St Nicholas's, with Bach himself directing the cantata or other concerted music. The second choir sang in the lesser service at the same two churches and, once a year, evidently joined the first choir in the Good Friday Passion. The third choir sang at the Neue Kirche, the fourth at St Peter's. Given the lack of any but the simplest music at this last church, Bach could stock the fourth choir with those who, in the words of the *Entwurff*, 'do not understand any music'. Everyone in the other three groups, however, had to have at least enough ability to sing a motet – one of the relatively straightforward pieces in Eberhard Bodenschatz's *Florilegium portense*, the standard repository in Leipzig for older polyphony; and the first and second choirs each had to include singers capable of negotiating the greater vocal demands of a cantata as well.

In addition to the singers and prefects, the music under Bach's purview also required a sufficient number of instrumentalists to perform one or even, on feast days, two cantatas. The city administration placed a group of eight musicians – seven salaried players and an apprentice – at his disposal. But as virtually everyone knows, his concerted music, even with the smallest possible string section, routinely demands more than this number. Hence Bach would have had to scramble repeatedly to bring the ensemble up to requisite size. In part, he could manage this by engaging musically competent students from the university on an ad-hoc basis. It would appear, however, that he could not get sufficient funds from the city to hire enough students to close the gap completely, and he had to fill the positions that remained with *alumni*. Yet doing this reduced the pool of singers on which he could draw – a pool already kept below its fullest possible level by an admissions policy at the Thomasschule that granted a substantial share of places to boys of presumably high academic ability but no musical talent whatever. The system, in other words, placed Bach in a constant bind. After seven years, he obviously found the strain more than he could bear in silence; his protest took the form of the *Entwurff*. The full title of the document [see above, Appendix 3] describes its contents and intent with admirable precision. One may best translate the first clause as 'Short but most necessary outline of a properly appointed church music', with the word 'appointed' meaning, in English as in the original German, both 'outfitted' and 'engaged', and the term 'church music' understood as a performing body, not the compositions that they presented. The second clause reads, 'together with some modest reflections on the decline of the same', transforming the musical establishment previously spoken of in rather abstract terms into the very real body of singers and instrumentalists maintained by the city.

Although the *Entwurff* lacks the crystalline formal logic that we prize in so much of Bach's music, it nevertheless has a coherent structure more than adequate to its purpose. As I suggest in Table IV, we may divide the document into four sections. The third, and by far the longest – which itself falls into a number of subsections – presents the core of Bach's argument, detailing the effects of the city's inadequate provision for the hiring of instrumentalists. Sections II and IV frame this centerpiece with background material clearly meant to buttress those points specifically related to the inroads that the situation had made on the number of *alumni* available for duty as singers. Finally, Section I provides a sort of crash course in musical personnel as a necessary preamble to a document whose audience might otherwise have had trouble understanding it.

Schering's reconstruction of Bach's chorus – meaning, of course, the group that sang the cantata each week at St Thomas's or the Nikolaikirche – derives from two different passages in the *Entwurff*. The first of these occupies most of the opening section, the other the second half of Section II. [The passages specifically discussed here are ¶¶2–5, in Rifkin's Section I, and ¶¶8–9, in his Section II.] Read casually, the two sets of remarks could indeed give the appearance of supporting the inferences that Schering drew from them, as both describe a choir consisting normally of twelve singers, three of each voice type. Yet a more careful examination of both the passages themselves and their relation to the document as a whole reveals that Schering's inferences in fact rest on an extremely shaky foundation.

Table IV *Kurtzer, iedoch höchstnöthiger Entwurff einer wohlbestallten Kirchen Music, nebst einigem unvorgreiflichen Bedencken von dem Verfall derselben*: conspectus

I.   Basic elements of an ecclesiastical musical establishment
II. Division of Thomasschule pupils into four choirs for four churches; requisites for composition of first three choirs and total number of pupils who must 'understand music'
III. (a) Instrumentalists required; instrumentalists regularly engaged by city; instruments lacking regular performers
     (b) Use of university students (paid individual honoraria) and Thomasschule pupils to make up shortage; loss of singers caused by latter
     (c) Pool of singers kept too low by admissions policy of Thomasschule; hiring of students not as well supported as in time of Schelle and Kuhnau
     (d) Changes of musical situation since then with attendant higher demands on musicians' skills; higher, not lower level of support thus needed
IV. List of Thomasschule pupils ranked in three classes according to musical ability

To begin with, we must recall that the two passages, although close to each other in location, belong to portions of the *Entwurff* divergent in function. We cannot, therefore, necessarily treat them as a pair of interlocking statements. The particular function of the first section, moreover, casts its references to concertists and ripienists in a light substantially different from that in which Schering and others have seen them. As part of a guide to basic terminology and procedure, Bach's remarks have a clearly instructional nature: the usual vocal ensemble contains voices of four sorts, soprano, alto, tenor, and bass; if the ensemble – assuming that it has more than one representative of each voice type – performs a cantata, one must arrange the singers into two further classes, concertists and ripienists. None of this, however, says that Bach regularly had ripienists among his own vocal forces, any more than the mention of trumpets, timpani, and flutes in the final sentence of the section tells us that he made use of these instruments in every one of his cantatas.

In any event, anything more than a provisional interpretation of this passage will have to await the consideration of other evidence – above all, for the moment, of material elsewhere in the *Entwurff*. This brings us back to the second passage [¶¶8–9]. As I have already intimated, this passage does not really dovetail with that in the first section; for while the earlier comments, whatever their precise meaning, clearly take concerted music as their frame of reference, those here just as clearly do not. For one thing, the material directly surrounding them shows that the words 'musical choir' refer equally to the first, second, and third choruses – ensembles with a common denominator of motet singing, not cantatas. The connection with the motet, moreover, becomes fully explicit in the reason that Bach gives for stipulating the particular composition of these groups: each must have sufficient forces in reserve for it to perform the eight-part works typical of the Bodenschatz repertory even in the frequent event that one of the singers falls ill. Admittedly, Bach's specifications do still seem to imply that the choirs participating in services at the Neue Kirche, the Nikolaikirche, and the Thomaskirche would indeed have had twelve members, at least in principle. Yet this hardly rescues Schering's case; for not only does the figure of twelve singers lack any external verification, but as Bach reveals in the final portion of the *Entwurff*, only a limited portion of either the first or the second choir can actually have sung in the cantatas.

The fourth section of the *Entwurff* begins, 'In conclusion I find myself obliged to append the roster of the present *alumni*, to indicate the skill of each in music, and thus to leave it to riper reflection whether in such circumstances the music' – meaning, again, the performing establishment – 'can further survive or whether its still greater decline is to be feared'. Bach then provides a list of fifty-four names divided into three classes: those whom he calls 'usable', which plainly means those whom he can employ in cantatas and similar works; the 'motet singers, who must first perfect themselves still further in order to be used in figural music'; and those who 'are not musicians at all'. If we take the *Entwurff* literally – and we can scarcely base any conclusions on it if we do not – then only the 'usable' pupils would have performed concerted pieces; we might thus more conveniently call them 'cantata singers'. In the present context, they will obviously occupy the center of our interest.

The *Entwurff* lists a total of seventeen cantata singers, three of them prefects. Bearing in mind that one of the prefects had to conduct the third choir, we see that Bach would have had no more than sixteen cantata singers to assign to the first and second choirs. If, as suggested in Table V, we assume that he placed only four of those singers in the second ensemble – with the prefect thus functioning as singer and conductor simultaneously – we can still imagine a first choir conforming to what has become the standard picture of twelve cantata singers. We must recall, however, that Bach had to use some of his choir members as instrumentalists. Section III of the *Entwurff* states that the shortage of regularly salaried players 'has had to be made up partly by *studiosi*' – musicians from the university – 'but mostly by *alumni*'. In greater detail, Bach subsequently writes, 'It is further to be remembered that (in the absence of more capable persons) I have usually had to fill the second violin, and always the viola, violoncello, and violone, with *alumni*; it is easy to judge what the vocal choir has been deprived of thereby.' These last words clearly refer to the cantata singers, since the use of motet singers as instrumentalists could hardly have depleted a vocal ensemble to which they would not otherwise have belonged. Even if we restrict our calculations to only the three instruments 'always'

Table V   Bach's first three choirs as suggested by *Entwurff*, Section IV
(C = cantata singer; M = motet singer; P = prefect)

CHOIR

I	C/P	C	C	C	C	C	C	C	C	C	C
II	C/P	C	C	C	M	M	M	M	M	M	M
III	C/P	M	M	M	M	M	M	M	M	M	M

Table VI   First choir in light of *Entwurff*, Section IIIb (i = cantata singer playing instrument)

C/P	C	C	C	C	C	C	C	C	i	i	i

played by *alumni*, Bach's testimony yields a breakdown of forces no more favorable than that shown in Table VI, which leaves a maximum of nine qualified vocalists in the first choir. This number, moreover, would not have enabled him to perform cantatas with even two singers on each line unless a pair of further best-case situations prevailed: that the nine singers remaining happened to include at least two sopranos, two altos, two tenors, and two basses; and that every one of the singers remained in constant good health. In sum, therefore, the *Entwurff*, far from proving that Bach presented his Leipzig sacred music with a chorus of twelve singers, creates a strong impression that he would have had difficulty having it sung by anything more than a quartet of soloists.

While the foregoing reading of the *Entwurff* surely does not represent the only possible interpretation of the document, it does, I think, make clear that Bach's text will not really support the assertions that Schering and others have confidently made on its basis. As I have already intimated, we have no further documents from the Leipzig period – no reports, for example, of actual performances – that go beyond the *Entwurff* on any points germane to our investigation. Outside Leipzig, what scant evidence survives does equally little to sustain the credibility of the performance configuration so long accepted as standard. Chapel registers from Weimar, the relevant portions of which I have summarized in Table VII, show that the regular vocal forces during Bach's years as ducal organist and concertmaster never exceeded eight singers and, indeed, fell below this total during the very time in which he wrote the bulk of his early cantatas. Given our experience with the *Entwurff*, moreover, we can no more assume without qualification that the singers would have performed together in cantatas than we can assume that football teams

Table VII   Singers in the ducal chapel at Weimar (— = not named but presumably present)

	6 Nov 1713	6 Apr 1714	between Apr 1714 and Dec 1716
Discant	—	—	J. P. Weichard
	—	—	J. C. Gerrmann
Alto	J. J. Graff	Graff	C. Bernhardi
	G. Blühnitz	Blühnitz	
Tenor	A. Aiblinger	Aiblinger	Aiblinger
	J. Döbernitz	Döbernitz	Döbernitz
Bass	G. E. Thiele	'Vice-Cantor'	Thiele
		C. Alt	Alt

routinely put forty-five men on the field. The only remaining information on the vocal component of any ensemble with Bach had some sort of association comes from the electoral court in Dresden, for which he wrote his Missa of 1733 – the Kyrie and Gloria of what ultimately became the B Minor Mass. Here, the registers show a generally impressive body of forces, especially in the instrumental domain; but at no time from the late 1720s to the late 1730s does the court appear to have maintained more than a single tenor on its rolls.

Faced, then, with both a careful scrutiny of the documents and the admittedly negative, but nonetheless suggestive evidence of the musical sources as we have examined them so far, the entire paradigm of three singers reading from each of Bach's parts simply evaporates for want of substance. This leaves us, of course, with the question of how many actually did sing from each part, and thus how many actually sang in the works themselves. Considering the limitations of the documentary record, it would seem obvious that the search for an answer has no choice but to return to the performing materials for a second, and more extended, look at the information that they provide. Original materials exist for just under a hundred fifty of Bach's works that we would today regard as choral – works, in other words, containing at least one movement for four or more different voices. Most of the parts offer no positive clues to their manner of use, since they bear no title beyond their voice type and contain no internal markings other than the designations of genre that we have already discussed. But in a significant number of cases – something over one work out of eight – the manuscripts provide more definite indications of what Bach intended; and analysis of this evidence leads inescapably to the conclusion that he always meant his voice parts for one singer and one singer only.

Given the amount of time available to us, we obviously cannot consider the evidence in its entirety. That portion of it which we shall consider divides into three strands. The first of these comes from the materials to the cantatas BWV 55, 56, 84, and 169 [cf. above, p. 39]. An examination of the parts themselves reveals nothing out of the ordinary: each set contains the usual four vocal parts, all labeled in the customary fashion and conforming in every other way to the norm that we have already encountered. But the wrappers in which Bach kept the parts deviate from his usual practice in one significant respect. Like countless others of their sort, these wrappers have autograph inscriptions specifying the liturgical function title, and scoring of the music that they preserve. In most such instances, Bach did not enumerate the vocal forces called for beyond the summary formulation 'à 4 voci'. Yet even though the present cantatas all require a total of four voices, their wrappers show neither the standard rubric nor some other conventional designation such as 'à Soprano, Alto, Tenore e Basso'. The reason clearly lies in the rather uncommon distribution of voices within the works themselves. Each cantata, although ending with a four-part chorale, otherwise calls for only one singer throughout – a soprano in BWV 84, alto in BWV 169, tenor in BWV 55, and bass in BWV 56. A reference to four voices without any distinction among them, therefore, would have seriously obscured the fundamental nature of the music.

Bach's solution to this problem proves illuminating. [The list on p. 39 above] cites the relevant portions of the four wrappers; we may take BWV 84 as a representative for closer inspection. Since Bach speaks plainly of a soprano soloist without mentioning a further soprano, it would appear self-evident that he envisioned only one singer reading from the corresponding part in the set, even in the chorale; and given the homogeneous texture of this movement, it seems equally clear that he meant the three remaining parts – the *ripieni* listed on the wrapper – for solo performance as well. Hence all four parts, whose utterly normal appearance I must again stress, served for use by one singer each.

The second strand of evidence that we have to consider involves a practice already familiar to us from the *Coffee Cantata*: the addition of a character designation to the usual nomenclature of one or more voice parts within a set. Apart from the *Coffee Cantata* itself – whose use of fewer than four voices removes it from our immediate field of concern – such additions occur in the five works listed in Table VIII. For the moment, I shall discuss only three of these pieces, BWV 249, 57, and 244.

Table VIII   Works with character designations in original voice parts (dates = first performances; later performances indicated only if these involve significant changes in performing materials)

BWV 57   *Selig ist der Mann* (26 Dec 1725)
BWV 201   *Geschwinde, geschwinde, ihr wirbelnden Winde* (1729)
BWV 244   St Matthew Passion (11 Apr 1727?; 30 Mar 1736)
BWV 245   St John Passion (7 Apr 1724; 30 Mar 1725; 1728–31; late 1740s)
BWV 249   *Easter Oratorio* (1 Apr 1725)

BWV 249, the *Easter Oratorio*, originated as an adaptation of a secular *dramma per musica* that Bach had composed only a short time before. Although the vocal parts of the original work no longer survive, the libretto plainly associates each singer with a specific character in the action; and the text of the sacred version maintains these associations while transferring them from a pastoral to a biblical plane: the soprano, formerly Doris, becomes Maria Jacobi; the alto, originally Sylvia, becomes Maria Magdalena; and the tenor and bass undergo similar changes. The materials for the first performance of the oratorio make the connection of singer and role fully explicit: each of the four voice parts bears the name of its character alongside the specification of its range. Since none of the parts contains anything that could so much as hint at the presence of additional singers, we surely have no option but to take this labeling at face value – which means, obviously, imagining the entire work, including its brilliant final movement, performed with no more than four singers from start to finish.

While one might conceivably argue that a work like BWV 249 does not really have much consequence for the interpretation of voice parts not distinguished by such special labeling, BWV 57 and BWV 244 make this argument impossible to sustain. The former work calls for four voices in all; but with the exception of the final chorale, it uses only two singers, soprano and bass, who set forth a dialogue between Jesus and the soul. The scribe who copied the original voice parts labeled them in the usual neutral manner. In revising the materials, however, Bach took pains to underscore the dramatic function of the two principal voices by inscribing their parts 'Anima' and 'Christus', respectively. Once again, this surely means that he envisioned only one singer performing from each part throughout the entire work, including the chorale; hence – as we already saw with the cantatas discussed earlier – the remaining parts must also have served for only one singer each.

An even more striking instance of the same principle confronts us in the materials to the St Matthew Passion BWV 244. The vocal component of this source consists primarily of eight parts, four for each choir, all headed with a designation of voice type and the group to which they belong: 'Soprano 1. Chori', 'Alto Chori II', and so forth. The tenor and bass of Chorus I, however, carry the supplementary inscriptions 'Evangelista' and 'Jesus', respectively. It would take some fancy semantic footwork indeed to make these headings mean anything but that Bach intended no more than a single performer to sing from each of these two parts – which contain the entire sequence of choruses, chorales, recitatives, and arias involving their particular voice as well as the Gospel passages for the characters whose names they bear; and since what holds true for these parts must surely hold true for the other six as well, we see that the two choruses in the Passion would have numbered a total of only eight singers.

Although these conclusions receive what amounts to positive confirmation from the materials to a work that we have yet to consider, I might also point to some corroborating evidence for them within the Passion itself. In addition to the eight parts that we have already encountered, the materials for the Passion include a handful of isolated leaves containing music not assigned to members of either choir: the 'Soprano in Ripieno' in the opening and closing numbers of the first half, and the utterances of such characters in the drama as Peter, Pilate, and Pilate's wife. While the provision of a separate part for the Soprano in Ripieno makes perfect sense, as this voice functions outside the two 'regular' choirs, the similar treatment accorded the minor interlocutors does not – not, at least, if we regard it in the light of traditional theories. For example, Pilate, a bass, sings in dialogue with the Evangelist and Jesus, always accompanied by the same continuo group as they; strictly speaking, therefore, he should belong to Chorus I. If Bach had had more than one singer reading from the bass part of that chorus – in other words, from the part marked 'Jesus' – we could surely expect him to have placed Pilate's music in that part, especially as this would have allowed the singer representing Pilate to perform in all the choral numbers. Yet not only does Pilate's music appear in one of the extra parts, but the part in question expressly marks every chorus and chorale occurring within its boundaries 'tacet'.

In the sources that we have examined until now, the practice of writing a separate part for each singer in the ensemble has at the same time meant having only one singer perform each line of the vocal texture. It takes little effort to recognize, however, that the same notational procedure could just as well result in the 'choral' sonority to which we have long since become accustomed. Put simply, when a composer had the opportunity and the desire to double his principal singers with supporting voices, he merely copied additional parts – usually distinguished from the main set by the presence of the words 'capella' or 'ripieno' in the title – for the extra performers. This convention reached back into the seventeenth century and continued until at least the time of Mozart and Haydn. In the preface to his *Musicalische Exequien* of 1636, for example, Heinrich Schütz wrote, 'This . . . concerto is, strictly speaking, for six voices or rather six concerted singers with organ . . . From these six concerted parts . . . one may write out (where the word *Capella* appears) six further parts . . . and thus set up and add a special extra chorus or *capella*'. Significantly, the voices described by Schütz as 'concerted' bear no designation in the actual parts beyond the usual headings 'Cantus', 'Altus', 'Tenor', and the like.

Significantly, too, Schütz does not suggest that one achieve the richer texture that he proposes by having additional singers read from the concertists' parts. At the other end of the chronological spectrum, the original materials to Haydn's *Harmoniemesse* of 1802 include a total of eighteen voice parts, four marked 'concertato' and containing all the music for their respective voices, the rest labeled 'ripieno' and omitting all the solo passages.

These remarks bring us to the final strand of evidence in Bach's materials that we have to consider. Nine works [listed in Table 3A, p. 61 above] stand out within Bach's output by the inclusion of specially written *ripieno* parts among their original sources. Paradoxically, the very compositions whose sonority most closely approaches our present-day conception of Bach's performances offer the most telling arguments against the assumption that concertists and ripienists shared the same music – and, with that, the assumption that the ripienists formed a regular part of Bach's vocal ensemble.

Once again, we can deal only with selected examples. Let us start with the earliest work on the list, the cantata BWV 71. The largely autograph materials from the first performance include eight voice parts, four labeled simply according to range, the others bearing the additional inscription 'in ripieno'. The *ripieni* do not double the main parts throughout the entire composition but join the ensemble only in more densely scored passages. This manner of writing all but unquestionably presupposes that only one singer would perform from each of the 'regular' parts.

One could perhaps argue, of course, that Bach regarded the notated ripieno parts as simply a more careful means of accomplishing an end that he would reached anyway – by having additional singers read from each of the main parts. But aside from the absence of any real evidence supporting this proposition, not to speak of the enormous impracticalities that it would have created, Bach himself pulls the ground out from under it with a notice at the head of the autograph score. The summary of the work's forces there reads 'âb 18 è se piace 22' – in eighteen or twenty-two parts. As both the nature of the music itself and comparison with many similar examples from the seventeenth and eighteenth centuries reveal, the two options mean that performers could include or omit the ripieni at will; and this, in turn, surely means that Bach considered these voices as supplementary, not integral, to the basic texture of the cantata. Clearly, therefore, the internal constitution of that texture would have remained unaffected by the presence or absence of the ripieni; hence the association of the four neutrally headed parts with concertists alone would have prevailed in either of the performance circumstances implied by Bach's inscription.

A further, if less direct, indication of both the supplementary character of the ripienists and the essentially soloistic nature of the primary voice parts comes from the substantially later cantata BWV 110. At the first performance of the work, in 1725, the materials included only the usual four voice parts, all labeled in the usual manner; for the second performance, some time between 1728 and 1731, Bach added a set of autograph ripieno parts, only the upper three of which survive. The new parts include only the opening chorus and the final chorale, omitting the intervening arias and recitatives. In the first movement, Bach again uses the ripienists to 'register' the texture, introducing them only in fully scored sections and leaving them out at lighter passages. Again, too, this procedure clearly means that he assigned the four main parts to his concertists alone – at least in the second performance of the cantata. But in the absence of any tangible evidence, we have no real warrant for

assuming that he would have used these parts any differently at the earlier performance. A parallel may help bear out this point. The cantata BWV 172 includes an
aria with an *obbligato* accompaniment of unison violins and violas. At the second
presentation of the work, Bach had the strings doubled at the upper octave by a
flute, for which he naturally provided an individual part. Surely, we may take it as
doubtful in the extreme that he had conceived the aria with flute from the outset
and previously had the player read from the violinists' music.

A third of Bach's works with *ripieno* parts, the cantata BWV 195, has particular significance in clarifying a potentially misleading aspect of his practice with regard to
materials for extra singers. For this composition we have four voice parts called simply 'Soprano', 'Alto', 'Tenore', and 'Basso', respectively, and, four corresponding
parts marked 'in Ripieno'. In contrast to the situation with BWV 110, the *ripieno* parts
belong to the earliest layer of the cantata's history. Indeed, their origin precedes that
of the extant main parts, which date from a performance near the end of Bach's life.
This does not, however, affect the outcome of our inquiry in any substantive fashion, since the scribes of the main parts seem to have copied them directly from the
now-lost earlier set and accurately reproduced the readings of that material in all
but the most minute particulars.

The opening number of BWV 195 consists, in essence, of two fugues, each with two
expositions. In both fugues, the four principal voices alone carry the first exposition, while the second exposition adds the ripienists to them in unison. In the first
fugue, however, Bach complicates matters by prefacing each entry of the subject
with a brief homophonic fanfare involving all four voice lines [see Ex. 13, pp. 85ff
above; here, Rifkin's music example illustrated just 'the first entry of the soprano,
with two measures of homophony, then the subject proper']. The ripienists double
the main voices in the homophonic outbursts – not always with literal exactness.

Once again, the presence of *ripieno* parts surely means that Bach intended the
principal parts solely for concertists, and the variants between concertists and ripienists in passages like the one just described from BWV 195 only strengthen this
conclusion – after all, one could hardly have expected a second singer reading from,
say, the soprano or alto part to infer the delicate adjustments to both text and music
made in the *ripieno* parts. Moreover, the main parts leave no doubt as to what kind
of sonority Bach had in mind for those sections where the *ripieno* parts remain
silent, for at the start of the second fugue they all bear the marking 'solo'; indeed,
this marking appears in the second chorus of the cantata as well, again at passages
where the *ripieni* do not sing.

At the same time, however, the main parts also carry the indication 'tutti' at several places, each time coinciding with the entry of the ripienists. We have, of course,
seen already that the word itself does not necessarily have the implications that
some may wish it to have in the present context; the absence, moreover, of tutti
markings corresponding to the interjections of the ripienists at the start of the first
movement suggests that those markings that do occur cannot have had any direct
relevance for the performance of the music. Nevertheless, the mere appearance of
the word 'tutti' in the voice parts to a composition like BWV 195 constitutes a puzzle
that neatness, if nothing else, demands that we solve.

The solution, in fact, proves fairly simple. I shall begin with a reminder that the
main parts as we have them served as replacements for an earlier set that no longer
exists, and I shall make two assumptions about that earlier set: first, that the tenor

of the group included a 'tutti' marking at bar 35 [cf. Ex. 13]; and, second, that Bach himself most likely added the words 'solo' and 'tutti' to the parts after their copying. As we shall see, simple common sense dictates the first assumption; the second depends on parallel instances in other materials that time does not permit me to mention here.

As you can observe [in the figure below], the main parts in the first fugue do not have the inscription 'tutti' – indicated in the figure by a capital 'T' – until the start of the second exposition. You can also observe that only at this spot do the ripienists begin to double the principal voices literally, which they do from now on whenever they appear. Finally, you can see that Bach divided the preparation of the *ripieno* parts between himself and a group of copyists, each of whom started work precisely where the doubling becomes exact. Putting together the evidence of the script and the music, we obtain the following picture: As he always did with supplementary parts, Bach had those of the *ripieno* group copied directly from the main parts. While he would normally have entrusted such a lower-order task entirely to copyists, no one but he could make the subtle adjustments necessitated by the homophonic passages of the first exposition, so he took over this job himself. From the start of the second exposition, however, he could readily leave things to his helpers, who needed nothing more than a guide to where the ripienists should sing and remain silent. Obviously, the 'solo' and 'tutti' markings entered in the main parts functioned as this guide – and, so far as we can tell, had no other function whatever. Although time does not permit us to discuss any other instances of this practice, I should note in passing that BWV 21 and 76 in fact present situations directly parallel to the one described here.

	13	17	22	25	30^2	34	37^2	41
S								T
A							T	
T						[T?]		
B					T			
S rip.								
A rip.								
T rip.								
B rip.								

AUTOGRAPH

COPYIST

〜〜	= homophony
——	= subject
----	= counter-subject (or free)
( )	= identity not literal
T	= *tutti* in source

I should like to conclude this portion of our discussion with a look at a single work that weaves together virtually all the different strands of evidence that we have until now considered in isolation: the St John Passion BWV 245. The materials to the Passion document a particularly complex history of re-use and change; as you can see from Table IX, the surviving voice parts originated or underwent revision at some four different times in a period of more than two decades. Precisely this intricate pattern of chronological layers makes them a uniquely valuable witness to the nature of Bach's vocal forces and the manner in which he deployed them.

The Passion has the usual four main voice parts. Although the exemplars presently known date from the second performance of the work, internal evidence suggests that they do not deviate from their lost predecessors of a year earlier in any way significant to our investigation. The soprano and alto parts contain all the music falling within their respective ranges; the tenor and bass, like their opposite numbers in the St Matthew Passion, include choruses, chorales, recitatives, arias, and the Gospel recitatives for the Evangelist and Jesus respectively, but omit the music for the other male interlocutors: the Servant, a tenor; and Peter and Pilate, basses. The scribe who copied the parts gave each one the customary labels – 'Soprano', 'Alto', etc. – at the top of its first page. Beneath the first stave of music in the tenor, however, he inserted the inscription 'Evangelista'. Given what we have already seen of such character designations, this entry surely means that Bach meant the part – and, by obvious extension, its companions as well – for only one singer. Bach himself furnishes what looks like direct confirmation for this assumption in a set of replacement pages, prepared for the third performance, on which he substituted a different opening movement for the one initially entered into the four parts. The new pages contain new, autograph captions. That for the tenor explicitly reads 'Tenore Evangelista', that for the bass, 'Basso. Jesus'. Perhaps more important, the two upper parts now become, respectively, 'Soprano Concert.' and 'Alto Concert.' – as conclusive a demonstration, it would appear, as one could wish that Bach intended them for solo performance throughout.

A remote chance could seem to exist, however, that the inscription 'concertato' denotes a change in Bach's intentions concerning the soprano and alto parts – meaning that they, together with the tenor and bass, could earlier have served for three singers each. Yet we can eliminate this possibility in two ways. The apportionment of the Servant, Peter, and Pilate to parts other than the principal tenor and bass – a matter to which I shall return – provides the first. As with the St Matthew Passion, this procedure hardly squares with the assumption of three singers reading from either the main tenor or the main bass part at any time.

More conclusive evidence for the use of the main parts by concertists alone even before the third performance comes from the *ripieno* parts listed in Table IX. The very existence of these parts, of course, proves highly suggestive; but the information that they offer goes considerably beyond that. The movement numbered 32 in the *Neue Bach-Ausgabe* text of the Passion combines, in effect, a bass aria and a four-part chorale. As we can see from the example [opposite], Bach arranged the vocal parts of the piece in such a way as to give the chorale the full texture of combined concertists and ripienists that he used for other chorale settings in the Passion. The attempt breaks down with the lowest line, however, which goes to Basso Ripieno alone, while the principal bass – Jesus' part – has the solo line.

Table IX   BWV 245: original voice parts

Main parts (1725; new first pages 1728–31)

Title 1725	Title 1728–31
Soprano	Soprano Concert.
Alto	Alto Concert.
Tenore (beneath first stave: Evangelista)	Tenore Evangelista
Basso	Basso. Jesus

Ripieno parts (1724)
   Soprano ripieno
   Alto Ripieno
   Tenore Ripien:
   Basso Ripien: (includes Petrus)

Interlocutors
   [Basso Pilatus, fragment] (1725?)
   Tenore Servus (late 1740s)
   Basso Petrus & Pilatus (late 1740s)

J. S. Bach, St John Passion BWV245/32 ('Mein teurer Heiland'), bars 4–6

Clearly, if even one ripienist as well as the bass soloist had used this part, Bach would have found a way to have that singer double the chorale line, either by entering that line together with the solo in the same part or by some sort of directive sending the singer to the part used by his ripienist colleague. Hence the *ripieno* parts presuppose only one voice on each of the main parts; and since they belonged to the materials for the Passion from its very first presentation, they remove any conceivable doubt that Bach meant the main parts for concertists, and concertists alone, right from the start. Seen against this background, Bach's subsequent decision to give the soprano and alto of the principal set the description 'concertato' has no more motive behind it than the wish to make absolutely clear the distinction between these parts and the corresponding members of the *ripieni*.

Naturally, those who wished at all costs to uphold the theory of the ever-present ripienists might contend that the St John Passion has only limited bearing on other works by arguing that the association of its main parts with concertists alone depends exclusively on the presence of the *ripieno* parts – that without such parts, the 'normal' materials would revert to the sort of use posited for them by Schering. Aside, however, from the implausibility of this thesis in light of a piece like BWV 71, the argument receives a virtually fatal blow from a previously unnoticed detail in the history of the materials. The *ripieno* parts show not a trace of the revisions entered into every other surviving part of the set at the time of the Passion's last performance; moreover, the part for the bass ripienist, which contains the music for Petrus along with the usual *ripieno* material, does not have these solo passages deleted, despite the existence of a newly written 'Basso Petrus & Pilatus'. Given the thoroughness with which Bach otherwise revised cues, 'tacet' markings, and transposition indications in connection with the performance in question, it would appear obvious that he simply did not use the *ripieno* parts on this occasion; and their omission has no rational explanation other than that he did not use the ripienists themselves.

A final question posed by the materials to the Passion concerns the number of singers whom Bach would have had reading from each of the *ripieno* parts. The word 'ripieno' itself does not imply more than one singer – properly speaking, as we saw with the cantatas listed [on p. 39], it refers to function, not numbers. Moreover, there seems no reason to posit a different manner of performance from ripienists' parts than from concertists' parts. Again, however, the materials themselves shed some light on this matter. We have seen that Basso Ripien: contains the role of Petrus. Pilatus, however, does not appear in either this part or Jesus'. In earlier performances, Bach seems to have assigned the role to a singer reading from a third bass part; in the last performance, when he omitted the ripienists, he combined Pilate and Peter into a single part – which, incidentally, contains 'tacet' markings for all the choruses and chorales occurring within the span of the piece that it covers. Once again, we may assume that if Bach had two ripienists reading from the same music, he would have put both Pilate and Peter in their shared parts. In all probability, therefore, the *ripieno* parts, like those for the concertists, served for only one singer each. This means that the total vocal forces in the choruses and chorales of the St John Passion numbered only eight singers.

This conclusion has twofold significance. We must recall, first of all, that the Passion on Good Friday united Bach's first and second choirs. Clearly, therefore, the four concertists in the work represented the first choir, the four ripienists, the second – and each choir had only four singers each. We now see, too, a previously unsuspected parallel between the St John Passion and the St Matthew Passion. Since the materials to the later work, as we already know, parallel those to the earlier one in every particular except the presence of *ripieno* parts, we cannot realistically doubt that the St Matthew Passion, too, called for only one singer for each of its voice parts – which again, barring such 'extras' as the Soprano in Ripieno and the interlocutors, yield a total of eight singers for the bulk of the work. The double-chorus layout of the St Matthew Passion, therefore, does not represent an amplification of the vocal forces used in the St John Passion but merely a re-disposition of essentially the same body. Finally, if Bach had no more than eight singers for his two surviving Passions – the works for which he could apparently call on a larger vocal group than he normally could at any other point in the Leipzig liturgical year – how can one seriously contend that he normally had more than that number for regular Sunday cantatas? In sum: We have no solid evidence – documentary, theoretical, or notational – to support the assumption that Bach ever had more than one singer reading from each of his vocal parts, while every piece of evidence that we do have speaks strongly for one singer alone. Given the state of his performing materials, cautious scholarship hardly leaves us any option but to imagine the greater part of his vocal performances – in or out of church, in Leipzig or elsewhere – as involving nothing more than a quartet of singers.

As I have already intimated in passing, the practice that I have sought to demonstrate in connection with Bach in fact constituted a normal – indeed, *the* normal – procedure for the notation and performance of vocal music from 1600 to at least 1800. Analysis of notational and documentary evidence for composers as diverse as Schütz, Monteverdi, Biber, Telemann, Graupner, Mozart, and Haydn indicates that they invariably provided separate parts for every singer called for in any piece that they wrote. Hence Bach, rather than deviating from the norm, in fact agrees with it in every particular.

We might, in closing, pause for a final moment on the matter of *ripieno* parts. It lay entirely within the realm of Baroque custom to add such parts to a work originally written without them. We have seen Bach do this in the case of BWV 110; but the process did not necessarily require the composer's intervention. Indeed, in the decades after Bach's death, other musicians amplified the original materials to several of his cantatas with extra voice parts for the choruses and chorales. The performances that resulted would, of course, have sounded more or less exactly the way we have traditionally imagined Bach's own to have sounded. Obviously, these posthumous adaptations provide the missing link between what we can now recognize as his actual practice and the conception of it that we have inherited. As choirs grew in both their size and their importance in the broader musical community, performances of Bach's music inevitably involved a steadily larger number of voices, whose addition to the texture could readily follow those eighteenth-century precedents still no doubt known to virtually any musician. By the time scholars began to investigate the historical conditions under which Bach presented his work, therefore, the sound of his 'great choral frescoes' had become an integral part of general musical awareness; at the same time, however, the details of the process that had engendered that sound had faded from view. Hence Schering and others could scarcely fail to read the documents and musical sources within an unconscious bias towards extracting the maximum possible number of performers from the evidence. But if we now understand the origins of that bias, and can even trace its roots back to Bach's own time, the misconceptions that flow from it remain misconceptions nevertheless. So long as we define 'chorus' in the conventional modern sense, then Bach's chorus, with few exceptions, simply did not exist.

Appendix 7

Twentieth-century discussions
of Bach's choir

The arrangement of this checklist is mainly chronological, but where an item was written primarily to answer another, it is marked • and placed after the contribution which prompted it. See also Smithers 1997 (pp. 77–81) for a 'Bibliographical checklist of the minimalist argument and contrary evidence with regard to the original performing resources for music by J. S. Bach' (54 entries).

Bernhard Friedrich Richter, 'Stadtpfeifer und Alumnen der Thomasschule in Leipzig zu Bachs Zeit', *Bach Jahrbuch*, 4 (1907), pp. 32–78

Arnold Schering, 'Die Besetzung Bachscher Chöre', *Bach Jahrbuch*, 17 (1920), pp. 77–89

Arnold Schering, *Johann Sebastian Bachs Leipziger Kirchenmusik* (Leipzig, 1936; ²/1954)

Wilhelm Ehmann, '"Concertisten" und "Ripienisten" in der h-moll-Messe Joh. Seb. Bachs', in Ehmann, *Voce et tuba* (Kassel, 1976), pp. 119–77 [first published in *Musik und Kirche*, 30 (1960), pp. 95–104, 138–47, 227–36, 255–73, 298–309]

Alfred Dürr, 'Zum Problem "Concertisten" und "Ripienisten" in der h-Moll-Messe', Musik und Kirche 32 (1961), pp. 232–6

Joshua Rifkin, 'Bach's chorus': see Appendix 6 above

  • Nicholas Kenyon, 'Further events: Solos', *The New Yorker*, 14 Dec 1981, pp. 189, 195–6, 198 [a report of events at the American Musicological Society meeting in Boston]

Joshua Rifkin, 'Bach's chorus: A preliminary report', *Musical Times*, 123 (Nov 1982), pp. 747–54 [revised as 'Bachs Chor: ein vorläufige Bericht', *Basler Jahrbuch für Historische Musikpraxis*, 9 (1985), pp. 141–55]

  • Robert L. Marshall, 'Bach's chorus: A preliminary reply to Joshua Rifkin', *Musical Times*, 124 (Jan 1983), pp. 19–22

Joshua Rifkin, 'Bach's "choruses": Less than they seem?', *High Fidelity*, 32/9 (Sept 1982), pp. 42–4

- Robert L. Marshall, 'Bach's "choruses" reconstituted', *High Fidelity*, 32/10 (Oct 1982), pp. 64–6, 94
- Joshua Rifkin, 'Bach's "choruses": The record amplified', special supplement to *High Fidelity*, [Dec 1982]
- Joshua Rifkin, 'Bach's chorus: A response to Robert Marshall', *Musical Times*, 124 (Mar 1983), pp. 161–2

Donal Henahan, 'Choral conductors forum: Minimalism', *American Choral Review* (July 1983), pp. 12–15
- Joshua Rifkin, 'Minimalism: A reply', *American Choral Review* (Jan 1984), pp. 24–5

Don Smithers, 'Abiding discrepancies between historical fact and present-day practice in performances of music by J. S. Bach', *Beiträge zur Bachforschung*, 2 (Leipzig 1983)

Joshua Rifkin, ' ". . . wobey aber die Singstimmen hinlänglich besetzt seyn müßen ...": zum Credo der h-moll-Messe in der Aufführung Carl Philipp Emanuel Bachs', *Basler Jahrbuch für Historische Musikpraxis*, 9 (1985), pp. 157–72

Günther Wagner, 'Die Chorbesetzung bei J. S. Bach und ihre Vorgeschichte: Anmerkungen zur "hinlänglichen" Besetzung im 17. und 18. Jahrhundert', *Archiv für Musikwissenschaft*, 43 (1986), pp. 278–304

Gerhard Herz, 'Concertists and ripienists: An old performance problem revisited', *American Choral Review*, 29/3–4 (Summer–Fall 1987), pp. 35–51

Joshua Rifkin, 'Bach's choral ideal', a paper first presented in April 1990 at the Royal Musical Association Annual Conference

Hans-Joachim Schulze, *Bach stilgerecht aufführen*, Societas Bach Internationalis: Jahresgabe 1990 der Internationalen Bach-Gesellschaft Schaffhausen (Wiesbaden, 1991)

Peter Reidemeister, 'Bachs Chorbesetzung: zur Aufführungspraxis der geistlichen Werke', *Wege zu Bach. Fünf Aufsätze* (Wiesbaden 1992), pp. 34–9

Joshua Rifkin, 'Bach's chorus: Some red herrings', *Journal of Musicological Research*, 14 (1995), pp. 223–34 (with an appended reply by George B. Stauffer, p. 234) [a response to earlier comments by Stauffer]

Andrew Parrott, 'Bach's chorus: A "brief yet highly necessary" reappraisal', *Early Music*, 24 (1996), pp. 551–80

Joshua Rifkin, 'From Weimar to Leipzig: Concertists and ripienists in Bach's *Ich hatte viel Bekümmernis*', *Early Music*, 24 (1996), pp. 583–603

Ton Koopman, 'Recording Bach's early cantatas', *Early Music*, 24/4 (Nov 1996), see esp. pp. 612–17
- Andrew Parrott, 'Bach's chorus: Who cares?', *Early Music*, 25 (1997), pp. 297–300
- Joshua Rifkin, 'Bassoons, violins and voices: A response to Ton Koopman', *Early Music*, 25 (1997), pp. 302–7
- Ton Koopman, 'One-to-a-part? Who then turns the pages? – More on Bach's chorus', *Early Music*, 25 (1997), pp. 541–2
- Joshua Rifkin, 'Page turns, players and ripieno parts: More questions of scoring in Bach's vocal music', *Early Music*, 25 (1997), pp. 728–34

George B. Stauffer, *Bach, the Mass in B Minor: The Great Catholic Mass* (New York, 1997), esp. pp. 206–16

John Butt, 'Bach's vocal scoring: What can it mean?', *Early Music*, 26 (1998), pp. 99–107

Ton Koopman, 'Bach's choir, an ongoing story', *Early Music*, 26 (1998), pp. 109–21

- Joshua Rifkin, 'Bach's chorus: A neverending story?' (letter), *Early Music*, 26 (1998), pp. 380–1
- Christoph Wolff, 'Bach's chorus: Stomach aches may disappear!', (letter), *Early Music*, 26 (1998), pp. 540–1 (with an appended reply by Joshua Rifkin, pp. 541–2)
- Christoph Wolff, 'Bach's chorus: An amplification' (letter), *Early Music*, 27 (1999), p. 172
- Joshua Rifkin, 'Bach's chorus: Not again!' (letter), *Early Music*, 27 (1999), p. 350

Andrew Parrott, 'Bach's chorus: Beyond reasonable doubt', *Early Music*, 26 (1998), pp. 637–58

Don Smithers, 'The Emperor's new clothes reappraised: or Bach's musical resources revealed', BACH: *The Journal of the Riemenschneider Bach Institute*, 28 (1997), pp. 1–81 ['A detailed and documented repudiation of the historically anomalous views of Joshua Rifkin and Andrew Parrott . . .']

- Joshua Rifkin, 'The Emperor's headgear: A brief response to Don Smithers', BACH: *The Journal of the Riemenschneider Bach Institute*, 30 (1999), pp. 70–3

Matthias Hengelbrock, 'Das Problem der solistischen Besetzung von Bachs Chören', in *Musik und Kirche*, 69 (1999), pp. 274ff

- Joshua Rifkin, 'Zu Matthias Hengelbrocks Artikel "Das Problem der solistischen Besetzung von Bachs Chören", MuK 4/1999, S. 274ff', *Musik und Kirche* 69 (1999), p. 360

Bernard D. Sherman, 'Rifkin's pesky idea', *Early Music America*, 5/2 (Summer 1999), p. 48

- Joshua Rifkin, 'Schering's wacky theory', *Early Music America*, 5/3 (Fall 1999), p. 48

Andrew Parrott, 'How many singers . . .', *BBC Music Magazine*, Jan 2000, pp. 38f

Joshua Rifkin, 'Zelenkas Chor: Der Blick von 1725', *Provokation und Tradition: Erfahrungen mit der Alten Musik*, ed. Hans-Martin Linde and Regula Rapp (Munich, 2000), pp. 241–68

Bibliography

Agricola 1757 — Johann Friedrich Agricola, *Anleitung zur Singkunst* (Berlin, 1757; R/1966). Cf. Baird 1995

Bach 1773 — C. P. E. Bach, Autobiographical sketch, in *Carl Burney's der Musik Doctors Tagebuch seiner musikalischen Reisen*, trans. C. D. Ebeling, ii, iii (Hamburg, 1773); trans. W. S. Newman as 'Emanuel Bach's Autobiography', *Musical Quarterly*, 51 (1965), pp. 363–72

Bacilly 1668 — Bénigne de Bacilly, *Remarques curieuses sur l'art de bien chanter* (Paris, 1668)

Baird 1995 — Julianne C. Baird, trans. and ed., *'Introduction to the Art of Singing' by Johann Friedrich Agricola* (Cambridge, 1995)

Barclay 1998 — Robert Barclay, 'A new species of instrument: The vented trumpet in context', *Historic Brass Society Journal*, 10 (1998), pp. 1–13

BD I — *Bach-Dokumente*, i: *Schriftstücke von der Hand Johann Sebastian Bachs*, ed. W. Neumann and H.-J. Schulze (Kassel etc., 1963)

BD II — *Bach-Dokumente*, ii: *Fremdschriftliche und gedruckte Dokumente zur Lebensgeschichte Johann Sebastian Bachs 1685–1750*, ed. W. Neumann and H.-J. Schulze (Kassel etc., 1969)

BD III — *Bach-Dokumente*, iii: *Dokumente zum Nachwirken Johann Sebastian Bachs 1750–1800*, ed. H.-J. Schulze (Kassel etc., 1972)

BD IV — *Bach-Dokumente*, iv: *Bilddokumente zur Lebensgeschichte Johann Sebastian Bachs*, ed. W. Neumann (Leipzig, 1978)

Bodenschatz 1603ff — Erhard Bodenschatz, *Florilegium Portense*, i (Leipzig, 1603/1618); ii (Leipzig, 1621)

Bösken 1937 — F. Bösken, *Musikgeschichte der Stadt Osnabrück* (Regensburg, 1937)

Boyd 1984 — M. Boyd, 'Bach's chorus' (Correspondence), *Early Music*, 12/3 (Aug 1984), p. 431. Cf. Rifkin 1984

Boyd 1990 — M. Boyd, *Bach*, The Master Musicians, 2nd edn (London, 1990)

Boyd 1995 — M. Boyd, 'Sacred Bach, *echt* and *unecht*' (recording review), *Early Music*, 23/2 (May 1995), p. 338

Boyd 1996 — M. Boyd, 'Bach and Handel: Crucifixion and Resurrection' (recording review), *Early Music*, 24/4 (Nov 1996), pp. 717f

Boyd 1999 — M. Boyd, ed., *J. S. Bach*, Oxford Composer Companions (Oxford, 1999)

BR — *The Bach Reader: A Life of Johann Sebastian Bach in Letters and Documents*, ed. H. T. David and A. Mendel, rev. edn (New York, 1966). Cf. *NBR*

Brown/Sadie 1989 — *Performance Practice: Music after 1600*, The New Grove Handbooks, ed. H. M. Brown and S. Sadie (London, 1989)

Butt 1991 — J. Butt, *Bach: Mass in B Minor*, Cambridge Music Handbooks, (Cambridge, 1991)

Butt 1994 — J. Butt, *Music Education and the Art of Performance in the German Baroque* (Cambridge, 1994)

Butt 1998 — J. Butt, 'Bach's vocal scoring: What can it mean?' *Early Music*, 26/1 (Feb 1998), pp. 99–107

Butt 1999 — J. Butt, Recording review in *Early Music Review*, 53 (Sep 1999), p. 32

Cavalieri 1600 — E. del Cavalieri, *Rappresentatione di Anima, et di Corpo* (Rome, 1600; ^{R}/1967)

Clark 1997 — *The Letters of C. P. E. Bach*, trans. and ed. S. L. Clark (Oxford, 1997)

Daw 1973 — S. Daw, 'German Lutheran choirs of Bach's time: Their constitution, performance practice and repertoire', *Organists' Review*, April 1973, pp. 13–15

Downey 1996 — P. Downey, 'On sounding the trumpet and beating the drum in 17th-century England', *Early Music*, 24/2 (May 1996), pp. 263–77

Dreyfus 1987 — L. Dreyfus, *Bach's Continuo Group: Players and Practices in His Vocal Works* (Cambridge, MA, 1987)

Engelke 1918–19 — B. Engelke, 'Die Rudolstädter Hofkapelle unter Lyra und Joh. Graf', *Archiv für Musikwissenschaft*, 1 (1918–19), pp. 594–606

Forkel 1802 — J. N. Forkel, *Über Johann Sebastian Bachs Leben, Kunst und Kunstwerke* (Leipzig, 1802); trans. C. S. Terry as *Johann Sebastian Bach: His Life, Art, and Work* (London, 1920)

Friderici 1618/1624 — D. Friderici, *Musica figuralis* (Rostock, 1618/1624)

Fröde 1984 — Christine Fröde, 'Zu einer Kritik des Thomanerchores von 1749', *Bach-Jahrbuch*, 70 (1984), pp. 53–8

Fuhrmann 1706 — M. H. Fuhrmann, *Musikalischer-Trichter* (Frankfurt an der Spree, 1706)

Geck 1967 — Martin Geck, *Die Wiederentdeckung der Matthäus-Passion im 19. Jahrhundert* (Regensburg, 1967)

Glöckner 1990 — A. Glöckner, *Die Musikpflege an der Leipziger Neukirche zur Zeit Johann Sebastian Bachs*, Beiträge zur Bach-Forschung, viii (1990)

Grove 1 — *Grove's Dictionary of Music and Musicians*, 1st edn (London, 1879–89)

Groschuff 1710 — *Unfehlbare Engel-Freude oder Geistliches Gesangbuch*, ed. Friedrich Groschuff (Leipzig, 1710)

Held 1894 — K. Held, *Das Kreuzkantorat zu Dresden* (Leipzig, 1894)

Keller ?1699 — G. Keller, *Six Sonatas* (Amsterdam, ?1699)

Kenyon 1981 — N. Kenyon, 'Further events: Solos', *The New Yorker*, 14 Dec 1981, pp. 189, 195f, 198 (see above, Appendix 7 and Appendix 6)

Knick 1963 — *St Thomas zu Leipzig, Schule und Chor: Stätte des Wirkens von Johann Sebastian Bach*, ed. B. Knick (Wiesbaden, 1963)

Knighton 1996 — T. Knighton, Editorial, *Early Music*, 24/4 (Nov 1996), p. 549

Köhler 1776 — J. F. Köhler, *Historia scholarum Lipsiensium* (Leipzig, 1776)

Koopman 1996 — T. Koopman, 'Recording Bach's early cantatas', *Early Music*, 24/4 (Nov 1996), pp. 604–19

Koopman 1997 — T. Koopman, 'One-to-a-part? Who then turns the pages – More on Bach's chorus' (Correspondence), *Early Music*, 25/3 (Aug 1997), pp. 541f

Koopman 1998 — T. Koopman, 'Bach's choir, an ongoing story', *Early Music*, 26/1 (Feb 1998), pp. 109–21

Kroesbergen/Wentz 1994 — W. Kroesbergen and J. Wentz, 'Sonority in the 18th century, *un poco più forte?*' *Early Music*, 22/3 (Aug 1994), pp. 482–95

Krüger 1933 — L. Krüger, *Die Hamburgische Musikorganisation im XVII. Jahrhundert* (Strassburg, 1933)

Küster 1996 — K. Küster, *Der junge Bach* (Stuttgart, 1996)

Marpurg 1754–78 — F. W. Marpurg, *Historisch—Kritische Beyträge zur Aufnahme der Musik* (Berlin), i (1754–5), ii (1756), iii (1757–8), iv (1758–9), v (1760–78)

Marshall 1983 — R. L. Marshall, 'Bach's chorus: A preliminary reply to Joshua Rifkin', *Musical Times*, 124 (Jan 1983), pp. 19–22

Mattheson 1713 — J. Mattheson, *Das neu-eröffnete Orchestre* (Hamburg, 1713; [R]/1997)

Mattheson 1722 — J. Mattheson, *Critica musica* (Hamburg, 1722; [R]/1964)

Mattheson 1728 — J. Mattheson, *Der musicalische Patriot* (Hamburg, 1728; [R]/1975)

Mattheson 1739 — J. Mattheson, *Der vollkommene Capellmeister* (Hamburg, 1739; [R]/1954)

Mattheson 1740 — J. Mattheson, *Grundlage einer Ehrenpforte* (Hamburg, 1740; [R]/1969)

Melamed 1995 — D. Melamed, *Johann Sebastian Bach and the German Motet* (Cambridge, 1995)

MGB IV/2 — *Musikgeschichte in Bildern*, iv/2, ed. H. W. Schwab (Leipzig, 1971)

Michael 1637 — T. Michael, *Musicalische Seelen-Lust*, ii (Leipzig, 1637)

Mizler 1754 — L. C. Mizler [von Kolof] *et al.*, *Musikalische Bibliothek*, iv/1 (Leipzig, 1754; [R]/1966)

Nausch 1954 — A. Nausch, *Augustin Pfleger: Leben und Werke*, Schriften des Landesinstitut für Musikforschung Kiel, iv (Kassel and Basel, 1954)

NBR — *The New Bach Reader*, ed. H. T. David and A. Mendel, rev. and enlarged C. Wolff (New York, 1998). Cf. *BR*

Neumann 1971 — W. Neumann, *Handbuch der Kantaten Johann Sebastian Bachs*, 4th edn (Leipzig, 1971)

New Grove — *The New Grove Dictionary of Music and Musicians*, ed. S. Sadie (London, 1980)

Niedt 1706 — F. Niedt, *Die musicalische Handleitung*, Part 2 (Hamburg, 1706; ²/1721)

Niedt 1717 — F. Niedt, *Die musicalische Handleitung*, Part 3 (Hamburg, 1717); trans. P. L. Poulin and I. C. Taylor as *The Musical Guide* (Oxford, 1989)

Noack 1967 — E. Noack, *Musikgeschichte Darmstadts von Mittelalter bis zur Goethezeit* (Mainz, 1967)

Ordnungen — *Die Thomasschule Leipzig zur Zeit Johann Sebastian Bachs: Ordnungen und Gesetze 1634, 1723, 1733*, ed. H.-J. Schulze (Leipzig, 1987)

Owens (forthcoming) — Samantha Owens, 'Professional women musicians in early 18th-century Württemberg', *Music & Letters* (forthcoming)

Parrott 1996 — A. Parrott, 'Bach's chorus: A "brief yet highly necessary" reappraisal', *Early Music*, 24/4 (Nov 1996), pp. 551–80

Parrott 1997 — A. Parrott, 'Bach's chorus: Who cares?' (Observation), *Early Music*, 25/2 (May 1997), pp. 297–300

Parrott 1998 — A. Parrott, 'Bach's chorus: Beyond reasonable doubt', *Early Music*, 26/4 (Nov 1998), pp. 636–58

Petri 1767 — J. S. Petri, *Anleitung zur praktischen Musik* (Lauban, 1767; R/Leipzig, 1782)

Praetorius 1619 — M. Praetorius, *Syntagma musicum*, iii (Wolfenbüttel, 1619; R/1958)

Printz 1678 — W. C. Printz, *Musica modulatoria vocalis* (Schweidnitz, 1678)

Rauschning 1931 — H. Rauschning, *Geschichte der Musik und Musikpflege in Danzig* (Danzig, 1931)

Richter 1907 — Bernhard Friedrich Richter, 'Stadtpfeifer und Alumnen der Thomasschule in Leipzig zu Bachs Zeit', *Bach Jahrbuch*, 4 (1907), pp. 32–78

Rifkin 1981 — J. Rifkin, 'Bach's chorus', paper prepared for the Annual Meeting of the American Musicological Society, Boston, 1981 (= Appendix 6 above)

Rifkin 1982 — J. Rifkin, 'Bach's chorus: A preliminary report', *Musical Times*, 123 (Nov 1982), pp. 747–54 (revised as 'Bachs Chor: Ein vorläufige Bericht', *Basler Jahrbuch für historische Musikpraxis*, 9 (1985), pp. 141–55)

Rifkin 1983 — J. Rifkin, 'Bach's chorus: A response to Robert Marshall', *Musical Times*, 124 (Mar 1983), pp. 161f

Rifkin 1984 — J. Rifkin, [Untitled response to Boyd 1984], *Early Music*, 12/4 (Nov 1984), p. 591

Rifkin 1985 — J. Rifkin, '". . . wobey aber die Singstimmen hinlänglich besetzt seyn müßen . . .": Zum Credo der h-Moll-Messe in der Aufführung Carl Philipp Emanuel Bachs', *Basler Jahrbuch für historische Musikpraxis*, 9 (1985), pp. 157–72

Rifkin 1987–8 — J. Rifkin, review of facsimiles of the Mass in B Minor BWV 232, *Notes*, 44 (1987–8), pp. 787–98

Rifkin 1990 — J. Rifkin, 'Bach's choral ideal', paper presented at the Royal Musical Association Annual Conference, April 1990

Rifkin 1991 — J. Rifkin, 'More (and less) on Bach's orchestra', *Performance Practice Review*, 4 (Spring 1991), pp. 5–13

Rifkin 1995a — J. Rifkin, 'Bach's chorus: Some red herrings', *Journal of Musicological Research*, 14 (1995), pp. 223–34. Cf. Stauffer 1995

Rifkin 1995b — J. Rifkin, 'Some questions of performance in Bach's *Trauerode*', in *Bach Studies 2*, ed. D. K. Melamed (Cambridge, 1995), pp. 119–53

Rifkin 1996a — J. Rifkin, 'From Weimar to Leipzig: Concertists and ripienists in Bach's *Ich hatte viel Bekümmernis*', *Early Music*, 24/4 (Nov 1996), pp. 583–603

Rifkin 1996b — J. Rifkin, 'The violins in Bach's St John Passion', in *Critica musica: Essays in Honor of Paul Brainard* (*Musicology*, 18), ed. J. Knowles (Amsterdam, 1996), pp. 307–32

Rifkin 1997a — J. Rifkin, 'Bassoons, violins and voices: A response to Ton Koopman' (Observation), *Early Music*, 25/2 (May 1997), pp. 302–7

Rifkin 1997b — J. Rifkin, 'Page turns, players and ripieno parts: More questions of scoring in Bach's vocal music' (Observation), *Early Music*, 25/4 (Nov 1997), pp. 728–34

Rifkin 1998a — J. Rifkin, 'Bach's chorus: A neverending story?' (Correspondence), *Early Music*, 26/2 (May 1998), pp. 380f

Rifkin 1998b — J. Rifkin, [Untitled response to Wolff 1998] (Correspondence), *Early Music*, 26/3 (Aug 1998), pp. 541f

Rifkin 1998c — J. Rifkin, 'Bach's violins: A progress report', paper presented to the American Bach Society, April 1998

Rifkin 1999a — J. Rifkin, 'Bach's chorus: Not again!' (Correspondence), *Early Music*, 27/2 (May 1999), p. 350

Rifkin 1999b — J. Rifkin, 'Schering's wacky theory', *Early Music America*, 5/3 (Fall 1999), p. 48

Rifkin 2000 — J. Rifkin, 'Zelenkas Chor: Der Blick von 1725', in *Provokation und Tradition: Erfahrungen mit der Alten Musik*, ed. Hans-Martin Linde and Regula Rapp (Munich, 2000), pp. 241–68

Scheibe 1745 — J. A. Scheibe, *Der critische Musikus*, 2nd edn (Leipzig, 1745; ^R/1970)

Scheibel 1721 — G. E. Scheibel, *Zufällige Gedancken von der Kirchen-Music* (Frankfurt and Leipzig, 1721)

Schering 1920 — 'Die Besetzung Bachscher Chöre', *Bach-Jahrbuch*, 17 (1920), pp. 77–89

Schering 1926 — A. Schering, *Musikgeschichte Leipzigs*, ii (Leipzig, 1926)

Schering 1936 — A. Schering, *Johann Sebastian Bachs Leipziger Kirchenmusik* (Leipzig, 1936; ²/1954)

Schering 1941 — A. Schering, *Musikgeschichte Leipzigs*, iii (Leipzig, 1941)

Schiffner 1987 — M. Schiffner, 'Die Arnstädter Hofkapelle – regionales Zentrum der Musikpflege im historischen und zeitgenössischen Umfeld des jungen Bach', *Beiträge zur Bach-Forschung*, 6 (Leipzig, 1987), pp. 37–53

Scholz 1911 — Hans Scholz, *Johann Sigismund Kusser (Cousser): Sein Leben und seine Werke* (Leipzig, 1911)

Schulze 1977 — *Katalog der Sammlung Manfred Gorke. Bachiana und andere Handschriften und Drucke des 18. und frühen 19. Jahrhunderts*, Bibliographische Veröffentlichungen der Musikbibliothek der Stadt Leipzig, viii, ed. Hans-Joachim Schulze (Leipzig, 1977)

Schulze 1984 — H.-J. Schulze, 'Studenten als Bachs Helfer bei der Leipziger Kirchenmusik', *Bach-Jahrbuch*, 70 (1984), pp. 45–52

Schulze 1989 — H.-J. Schulze, 'Johann Sebastian Bach's orchestra: Some unanswered questions', *Early Music*, 17/1 (Feb 1989), pp. 3–15

Schulze 1991 — H.-J. Schulze, *Bach stilgerecht aufführen*, Societas Bach Internationalis: Jahresgabe 1990 der Internationalen Bach-Gesellschaft Schaffhausen (Wiesbaden, 1991)

Schünemann 1918–19 — G. Schünemann, 'Die Bewerber um das Freiberger Kantorat 1593–1798', *Archiv für Musikwissenschaft*, 1 (1918–19), pp. 179–204

Schütz 1619 — H. Schütz, *Psalmen Davids* (Dresden, 1619)

Schütz 1636 — H. Schütz, *Musicalische Exequien* (Dresden, 1636)

Schütz 1650 — H. Schütz, *Symphoniae sacrae*, iii (Dresden, 1650)

Sherman 1997 — B. D. Sherman, *Inside Early Music: Conversations with Performers* (New York and Oxford, 1997)

Siegele 1978 — U. Siegele, 'Bachs Endzweck einer regulierten und Entwurf einer wohlbestallten Kirchenmusik', in *Festschrift Georg von Dadelsen zum 60. Geburtstag*, ed. T. Kohlhase and V. Scherliess (Neuhausen—Stuttgart, 1978), pp. 315–51

Siegele 1997 — U. Siegele, 'Bach and the domestic politics of Electoral Saxony', in *The Cambridge Companion to Bach*, ed. J. Butt (Cambridge, 1997), pp. 17–34

Sittard 1890 — J. Sittard, *Geschichte des Musik- und Concertwesens in Hamburg vom 14. Jahrhundert bis auf die Gegenwart* (Altona and Leipzig, 1890)

Sittard 1890–1 — J. Sittard, *Zur Geschichte der Musik und des Theaters am Württembergischen Hofe* (Stuttgart, 1890–1)

Smend 1951 — Friedrich Smend, *Bach in Köthen* (Berlin, [1951])

Smithers 1997 — Don Smithers, 'The Emperor's new clothes reappraised: or Bach's musical resources revealed', *Bach*: The Journal of the Riemenschneider Bach Institute, 28 (1997), pp. 1–81

Snyder 1987 — Kerala Snyder, *Buxtehude* (New York, 1987)

Spitta 1880 — P. Spitta, *Johann Sebastian Bach*, ii (Leipzig, 1880). Trans. as Spitta 1889 below

Spitta 1889 — P. Spitta, *Johann Sebastian Bach*, ii, trans. C. Bell and J. A. Fuller-Maitland (London, 1889)

Stauffer 1995 — G. Stauffer, [Untitled response to Rifkin 1995a], *Journal of Musicological Research*, 14 (1995), p. 234

Stemler 1765 — Christoph Gotthelff Stemler, *Abhandlung aus der Kirchengeschichte von der Currende und denen Currendanern* (Leipzig, 1765)

Stiller 1984 — G. Stiller, *Johann Sebastian Bach and liturgical life in Leipzig*, trans. H. J. A. Bauman, D. F. Poellet and H. C. Oswald, ed. R. A. Leaver (St Louis, 1984). Translation of *Johann Sebastian Bach und das Leipziger gottesdienstliche Leben seiner Zeit* (Berlin, 1970)

Swack 1999 — J. Swack, '"Telemann's chorus": Vocal forces in Telemann's Frankfurt cantatas and the implications for the "one on a part" controversy', paper presented at the Annual Meeting of the American Musicological Society, Kansas City, 1999

Telemann [I] — G. P. Telemann, *Briefwechsel*, ed. H. Grosse and H. R. Jung (Leipzig, 1972)

Telemann [II] — G. P. Telemann, *Singen ist das Fundament zur Music in allen Dingen: Eine Dokumentensammlung* (Wilhelmshaven, 1981)

Tennent 1971 — R. M. Tennent (ed.), *Science Data Book* (Edinburgh, 1971)

Trömer 1745 — Johann Christian Trömer, *Die Avantures von Deutsch Francos* (Dresden, [1745]; R/1954)

Van Tassel 1999 — E. Van Tassel, 'Schütz and his contemporaries' (recording review), *Early Music*, 27/1 (Feb 1999), pp. 148–53

Vogler 1780 — G. J. Vogler, *Betrachtungen der Mannheimer Tonschule*, iii/1 (Mannheim, 1780)

Wagner 1986 — G. Wagner, 'Die Chorbesetzung bei J. S. Bach und ihre Vorgeschichte: Anmerkungen zur "hinlänglichen" Besetzung im 17. und 18. Jahrhundert', *Archiv für Musikwissenschaft*, 43 (1986), pp. 278–304

Walther 1732 — J. G. Walther, *Musikalisches Lexikon* (Leipzig, 1732)

Webber 1996 — G. Webber, *North German Church Music in the Age of Buxtehude* (Oxford, 1996)

Werner 1933 — A. Werner, *Vier Jahrhunderte im Dienste der Kirchenmusik* (Leipzig, 1933)

Wolf 1787 — G. F. Wolf, *Kurzgefasstes musikalisches Lexicon* (Halle, 1787)

Wolff 1995 — C. Wolff, 'J. S. Bach and the legacy of the seventeenth century', in *Bach Studies 2*, ed. D. K. Melamed (Cambridge, 1995), pp. 192–20

Wolff 1996 — C. Wolff, *Bach: Essays on His Life and Music* (Cambridge, Mass., 1991, ²/1996)

Wolff 1997 — *The World of the Bach Cantatas*, ed. C. Wolff (Amsterdam, 1995; New York, 1997)

Wolff 1998 — C. Wolff, 'Bach's chorus: Stomach aches may disappear!' (Correspondence), *Early Music*, 26/3 (Aug 1998), pp. 540f

Wolff 1999 — C. Wolff, 'Bach's chorus: An amplification' (Correspondence), *Early Music*, 27/1 (Feb 1999), p. 172

Wollny 1997 — P. Wollny, 'Neue Bach-Funde', *Bach-Jahrbuch*, 83 (1997), pp. 7–50

Young 1949 — P. Young, *The Oratorios of Handel* (London, 1949)

Index

[*] illustration; ⁺ music example

Agricola, J. F., 13n, 15n, 35f, 109, 114, 175f
Alt-Bachisches Archiv, 46
Altnickol, J. C., 14, 108ff
Arnstadt, 14, 41
Augsburg, 123, 125*, 128

Bach, C. P. E., 46, 106, 114, 175f
Bach, J. S.:
    Brandenburg Concerto No. 1 BWV046, 131n
    Brandenburg Concerto No. 2 BWV1047, 132
    Christen, ätzet diesen Tag BWV63, 61, 62,
        68, 75n, 180n
    Christmas Oratorio BWV248, 187n, 190f, 192
    Christum wir sollen loben schon BWV121,
        183n
    Christus, der ist mein Leben BWV95, 75n
    Coffee Cantata (*Schweigt stille, plaudert
        nicht*) BWV211, 192f, 199
    Dem Gerechten muß das Licht BWV195,
        60*, 61, 65, 70, 72f⁺, 85–92⁺, 202f
    Der Streit zwischen Phoebus und Pan: see
        *Geschwinde, geschwinde, ihr wirbel-
        nden Winde* BWV201
    Die Elenden sollen essen BWV75, 48, 62, 71
    Die Himmel erzählen die Ehre Gottes
        BWV76, 48, 59n, 61, 64, 68, 181, 203
    Dramma per musica: see *Geschwinde,
        geschwinde, ihr wirbelnden Winde*
        BWV201; *Vereinigte Zwietracht der
        wechselnden Saiten* BWV207
    Du wahrer Gott und Davids Sohn BWV23,
        61n, 75, 178
    Easter Oratorio BWV249, 199
    Ein ungefärbt Gemüte BWV24, 48, 62, 71
    Erschallet, ihr Lieder BWV172, 190, 202
    *Geschwinde, geschwinde, ihr wirbelnden
        Winde* BWV201, 61, 63⁺, 69, 186n, 199
    Gloria in excelsis Deo BWV191, 62, 71, 84n
    Gott ist mein König BWV71, 36, 37*, 53, 59,
        61, 64, 66f⁺, 68, 134, 141f, 181n, 201
    Gott soll allein mein Herze haben BWV169,
        39, 63n, 198
    Gottes Zeit ist die allerbeste Zeit BWV106,
        134, 135⁺
    Himmelskönig, sei willkommen BWV182,
        185n
    Hunting Cantata: see *Was mir behagt, ist
        nur die muntre Jagd* BWV208

Ich armer Mensch, ich Sündenknecht
    BWV55, 39, 63n, 198
Ich bin vergnügt mit meinem Glücke
    BWV84, 39, 63n, 198f
Ich glaube, lieber Herr BWV109, 75, 82⁺
Ich hatte viel Bekümmernis BWV21, 48, 61,
    64f, 69, 74⁺, 76f⁺, 178n, 203
Ich will den Kreuzstab gerne tragen
    BWV56, 39, 198
Jesus nahm zu sich die Zwölfe BWV22, 61n,
    62, 71, 74f, 81⁺, 128
Laß, Fürstin! laß noch einen Strahl: see
    Trauer Ode BWV198
Laßt uns sorgen, laßt uns wachen BWV213,
    186n
Liebster Gott, wenn werd ich sterben
    BWV8, 177n
Lobe den Herrn, meine Seele BWV69, 45,
    47*
Magnificat BWV243, 84n, 117
Mass in B Minor BWV232, 34, 45*, 64, 75,
    84⁺, 138n, 149n, 190, 191, 198
Missa in A Major BWV234, 62, 71
St John Passion BWV245, 40, 61, 69, 80f,
    83, 127n, 128f, 172, 187n, 199, 204ff⁺,
    207
St Matthew Passion BWV244, 3, 40, 80f,
    83, 138n, 187n, 191, 192, 199f, 204,
    207
Schweigt stille, plaudert nicht: see *Coffee
    Cantata* BWV211
Sei lob und Ehr dem höchsten Gut BWV117,
    128
Selig ist der Mann BWV57, 199
Suite (Ouverture) in C Major BWV1066,
    192
Trauer Ode (*Laß, Fürstin! laß noch einen
    Strahl*) BWV198, 172
Unser Mund sei voll Lachens BWV110, 61,
    69, 128, 201f
*Vereinigte Zwietracht der wechselnden
    Saiten* BWV207, 119n, 127n 128, 186n
Was mir behagt, ist nur die muntre Jagd
    BWV208, 134f
*Wer mich liebet, der wird mein Wort
    halten* BWV59, 190
Wir danken dir, Gott, wir danken dir
    BWV29, 61, 62, 63f, 65⁺, 70

Bach, W. F., 46, 106
Bach Reader, The, 93f
Bacilly, B. de, 13n
Bammler, J. N., 15
Barclay, R., 131n
Bassani, G. B., 62
Beer, J., 118, 119
Berlin, 101n, 118n
Beyer, J. S., 17n, 175
Biber, H. I. F. von, 207
Birnbaum, J. A., 1, 174f
Bodenschatz, E.: see *Florilegium Portense*
Bokemeyer collection, 32
Born, J., 95n
Boyd, M., 149n
Breslau, 118n
Brown, P. G. McC., 174
Brunswick (Braunschweig), 118n
Bütner, C., 33
Butt, J., 38n, 145n, 150
Buxtehude, D., 33

Calvi, L., 31, 32, 51
Calvisius, S., 101n
capella, 'da capella', 4, 21, 31ff, 35f, 38, 41, 51f,
    61, 64, 102n
Cavalieri, E. del, 40n
coro favorito, 4, 35
Croce, G., 22, 30
Currende (*Kurrende*): see street singing

Danzig (Gdańsk), 114
Darmstadt, 112f
Daw, S., 13n
Demantius, J. C., 35
Devrient, E., 3
Doles, J. F., jr, 13n
Dresden, 84, 111n, 166, 169, 172f, 175, 198
Dreyer, J. C., 14n, 98n
Düben collection, 32, 59

Eisenach, 14
Erhardi, L., 35
Ernesti, J. A., 10, 12n, 13n, 18, 101
Ernesti, J. H., 10n
Falck, G., 35
Florilegium Portense, 21f, 23*, 193f
Forkel, J. N., 175
Förtsch, J., 33
Frankfurt, 44, 97f
Freeman-Attwood, J., 149n
Freiberg, 9n, 17n, 56f*, 119, 122*
Friderici, D., 54n

Fuhrmann, M. H., 13, 38, 41,

Gengenbach, N., 35
Gentzmer (Genßmar), J. C., 129n, 164, 168
Gerber, C., 172f
Gerlach, C. G., 12, 59n, 109, 119, 136n
Gerstenbüttel, J., 33
Gesner, J. M., 136n, 173f
Gottsched, J. C., 172
Graun, C. H., 101, 133
Graun, J. G., 106
Graupner, C., 21, 144, 207
Groschuff: see *Unfehlbare Engel-Freude*
Güstrow, 14n, 111f

Hamburg, 14*, 32, 102n, 113n, 118, 123, 124*,
    128
Hammerschmidt, A., 23
Handel, G. F., 142
Handl, J., 22, 24[+], 26f[+]
Hanover, 14n
Harrer, J. G., 114n
Harris, E. T., 3
Hasse, J. A., 133
Hassler, H. L., 23*
Haydn, F. J., 201
Herreweghe, P., 151n
Hoffmann, M., 136
Hogarth, W., 43n

Jena, 123, 126*, 128

Keller, G., 132
Knighton, T., 118n
Knüpfer, S., 36
Koopman, T., 49n, 56n, 57n, 75n, 110n, 117n,
    143n
Krause, G. T., 12n, 13
Kuhnau, J., 7n, 18n, 19n, 80n, 95n, 99n,
    101n, 102n, 104, 107f, 110, 114, 119, 165,
    169, 172
Kusser, [Cousser] J. S., 15n
Leipzig:
    churches, 9, 12, 18, 20*, 21*, 94–7, 107,
        136, 137*, 157f, 163, 165, 167, 168, 172,
        192–7
    collegium musicum, 14, 18, 115, 135f
    große *Concert*-Gesellschafft, 15, 119, 120*,
        128
    Thomasschule, 11*, 49, 97 *et passim*; see
        also 155–62 *passim*, 163–9, 175, 193–7
        alumni (*inquilini/interni*), *externi*, 95f,
        104ff, 163, 165, 166, 167, 168, 169f, 196f
    prefects, 9–12, 25, 97n, 107n, 196f

Town Council, 17, 21, 61, 80, 93, 97, 101f, 103n, 106f, 111, 154*, 155–8, 165, 169
university students, 98f, 104, 106–10, 165, 168, 194, 196
Lipsius, J. C., 108n, 109
Lotti, A., 62
Ludewig, B. D., 109, 119n
Lüneburg, 14, 98n

Marshall, R., 46, 48, 149n
Mattheson, J., 33f, 35, 38, 52, 53f, 102n, 118, 128, 132, 133, 136n
Mecklenburg: *see* Güstrow
Meder, J. V., 114
Mendelssohn, F., 3
Mirampole, A. M. de, 13n
Mittendorff, J. C., 108, 109
Mizler, L. C., 175f
Monteverdi, C., 31f, 207
motet, 5, 10, 17, 20–25, 29, 32f, 35, 54, 95, 97, 133, 143, 164, 167, 195f; see also *Florilegium Portense*
Mühlhausen, 61, 141f
Munich, 123, 124*
Musik und Kirche, 150

Nagel, M., 13, 95n
New Bach Reader, The, 94
New Year singing: *see* street singing
Niedt, F. E., 22f, 53
Nietzsche, G. E., 106n
Nuremberg, 123, 127*

Osnabrück, 19n, 25n, 38, 48n, 113

Petri, J. S., 132n
Pfaffe, C. F., 14n
Pfleger, A., 14n, 18n, 111f
Pisendel, J. G., 136
Praetorius, M., 30, 34n, 36, 51f
Printz, W. C., 29, 48

Rifkin, J., 44, 94n, 103, 111, 117n, 127n, 147–51 *passim*, 152, 189–208 *passim*
Rudolstadt: *see* Stadtilm

Scarlatti, A., 192
Scheibe, J. A., 23, 25, 29, 98, 132ff, 174

Scheibel, G. E., 36, 38, 41, 144n
Schelle, J., 22, 101n, 108, 119, 165, 169
Schemelli, C. F., 13
Schering, A., 36, 51n, 54f, 189–208 *passim*
Schmidt, J. C., 62
Schneider, J., 119
Schulenberg, D., 134
Schulze, H.-J., 131n
Schütz, H., 3f, 44, 52, 53, 144, 200f, 207
Sebastiani, J., 33, 36n
Selle, T., 29, 32
Sicul, C. E., 172
Siegele, U., 99n
Smithers, D., 4n, 33n, 38n, 48n, 56n, 171n
Snyder, K., 33
Stadtilm, 53, 118f, 128
Stieglitz, C. L., 94, 159
stile antico, 21, 139; *see also* motet
Stölzel, G. H., 18n, 136, 192
street singing, 9n, 17, 49, 95, 105
Strodtmann, J. C., 38
Stuttgart, 114; *see also* Württemberg
Swack, J., 44, 59

Taverner Consort and Players, 84n
Telemann, G. P., 14, 18, 44, 97f, 101n, 107, 113n, 118, 123, 133, 136n, 144, 150, 207
Trömer, J. C., 136n, 171n
trumpet-playing, 131f

Unfehlbare Engel-Freude (Groschuff), 48n, 54, 55*, 119, 121*
Usper, F., 31

Van Tassel, E., 32n
Vatke, S., 19n, 25n
Vogler, G. J., 35

Walther, J. G., 35, 36, 49ff*, 64
Weimar, 135, 173, 197
Wilisch, C. F., 9n
Wolf, G. F., 34
Wolff, C., 75, 96n, 103, 104n, 106n, 111n, 142n, 144, 149n
Württemberg, 14, 15n, 41, 97

Zahn, G. P., 112f